Strategic Management in Nonprofit Organizations

William A. Brown, PhD

Associate Professor, Director Nonprofit Management

Texas A&M University

Bush School of Government and Public Service

College Station, Texas

JONES & BARTLETT
LEARNING

World Headquarters
Jones & Bartlett Learning
5 Wall Street
Burlington, MA 01803
978-443-5000
info@jblearning.com
www.jblearning.com

Jones & Bartlett Learning books and products are available through most bookstores and online booksellers. To contact Jones & Bartlett Learning directly, call 800-832-0034, fax 978-443-8000, or visit our website, www.jblearning.com.

Substantial discounts on bulk quantities of Jones & Bartlett Learning publications are available to corporations, professional associations, and other qualified organizations. For details and specific discount information, contact the special sales department at Jones & Bartlett Learning via the above contact information or send an email to specialsales@jblearning.com.

Production Credits

Executive Publisher: William Brottmiller
Publisher: Michael Brown
Associate Editor: Chloe Falivene
Editorial Assistant: Nicholas Alakel
Associate Production Editor: Rebekah Linga
Senior Marketing Manager: Sophie Fleck Teague
Manufacturing and Inventory Control Supervisor:
  Amy Bacus
Composition: Laserwords Private Limited, Chennai, India
Cover Design: Scott Moden
Photo Research and Permissions Coordinator:
  Amy Rathburn
Cover and Title Page Image: © BioMedical/Shutterstock, Inc.
Printing and Binding: Edwards Brothers Malloy
Cover Printing: Edwards Brothers Malloy

Library of Congress Cataloging-in-Publication Data

Brown, William A., 1964–
  Strategic management in nonprofit organizations / William A. Brown.
    pages cm
  Includes bibliographical references and index.
  ISBN 978-1-4496-1894-0 (paper.)
  1. Nonprofit organizations–Management. 2. Strategic planning. I. Title.
  HD62.6.B765 2015
  658.4'012–dc23

                                        2013038796

6048

Printed in the United States of America
18 17 16 15 14   10 9 8 7 6 5 4 3 2 1

This book is dedicated to my father, Elmo Charles Brown, who always enjoyed a good puzzle—forever seeking to find patterns in complex systems. Thanks to my kids, Linnea and Mic, as well as my lifelong friend and companion, Cheryl, without whom I could not have accomplished so much.

Table of Contents

Preface

Nonprofits provide public and social value, and yet the ability to define and measure that value is difficult to obtain. An often quoted management refrain is, "If you can't measure it, you can't manage it." So what is a nonprofit manager to do? There is no doubt that "not everything that counts can be counted and not everything that can be counted counts" (Cameron, 1963, p. 13). Nonprofits and managers worldwide who work in public service struggle to define how they create social value and often feel dissatisfied with outcome measures that obscure the spirit of their good work (Benjamin, 2012). Nevertheless, managers allocate resources and prioritize objectives to fulfill public benefit purposes. This text provides a glimpse into the uncertainties managers confront in making strategic choices. The text is based on classic strategic management framework (Hitt, Ireland, & Hoskisson, 2011), but with a twist. There is careful attention to the realities of operating a nonprofit organization—the challenges of muted markets and indeterminate performance expectations. This text is a modest attempt to inform the thinking of nonprofit managers and to bolster the rigor of nonprofit management education. I'll leave it to my esteemed and valued colleagues, students, and the nonprofit professionals who operate in complex, resource-limited, and political contexts to determine the text's success in achieving that objective.

The text begins with an introduction to nonprofit organizations as unique organizational forms that are distinct from for-profit enterprises and public organizations (governments). Chapters 2–7 introduce the fundamentals of strategic thinking, the analytic methods to understand environmental forces, and the methods to create comparative advantage. Using the adaptive cycle developed by Miles and Snow (1978), Chapter 2 suggests managers confront three "problems" when forming and implementing strategy: (1) defining the operating domain, (2) designing programs to create value, and (3) assessing performance. Chapter 3 reviews the features of the nonprofit operating environment. The text contends that managers confront two distinct operating domains: a public benefit domain and a resource domain. Chapter 4 reviews the resources and capabilities of nonprofit organizations and proposes the nonprofit value framework as the mechanism to create social value. Chapter 5 considers the public benefit practices managers utilize to create social value. The choices regarding program delivery options are reviewed and considered through the lens of business strategy literature. Chapter 6 considers methods to analyze the operating environment and the issues managers confront to understand the tendencies of organizations to compete or cooperate. Chapter 7 introduces the concept of corporate strategy, which is defined as the highest level of decision making in the organization. Chapters 8–10 unpack the methods by which managers implement strategic choices. Chapter 8 suggests that a theory of change, which is based on the logic of program delivery, can guide program and service activities to achieve public benefit outcomes. Chapter 9 recognizes the importance of operating in a sociopolitical domain, which includes advocacy activities. Chapter 10 reviews the funding and resource options available to nonprofit organizations. In particular the chapter considers how managers build relationships to sustain reliable revenue streams. Chapter 11 considers the challenges managers confront as they try to achieve programmatic and sociopolitical objectives through interorganizational relationships. Chapter 12 concludes the text by considering the role of leaders in creating a climate for success and guiding organizational choices.

William A. Brown
College Station, Texas

Benjamin, L. M. (2012). Nonprofits and outcome measurement: From tracking program activities to focusing on front line work. *American Journal of Evaluation, 33*(3), 431–447.

Cameron, W. B. (1963). *Informal sociology: A casual introduction to sociological thinking.* New York, NY: Random House.

Hitt, M. A., Ireland, R. D., & Hoskisson, R. E. (2011). *Strategic management competitiveness and globalization* (9th ed.). Mason, OH: South-Western Cengage.

Miles, R. E., & Snow, C. C. (1978). *Organizational strategy structure and process.* New York, NY: McGraw-Hill.

Acknowledgments

Numerous individuals contributed to the development of this text. Several graduate students, including Lauren Tolman, Nathan Louder, and Grace Norman, were diligent researchers and editors. They helped prepare and improve the material in the text. The students in my nonprofit management class have been at times unwilling victims to earlier versions of the text. Their thoughtful advice and perspective was invaluable as I created and refined this material. Special thanks to Dave Renz, who asked me to write a chapter for the *Jossey-Bass Handbook of Nonprofit Leadership and Management* (Brown, 2010) on strategic management, not planning but "strategy." That chapter launched my interest and imagination into the possibility of this book. I used Hitt, Ireland, and Hoskisson's *Strategic Management Competitiveness and Globalization* (2011) as a model. I do not presuppose that this text is anywhere near as thorough or insightful as theirs, but I diligently utilized that material to guide my work. It was a constant companion throughout the process. Thanks also to the anonymous reviewers who provided valuable insights, the editors and support staff at Jones & Bartlett Learning, and my colleagues at the Bush School at Texas A&M University, who allowed me the time to focus on this project and encouraged me to continue down this road.

Brown, W. A. (2010). Strategic management. In D. O. Renz (Ed.), *Jossey-Bass handbook of nonprofit management* (3rd ed., pp. 206–229). San Francisco, CA: Jossey-Bass.

Hitt, M. A., Ireland, R. D., & Hoskisson, R. E. (2011). *Strategic management competitiveness and globalization* (9th ed.). Mason, OH: South-Western Cengage.

The Nature of Nonprofit Organizations

Learning Objectives

- Describe the differences between government, for-profits, and nonprofits
- Explain the rationale and function of nonprofits in society
- Appreciate the range and variety of nonprofit organizations in U.S. society
- Understand the qualities of nonprofits and implications for strategic decision making

This text presents principles and practices to encourage effective operation of nonprofit organizations. It explores the strategic choices of 501(c)(3) tax-exempt organizations as defined by the U.S. Internal Revenue Service (IRS). It is necessary, therefore, to discuss briefly some of the unique attributes and characteristics of these organizations. The text draws on business management literature while blending public and nonprofit management literature to create a management system that is sensitive to the operational challenges nonprofit managers confront. Nonprofits are not businesses in the classic sense. They typically operate in markets that inherently lack the potential to earn a profit. Nonprofits meet the needs of their members or the community in a way that differs from for-profit businesses. The IRS definition of tax-exempt 501(c)(3) public charities states that they must operate for tax-exempt purposes:

> The exempt purposes set forth in section 501(c)(3) are charitable, religious, educational, scientific, literary, testing for public safety, fostering national or international amateur sports competition, and preventing cruelty to children or animals. The term *charitable* is used in its generally accepted legal sense and includes relief of the poor, the distressed, or the underprivileged; advancement of religion; advancement of education or science; erecting or maintaining public buildings, monuments, or works; lessening the burdens of government; lessening neighborhood tensions; eliminating prejudice and discrimination; defending human and civil rights secured by law; and combating community deterioration and juvenile delinquency.

Every nonprofit needs to explain how they achieve these exempt purposes. Nonprofits can earn income by "competing" and "marketing" their services, but they exist to produce a benefit for the public. This public benefit can also be referred to as social value (Brickson, 2007; Weerawardena, McDonald, & Mort, 2010). The overarching lens through which the organization makes decisions is related to this purpose or mission. As a buffer to ensure this orientation exists, nonprofits cannot distribute surplus funds (profit) to owners, leaders, or investors. There are not any owners in the typical sense. This nondistribution constraint is not sufficient, however, to guide operational decision making (Brody, 1996; Bushouse, 2011). That is the role of this text, to guide the decision making of nonprofit managers.

In a for-profit business there is always someone or some group that is intent on making a profit. In some instances, those intentions might be modest and their purposes might be honorable (Tom's Shoes). Businesses can and do exist to achieve some charitable purposes, but that is not their sole reason for being. To illustrate these differences, three idealized organizational entities—for-profit businesses, government entities, and nonprofits or social sectors organizations—are discussed (see **Figure 1-1**). These are legal categories and the entities within those categories can take different forms, for example there are local governments, state governments, and federal governments. Similarly, for-profit entities can be organized as sole-proprietor, partnerships, or corporations, and social sector organizations can be loose collaborations of individuals (e.g., voluntary groups) or organized as nonprofit corporations.

An Example: Providing Hot Food to a Low-Income Community

It is helpful to consider an example of how the three different sectors address the need or demand for hot food in a low-income community. Each entity (i.e., for-profit, nonprofit, and government) would likely approach the problem in a very different way, but there would also be some similarities. The basic idea of whether individuals in a particular community want or need hot meals is addressed by all three sectors. It is simple to consider

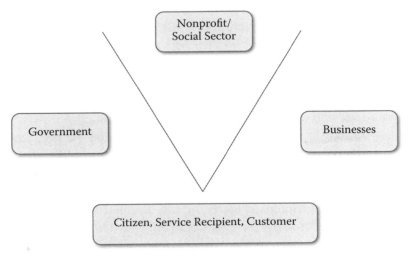

FIGURE 1-1 Organizational Types

how the different sectors confront the "problem" of providing hot food in different ways. For-profit entities might open a pizza shop, nonprofits might open a soup kitchen, and government might provide school lunches. Organizational entities in each sector frame the "opportunity" in ways that are functional for them. That framing is fundamentally different in stereotypical for-profit business, government entities, and nonprofits. One sector is not better than another. Entities in the different sectors confront opportunities for very different reasons and consider different issues before engaging and when deciding to disengage.

framing

A for-profit business would explore the range of potential customers and get some sense about their interest and their ability to pay for hot, prepared food. Part of those calculations would consider who else is providing a similar service or product. If it was decided that there was indeed a "market" for hot, prepared food, the business would consider a series of questions about what to provide and how to provide it (e.g., pizza, hamburgers, or something else). They would also consider things like start-up costs (i.e., how much it costs to get the space and equipment needed), and they would estimate how much it would cost to produce a unit of product. This is a basic for-profit business model. The customer pays a premium to have the hot food, and the revenue is sufficient to pay for all the business activities and have some leftover as profit. In order to acquire the equipment and space the owner must find financial capital. Those individuals (or corporations) who invest expect a financial return on their investment. They can monitor performance and with relative confidence make some judgments about the likelihood that they will reap financial rewards. At some point it will be determined if the business is profitable, and it will continue or discontinue based upon that calculation.

Nonprofit managers also consider the market for hot, prepared food, but they are less concerned about the ability of the potential customer to pay than they are about the "need,"—its depth and character. They are concerned about who has the need. For instance, children, elderly, or the disabled who may have limited capacity to pay for food would be of particular concern for a nonprofit. Nonprofits target populations that have the need for hot food irrespective of the capacity to pay. This is the charitable, or tax-exempt, purpose. Nonprofits can decide who they want to serve. Sometimes they serve everyone, while in other instances they may decide to serve a particular population (e.g., the elderly). There is also some philosophical or values-based premise on why the organization would provide this service. For example, faith-based entities provide services to the poor because they believe it is important to care for the less fortunate, but there are many potential values propositions that inspire individuals to serve low-income communities. Nonprofits as well must consider how the product or service will be provided (e.g., where and how). They too need to think about facilities and equipment or capital costs. Their ability to raise capital is severely constrained, how-ever, because the sources available to for-profit business are not typically available to nonprofits. Banks and investors are not nec-essarily interested in another "good cause." There are funds for nonprofits but the rationale for "investing" is different. It is ini-tially a moral or values proposition, not an opportunity to make money. Furthermore, the bottom line to determine success is usually quite a bit more difficult to determine. There is no single calculation to determine success. This simple example illustrates some of the issues managers confront when deciding what pro-grams to offer. To whom should the nonprofit provide services, and how is the organization going to sustain operations?

The government entity approaches the "opportunity" in a particular way as well. Government entities want to clarify the need and identify the characteristics of the potential recipients, and they are influenced by a political system that makes deter-minations about the appropriate role for any particular branch or division of government. Take for example a local city govern-ment that might empower a particular division to improve the condition of low-income community members. The scope of that authority is usually enacted in a political context. In other words, the city council has approved authority and budgetary alloca-tion to address this issue. Governments also must decide how to carry out the service. They may contract with an outside entity (for-profit or nonprofit) to provide these services or deliver the service themselves. If there are start-up costs, governments have access to debt and capital from the revenue of taxes and fees.

Again, these decisions are partially guided by political priorities. Governments are also constrained to provide services universally. So criteria to receive the hot food are determined based on some objective criteria (e.g., poverty line or disability status) that might or might not be present in nonprofits. Governments also have other roles in this area, such as creating and enforcing health safety rules and regulations. All businesses and nonprofits are concerned about quality and control issues, but only the government can authorize and sanction the existence of organizational entities.

Differences Between Organizational Types

This illustration of how businesses, government, and nonprofits approach the need for hot food in low-income communities reveals several features that differentiate the sectors (see **Table 1-1**). These features include differences related to ownership, revenue strategies, ability to acquire and use capital, the perspective of service beneficiaries, and the overall rationale for being. This last

TABLE 1-1 Fundamental Differences Between Organizational Types

Feature	For-Profit	Government	Nonprofit
Ownership	Individuals, partners, stockholders, etc.	Citizens/public	Nonspecific "public"
Revenue	Sales	Tax revenue, fees	Donated, contracted, or sales
Capital	Investors, public offering, or debt	Bonds (debt), tax revenue	Donated, limited debt
Customer or service beneficiary	Individual choice	Public or objective criteria	Some choice, but also nonprofit decides
Rationale for being/institutional logics	Market/economic	Public management or state bureaucracy	Values based or faith based

concept is sometimes referred to as "institutional logic." Institutional logic reflects the nature and character of the culture, identity, or ethos that guides decision making in the organization. The next sections discuss these differences in more detail.

Ownership

For businesses, ownership is the most obvious difference between the private and nonprofit sectors. In a business, either an individual or group owns the corporation. Decision making is driven by the underlying presumption that for-profit entities must generate a financial surplus that will at some point be returned to the owners. For government, ownership is more convoluted, but it is reasonable to consider that "the people" own the government. It is more problematic for decision making as the interests are much more complex than the financial bottom line in business. This is one role of elected officials, to interpret the interests of the "owners" and set parameters on operations. Nonprofits face similar ownership problems. Does the community own the nonprofit? Yes, to a degree nonprofits are quasi-public organizations that have public purposes and receive preferences that further recognize the public aspects of their work. In most instances, nonprofits are not anywhere near the size to suggest that they meet the needs of an entire community. Does the board or founder own the nonprofit? No, they serve as stewards of the mission and often are instrumental in the success of the organization, but they do not own the assets of the nonprofit. Those assets exist for public purposes and cannot be transferred to individuals for personal benefit. Consequently, nonprofits are often on the hunt to figure out to which "community" they are accountable. This principle underlies many nonprofit management challenges, because nonprofits don't know to whom they are accountable. They can prioritize different stakeholders but the clarity of "return on investment" is not easily determined. The ambiguity of ownership has significant implications for decision making and the systems of accountability that are created to guide operations (Connelly, Tihanyi, Certo, & Hitt, 2010).

Revenue

Revenue sources are another obvious difference among the three sectors. Businesses generate revenue through the provision of products or service. They make products or provide services, and consumers pay a premium that exceeds cost of production. Government can mandate its source of revenue through taxes or they can charge a fee. Most nonprofits can neither consistently charge a premium for services nor require support from the community. Nonprofits often provide services below cost, and as a result nonprofits seek funds based on the philanthropic interests of donors. Nonprofits rely on the good wishes of those in the community or they are contracted to fulfill a purpose predetermined by the government. Revenue is generated indirectly through services that meet needs in the community. Nonprofits can charge for services, but revenue generated through the direct provision of services often does not cover all the costs. If the organization is merely engaged in the provision of services for a fee, then the tax-exempt purposes are potentially in question. Why should an organization that generates all its revenue through payment from customers receive preferential treatment by the government unless the entity can clearly demonstrate charitable purposes? Excess revenue from services is not the only test because some industries do rely on fees for a significant portion of their revenue (e.g., education and health care), and a case is made that these entities provide public benefits in excess of the services fees charged. In summary, businesses primarily rely on revenue through sales, governments rely on revenue through taxation, and nonprofits rely on a mix of revenue streams that include fees for services, contracts with government entities, private foundation grants, and donations.

Capital

Access to capital is another fundamental difference among the sectors. Access to capital is a barrier to growth for all organizational entities. Nonprofits are the most disadvantaged in this area. Businesses access capital through investors or a public offering if they can merit that level of investment. Investors are engaged because they anticipate gaining returns from profits that are generated by the expanded ability to provide services or develop products. Businesses can also access capital through debt and bonds. The funds are loaned with the expectation that additional capital provides the capacity to increase revenue and profits, which form the basis of the arrangement. Businesses can also retain profits over time to build capital assets that can be used to expand the business. Governments can access capital through the bond markets because of the reliable tax revenue. They are constrained by the necessity to place large bond measures on the ballot and as a result must demonstrate the political as well as social benefit. Government expenditures on large capital expenses are often justified through the expectation that improved infrastructure facilitates business and residential development, which generates more revenue. Opportunities to raise capital are different for nonprofit managers. Nonprofits rely on the good will of donors to "invest" in their activities, but those "investments" do not generate financial returns to the investor. Rather, nonprofits must demonstrate a purpose or value that justifies the contributions. It is one of the most significant constraints for nonprofit managers as they try to expand services. Increased capital expands the ability to provide services but does not guarantee increased revenue. In most cases, the returns from investment are not financial. There is increased pressure from ROI donors to consider how investments in nonprofit infrastructures can generate quantifiable returns, but in most instances these returns are distant and difficult to quantify beyond a larger number of individuals served.

Citizen, Service Beneficiary, or Customer

Another difference has traditionally been the way individuals interact with the entities. In a for-profit context, the interaction is typically guided by exchange. There are exceptions, but in principle individuals engage with the business because they want what the business has to offer, and often they have choices concerning with which company they interact. That is, there is competition between companies to get customers. If you don't like Domino's Pizza you can go down the road and get pizza from Papa John's. With the government that is not the case. All citizens are required to register a vehicle to drive on public roads, and we are required to go to the Department of Motor Vehicles. The concept of customer choice is pervasive through capitalistic economies, and we have often grown to expect competition and choice. As citizens we have responsibilities toward the government, and we are accountable for our actions through the legal system. As citizens our engagement with government is complicated by the multiple roles governments play in our lives. For nonprofits, service recipients sometimes have a choice, but often there may be no other option. Consider for instance a program that delivers meals to homebound individuals. The meals are often delivered at very low or no cost to the recipient. There are typically more individuals who need the meals than the agency can accommodate, and there is very rarely an alternative service. Why would two organizations compete to give away meals? They don't. They typically coordinate their services and try to cover as many families as they can. If a recipient doesn't like the meals, they can complain, try to work with the system, or not take the meal. Related is the way different organizations approach the customer, the citizen, or the beneficiary. This will be discussed in more detail, but there is reason to suspect that many nonprofits (and governments) are not as directly aware or sensitive to service-recipient interests. This is true partly because nonprofits have conflicting demands that also influence how services are provided (e.g., funders).

Rationale for Being: The Influence of Institutional Logics

Institutional logics are cognitive frames that are broadly accepted by organizational stakeholders. These frames influence structures, guide behavior, and constrain options (Thornton & Ocasio, 2008). Institutional logics reflect the accepted way to do business in the organization. DiMaggio (1991) explored the different logics that exist in art museums, one related to artistic concerns of creativity and freedom of expression and the other to administrative concerns related to institutional sustainability.

Stone (1996) also provides a case study to explore how different institutional logics developed in a social service agency that grew from a small grassroots entity into a multimillion-dollar enterprise that was contracting with the state to provide social services. These conflicting logics ultimately lead to a split in the organization. There is growing research on hybrid organizations that recognize the need to understand and coordinate different logics. For example, microfinance organizations often have to balance the development (nonprofit) logic with the banking or capitalistic logic (Battilana & Dorado, 2010). While it is not possible to detail all the institutional logics that operate in organizations, this discussion recognizes some dominant logics that seem to compete for managers' attention. Identifying "pure" institutional logics and the influence on managing organizations is potentially useful (see **Table 1-2**). Broad metaphilosophies are often, although not exclusively, aligned with legal classifications.

Idealized institutional logics are rarely "pure," and the variations are complex as they are enacted in different organizations (Thornton & Ocasio, 2008). This is true in all types of organizations but it seems particularly true in nonprofits that exist to enact a wide range of philosophical purposes (Mullins, 2006) and confront complex resource challenges. A *market or economic logic*

TABLE 1-2   Idealized Institutional Logics

Features	Market/ Economic	Government/ State System	Values
Purpose	Profit accumulation	Creating and maintaining social systems	Philosophical and social
Strategy frame	Market share and dominance	Public benefit	Impact
Power and authority	Financial	Political	Social
Capital investment	Increased production and operations	Social infrastructure	Stability
Structural frame	Innovation and opportunity	Hierarchy and control	Inclusive and decentralized

suggests that the primary purpose of the organization is financial, which is enacted through profit and wealth accumulation. *Government and state systems* are primarily about creating and maintaining social systems that provide stability to society. A *values orientation* presupposes that the organization exists to promote a philosophical ideal that is often articulated in the mission of the organization. As a result of these different logics, managers make strategic choices and respond to different sources of power. These idealized institutional logics capture the rationale and purpose for organizational actions. The purpose is going to guide all kinds of organizational activities, for example, how funds are invested. Organizations with a market and economic orientation are going to invest in capital to improve production and achieve efficiencies. Government and state systems invest in public infrastructure. Values-focused organizations often invest to increase or obtain stability. For example, nonprofits build endowments (funds held and invested) to ensure that the organization can exist in perpetuity. These are idealized types and there is significant variety and rarely a pure system in an organization.

For-profit entities exist with a market or economic logic. They exist because they are able to provide a service or develop a product and then extract a profit from the exchange relationship. There are for-profit businesses that exist with high ideals and principles. For instance, Tom's Shoes ("TOMS Company Overview," n.d.) has a "buy-one, give-one" principle. For every shoe sold, Tom's Shoes provides a pair of shoes to an underprivileged child in a developing country. They sell one pair of shoes for a premium, and part of the surplus capital is used to provide a second pair of shoes to someone else. They are selling shoes *and* the philanthropic value of the product. It is a fascinating model and holds significant promise. Nevertheless, they have a superordinate proposition that requires the organization to generate sufficient profit to afford their charitable activities. Consumers have to be willing to purchase the shoes for a price that covers production costs and provides sufficient surplus to fulfill charitable and investor concerns. This is recognized as the logic of the market and includes wealth accumulation, ownership, competition, and efficiency as part of the system (Bryson, Crosby, & Stone, 2006).

Government entities are different because they exist for a broad range of public purposes. Some have described this as the state bureaucratic system or new public management. Bozeman (2007) discusses a spectrum that encapsulates economic influences on one axis and political influences and authority on another. This model illustrates that governments tend to be less economically based and are more responsive to political authority. Governments are about regulating markets and providing infrastructure (e.g., roads and bridges) in ways that are not addressed by either sector. Government entities are most directly influenced by the political context to achieve public value. This is characterized by elections that instill different leadership with different priorities. These priorities are translated into the other sectors through regulations or laws, but government entities enact those priorities and are constrained by political priorities in a way that is distinctive to that sector. Governments exist for broad public purposes, and choices are informed by political influences that are institutionalized into bureaucracies and legislation.

Nonprofits are heterogeneous entities operating in multiple industries, with a myriad of purposes. It is difficult to succinctly define the logic of nonprofits. As is the case with the name, considering what nonprofits are *not* is a starting point. There is a fairly identifiable logic toward the market and a second that reflects state bureaucracies. Scholars have described the remaining logics as "professional," "religious," "family," or "democratic," any of which might reflect some of how nonprofits approach their work. The logic of a nonprofit has to reflect a charitable purpose in some way. This purpose is captured in the organization's mission and might operate independent of economic or political influences. These charitable purposes are expressed through the mission and articulated in values that form the core of why the organization exists. The nature and character of those values reflect why the nonprofit exists. The translation of values into management practices is difficult and influenced by both economic and political forces.

Competing institutional logics are the reality for most managers. An example from health care illustrates the implications of different institutional logics. Healthcare organizations struggle with the balance of business/economic demands and clinical/service demands. An interesting illustration was revealed in an article exploring why healthcare costs were nearly twice as expensive in some regions of the country and yet health outcomes were not more impressive (Gawande, 2009). The author compared two regions with similar populations and health concerns: McAllen and El Paso, Texas. Both are border towns with similar population demographics and yet have significantly different per-patient Medicare costs. Gawande systematically reviews a series of explanations on why this might be the case. He concludes that there is a different philosophy about how to provide healthcare services in the two regions. In McAllen, there is a pervasive economic orientation. In other words, there was a subtle inclination to maximize revenue from the services provided. This resulted in extra tests or more aggressive utilization of advanced medical services. In El Paso, where costs were lower, that culture didn't seem as prevalent. It is appropriate to avoid judgment and highlight the distinctive decision-making styles. Health care is complex and it is not feasible to articulate all the subtleties of that industry. Economic realities are hard and fast and it is intriguing to consider why "softer" clinical values might rule when financial incentives are alluring.

There must be some system in place to protect the tendency to exploit a profit when markets are unable to control this behavior. Pure market forces can constrain excessive profits through competition and consumer choice. When those forces are muted, one of the fundamental challenges for nonprofit managers is creating and reinforcing organizational systems that support a values perspective (Bushouse, 2011). A nonprofit should create structures and institutional logics that promote impact and social value over financial returns (Bernardin, 1999; Place, 2007).

Summary of the Differences Between Organizational Types

Nonprofits are ownerless, rely on multiple revenue sources, and struggle to raise sufficient capital to achieve public benefits. Selecting and prioritizing the beneficiary and customer can also be a challenge. Mission becomes a defining rationale for these organizations because it is one way to solidify what they are doing. The mission distills the primary institutional logic and purpose of the organization. The mission is fundamental to distinguishing the nonprofit and is more than a marketing tool; it is central to defining the organization's identity. Without a hard and fast financial bottom line, which reflects an economic logic, nonprofits are relegated to utilizing performance indicators that are more elusive. Before exploring these management challenges and opportunities in detail, it is instructive to understand some theoretical explanations of why nonprofits exist.

Why Nonprofits Exist

A prominent explanation for why the nonprofit organizational form exists is called "market failure" (Jegers, 2008; Steinberg, 2006). In perfect markets, organizations compete and customers make choices. Through this process of competition, customer choice, and exchange customers get what they want/need and businesses generate profit. Markets work well for private goods (provide benefit to individuals exclusively) but less effectively for public goods (provide benefit to all with inability to exclude). Markets often fail to provide public goods because it is difficult for businesses to extract profits. If businesses are unable to extract profit from exchange opportunities then they are unlikely to provide that service. This is true irrespective of the demand or need for services. If businesses can't develop a model that allows them to provide the product *and* extract profit they are going to exit the field. Put another way, a hungry person does not guarantee an ability to make a profit. There are three types of market failures that are relevant to this discussion (see **Table 1-3**).

The first aspect of market failure relates to the idea that even though a community may "need" hot, prepared food, businesses may be unwilling to provide those goods or services. The market has failed to provide a particular level of service (under provision), which results in an unacceptable social condition. "Unacceptable social condition" is a normative and moral judgment, which shifts

TABLE 1-3 Theories of the Three Failures

Market "Failures"	Definitions	Government Response	Nonprofit Response/ Challenges
Under provision	Need exists but market does not provide	Direct provision or contract out	Provide services, difficult to discriminate needy
Contract failure	Information asymmetry	Regulate or educate	Sorting or "creaming" profitable clients
Exclusion limitations	Public/collective goods	Mandate or subsidize	Price discrimination

Data from Steinberg, R. (2006). Economic theories of nonprofit organizations. In W. W. Powell & R. Steinberg (Eds.), *The nonprofit sector: A research handbook* (2nd ed., pp. 117–139). New Haven, CT: Yale University.

and alters over time and societies. So does the method to address that social condition. Some societies decide that government entities are best able to fill that need, while others rely on family or philanthropic systems to fulfill that need. It is in this ambiguous moral and social space that nonprofits exist. The shifting conception of what is unacceptable is a fundamental aspect of nonprofit management. The manager's ability to articulate the social condition and the organization's ability to address that condition are the basis of philanthropic arguments. Tapping into the moral sense of unacceptable social conditions is often the basis of philanthropic requests.

An alternative explanation is called contract failure. This situation exists when services are too complex for consumers to effectively understand quality and cost. This is called information asymmetry, which means that the service provider knows more than the customer regarding quality, and the customer does not have an easy method to gather sufficient information to judge the appropriate level and type of service. Two examples are buying a used car and health care. When buying a used car it is often very difficult to accurately know everything regarding the condition of the automobile, and often the dealership (or former owner) is more knowledgeable regarding the condition of the automobile. There are a couple of solutions to this information challenge.

The buyer can request guarantees and warranties that provide assurance of quality. There are also modest methods to determine quality through a thorough inspection of the vehicle and access to historical records regarding the automobile. Through these efforts consumers are potentially protected from a lack of information, which might be exploited to gain excess profit. Government regulations have been developed to help protect consumers regarding poor quality cars (e.g., lemon laws). Health care is a much more complex service, and the idea of looking under the hood to determine quality is more difficult. The basis of decision making in health care is often framed as a matter of trust in the provider. It is very difficult to ascertain sufficient information and to fully understand options. In this case the nonprofit form exists to remove incentives to gain excess profit and support the trust relationship. By limiting the benefits an organization can extract from the exchange, the patient is hopefully protected, which is why the example discussed by Dr. Gawande (2009) is particularly interesting. Government regulation is instrumental in working to reduce information asymmetry problems.

The third failure is more difficult to explain, but reflects the limited ability to exclude participants when services are provided (exclusion failure). The most obvious example is national defense. It is not possible to protect some members of society and not protect others. It is impossible to exclude, so everyone must pay and in principle everyone benefits from those services. Often called a public good (Hess & Ostrom, 2003; Ostrom, 2003), these goods are typically provided by government entities. Nonprofits also provide some services that are more "public." Because it is difficult to discriminate participation or extract a profit, for-profit entities are reluctant to provide these services. Open space preserves and public art might be examples of elements that are provided by nonprofits, and enjoyed (theoretically) by everyone. Governments might incentivize nonprofits to provide these services because they provide public value. Land preservation provides aesthetic and environmental value that is available to society irrespective of who actually paid to preserve the land. Nonprofits might enact various methods to exclude access to these services so as to extract fees. For example, it is not uncommon that public space preserves might request donations or fees for entrance, but these fees rarely compensate for the cost of acquiring significant tracks of land.

This discussion recognizes that there is a continuum of goods and services provided and needed in society. Governments, businesses, and nonprofits negotiate and operate to address the production of these goods and services. Purely public goods are difficult to extract a profit from and are often provided by government entities (e.g., national defense). Conversely, purely private goods are amenable to extracting profit and so are often related to businesses and market economies (e.g., cars). There is, however, a whole range of goods and services that are not purely public or purely private. Health care, higher education, and numerous others have public value but also private purposes. For example, as a student gains an advanced degree, society benefits indirectly through an increasingly educated populous, while individuals (the students) benefit through the enhanced capacity to earn an income. Thinking about these explanations of why nonprofits exist suggests a number of roles or functions for nonprofits in society.

Functions of Nonprofit Organizations

It is possible to identify a few key functions of nonprofit organizations, especially in relation to government entities and business. As we discussed, there is a fundamental difference in the rationale for these organizations, and nonprofits are instrumental in meeting social needs when markets and businesses fail to provide needed services. Although there might be overlap in these functions across the different sectors of society, it is useful to consider five general roles that nonprofit organizations perform and explain how these roles are enacted (Anheier, 2005; Boris, 2006):

- Service provider
- Social and collective role
- Values guardian role (preservation)
- Innovator or vanguard role (creative and innovative)
- Advocacy role

A widely recognized function for nonprofit entities is that of *service provider.* They provide services to meet the needs and interests of individuals, groups, or communities. They might price these services in a way similar to for-profit corporations or they might operate in failed markets, which require donated or philanthropic support. Hansmann (1980) talks about donative nonprofits and commercial nonprofits, the latter of which are more dependent on fees to support service delivery. The more private the service (e.g., childcare, higher education), the more likely the organization is going to be able to charge a fee. Nonprofits commonly deliver social services the government identifies as useful or necessary but that it is unable/unwilling to provide itself. Nonprofits also provide services that are guided by private interests (e.g., religious schools). Ideological perspectives guide engagement of a number of providers. The motivation and the range of services are diverse (see the following discussion on size and scope) and reflective of the pluralistic society.

The *collective or social role* relates to the idea that nonprofits are an ideal form to help organize like-minded individuals. Sometimes these are formed as member benefit organizations (501[c][6]), or they may be organized as 501(c)(3) organizations that have dual purposes to provide member benefits and public value. Member associations and country clubs are examples of member controlled groups that are "owned" collectively by the members, and as a result only members benefit from the services and bear the costs. Governments might be motivated to provide incentives for these organizations to exist as they provide social value such as building social capital and potentially mitigating social needs. There are a number of public benefit nonprofits that are actively building social capital and these activities are reflective of the social roles nonprofits perform.

Another important function of nonprofit organizations is that of *values guardian and preservation.* Nonprofits are instrumental in the preservation of social, cultural, and historical artifacts. Religious organizations and faith-based providers promote and support values or religious beliefs. These values form the basis of their activities. They do not always have to be religious values. Many nonprofits are organized to promote ethical principles or standards that are defined by members. Cultural values are also nurtured and preserved by nonprofit organizations. Historical and environmental preservation are common domains for nonprofits to operate. They can be instrumental in highlighting value and holding these goods for the common benefit.

The fourth role is that of *innovator* or *vanguard*. This recognizes the ability of nonprofits to experiment with social innovations and invest in research and creative activities that are not dependent on market forces. Other sectors also support innovation, but nonprofits do have a role in innovation, especially social innovation (Anheier, 2005). Research and development initiatives might operate independent of market forces so as to free the research from personal preferences and biases. Healthcare research that seeks preventive measures, for example, might need public support because the direct market benefit is difficult to determine.

The final area is classified as the *advocacy* role. (Kramer, 1979, 1981). Nonprofits enact or promote concepts and ideas in a political and social context. Advocacy efforts are about coalescing like-minded individuals to influence social and institutional power elements. Through collective organizing, advocacy efforts highlight disparities in society so as to alter social systems. Nonprofit organizations are an appropriate organizing form as the incentives for engagement are increased social influence and not the accumulation of capital or, necessarily, the provision of direct goods and services to garner profit.

Size and Scope of the Nonprofit Sector

The number of nonprofit organizations continues to grow with an estimated 60% growth over the last 10 years to a total of over 1.5 million tax-exempt entities in the United States in 2012 (Roeger, Blackwood, & Pettijohn, 2012). This growth is not limited to the United States (Salamon, 1994) and does not seem to be abating. Reviewing the facts and figures for nonprofit entities in the United States provides a sense of the variety of entities that operate as nonprofits. This information is drawn from federal records and is compiled by the National Center for Charitable Statistics, a program of the Urban Institute. Tax-exempt entities in the United States are classified as 501(c) corporations. Of the 1.5 million tax-exempt entities in 2012, the vast majority are classified as 501(c)(3) charities or foundations, encompassing about 70% of the total (over 1 million). During that same time period, the number of 501(c) organizations in the other categories (e.g., labor unions, civic leagues, social clubs, and business associations) reduced in size by almost 8%. There is some concern that just about any group can get themselves recognized as a 501(c)(3) entity (Strom, 2009). The benefits of registering as a nonprofit include limited liability to taxes (e.g., most notably, property and income), but also the ability to accept donations that are deducted from personal income taxes. It is estimated that the $300 billion donated to charities in 2009 cost the U.S. government about $50 billion in revenue (Strom, 2009). Of the 1 million 501(c)(3) nonprofits, just a fraction actually file or report activities to the IRS (about 40% or just under a half million entities). Nonprofits with annual revenue less than $50,000 (prior to 2011 it was $25,000) are exempt from reporting (although some do file). Religious congregations (and many of the affiliated entities) are also exempt from reporting, although it is estimated that about half of the congregations in the United States register with the IRS.

The National Taxonomy of Exempt Entities (NTEE) identifies broad categories that cluster organizations by industry. There are four levels to the NTEE system. There are 10 broad categories (education, health, etc.), which can be subdivided into 26 major groups (see **Table 1-6** at the end of this chapter). Major categories are further subdivided into specific activity areas. For example, education is divided into higher education, secondary education, and so on. These subcategories are further subdivided into specific types of organizations. For example, higher education is divided by different types of colleges and universities (e.g., junior college, undergraduate). The final set of classifications defines specific activities carried out by the organization. These categorizations are useful for identifying other providers or potential funding sources. Nonprofits can also define their role in relation to the community they serve.

Using the IRS 990 Form (2009) and the NTEE classifications, it is possible to describe the size and scope of the sector. This includes the number of registered entities, the volume of financial activities (i.e., revenue and expenses), and the assets that the sector holds. **Table 1-4** details information on eleven categories, which include two significant subcategories (hospitals and higher education). Human services is the largest category, with just under 25% of the 501(c)(3) organizations classified as related to providing human services (265,951 entities). Religious-related organizations are the next largest category, reflecting just under 20% of the

TABLE 1-4 Major Subsectors of the Charitable (501[c][3]) Nonprofit Sector in the United States

Type	Frequency	Percentage of Total Number	Assets in Millions	Percentage of Total Assets
Arts, Culture	100,449	9.0%	$98,330.5	3.1%
Education				
Higher education	4229	0.4%	$552,073.5	17.5%
Other education	150,923	13.5%	$308,475.6	9.8%
Environment related	46,673	4.2%	$32,988.3	1.0%
Foundations	148,399	13.3%	$686,075.9	21.8%
Health				
Hospitals	6399	0.6%	$744,144.8	23.6%
Other health	73,392	6.6%	$254,062.4	8.1%
Human service	265,951	23.8%	$271,873.1	8.6%
International	15,089	1.4%	$31,336.1	1.0%
Religion	217,130	19.5%	$25,705.3	0.8%
Other charities	87,371	7.8%	$143,796.7	4.6%
Total	1,116,005	100.0%	$3,148,862.2	100.0%

Data from Internal Revenue Service. (2009, October). Exempt organizations business master file. The Urban Institute, National Center for Charitable Statistics. Retrieved from http://nccsdataweb.urban.org/

organizations (217,130 entities). Education-related entities and foundations are the next two largest categories, each accounting for about 13% of the 501(c)(3) organizations in the United States.

In relation to assets it is another story entirely. Reflecting less than 1% of the organizations (6399 entities) hospitals (including primary treatment centers) hold almost $700 billion in assets (23.6% of total assets). Institutions of higher education are second with a little under $600 billion in assets (4229 entities; less than 0.5% holding 17.5% of the assets), and foundations are third with over a half billion in assets, just over 20% of the total assets across 148,399 entities. These three subsectors combined hold about $2 trillion of the $3 trillion in assets held by 501(c)(3) organizations in the United States. The remaining $1 trillion in assets is scattered across a range of nonprofit organizations, which include the arts, human services, recreation, environment, research, and others. The vast majority of nonprofits are small; a few are quite large with significant assets and influence.

This text emphasizes those organizations that are engaged in activities to achieve public benefits. As the profile of the sector reveals, this entails a wide variety of industries, activities, and functions. This includes services (soup kitchen, counseling), advocacy activities, community building, and values preservation. Nonprofits operate in a wide range of industries and utilize a variety of activities to create public value. The character of the sector provides a common thread that informs management choices and challenges. The next section introduces organizational life stages as an additional consideration that constrains and informs strategic decision making.

Organizational Life Cycle Stages

Organizational life cycle stages refers to levels of development and professionalization in an organization. Organizations at different stages are going to present different managerial challenges (Mintzberg, 1978; Quinn & Cameron, 1983; Sirmon, Hitt, Ireland, & Gilbert, 2011). Although these life stages are not linear and organizations may remain in some stages indefinitely, it can be of value to consider some attributes of different stages of development (see **Table 1-5**). There is no universal agreement on what each "stage" entails, but in principle there is recognition that organizations tend to start as relatively informal entities that are based upon ideas or dreams and then evolve and develop through increasing levels of formalization and potentially growth (Hasenfeld & Schmid, 1989; Stevens, 2001). During the start-up phase, ideas and potential tend to guide activities. Sometimes it is the inspiration of a creative founder (Schein, 1995) or a small group. During the early start-up stage, the organization and leadership continue to create and define the purposes they hope to achieve

TABLE 1-5 Developmental Life Cycle Stages

	Start-up	Collective Stage	Formalization	Elaboration
Features	Idea based, innovative, and entrepreneurial	Bringing together support	Building increased professionalization	Expanding and growing
Strategic challenges	Finding stakeholder support	Fostering engagement	Increased effectiveness and efficiency	Strategically growing and expanding impact
Resources	Limited	Increased stability	Stabilized and diversified, increased capacity	Replication of resource portfolio to support growth
Public benefits	Potential for impact	Limited impact, increased production output	Consistency and expanding performance impact	Application of intervention model to more contexts
Structure	Unstructured, informal, emergent	Semistructured	Increased formal structures, accountability	Replication and expanding, increased specialization
Capacity	Limited	Specialized	Broad-based	Ability to replicate and grow

(Alexander, 2000). The structures are informal with few managerial processes. A key strategic challenge during this phase is gaining support from stakeholders.

As the organization moves to the second (collective) stage, administrative practices are developing and management roles are forming (Smith, Mitchell, & Summer, 1985). There is still tremendous reliance on a small core or even a single leader who helps define and enact the organization's purposes. The role of these founders or entrepreneurs is significant and often marks the nature and character of the development. If the organization can create a reasonable system to generate revenue through this second stage it is possible to further refine and "professionalize" the practices.

The third stage of formalization is characterized by increased stability and a broadening of involvement by participants at all levels of the organization. There is an increased stability that provides the opportunity and need for increased communication and coordination. The organization should be able to demonstrate consistent public benefit value. What was done hastily is refined and crafted to increase efficiencies. One of the challenges during this phase is to retain opportunities for innovation while creating systems and control mechanisms that are viable for the organization's future. There is also a need for long-term planning. Transitions in leadership during these early stages can have significant influence on organizational survival. Transitions in leadership are tricky, especially as long-time founders seek to redefine their roles. The fourth stage (elaboration) seeks to expand and grow the organization so as to increase impact. A significant challenge is the ability to replicate the resource portfolio so as to support growth and expansion.

Organizations can function for quite some time in the intermediate stages as systems are created to sustain the organization and long-term plans and strategies are enacted. Organizational decline is possible anywhere along the spectrum. An inability to address the significant strategic issues can result in decline and ultimately failure. If the organization experiences significant changes in the environment or there has not been significant development of leadership and management systems, then the organization can begin to experience organizational decline (Bailey & Grochau, 1993; Smith et al., 1985). Decline is marked by significant decreases in revenue and a tendency to rely on prior organizational practices that may or may not reflect current operating conditions. The inability to reassess market and resource opportunities ultimately can lead to decline and closure. If, however, the organization can reposition and reinvent practices, then they can experience growth and stability. At each stage, managers are challenged to define issues, negotiate resource demands, and coordinate activities. The specific risks and challenges are different, and successful choices are dependent on understanding the organizational demands reflected in different stages of organizational development.

Conclusion

There are over 1.5 million nonprofit organizations recognized by the Internal Revenue Service in the United States. That number has grown by over 60% in the last 10 years. The growth in the United States is paralleled by amazing growth internationally. Both developed and developing countries have experienced significant growth of social sector (nongovernmental) nonprofit organizations. These organizations operate between economically oriented enterprises and state bureaucracies. They exist to fulfill public purposes but are private entities created by individuals and groups to achieve objectives defined by those individuals. Those purposes are constrained by external influences. Nonprofit managers need to interpret those influences and design systems that exploit their capabilities to achieve mission objectives.

This text is about strategic choices managers have to make regarding social need, operational capacity, and accountability. Nonprofits face unique management challenges that require sophisticated skills and capabilities. **Figure 1-2** depicts the topics covered in the text. Chapter 2 presents a strategic management framework that helps decision makers consider the various environmental forces working on the organization and the potential response options. The opportunities experienced

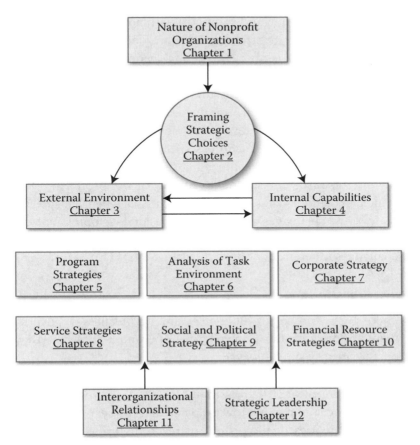

FIGURE 1-2 Strategic Management Topics

by nonprofit managers are complex and multifaceted. The text recognizes multiple operating contexts and defines the features and response options managers should consider to be successful. Chapter 3 introduces key facets of the external environment with particular attention to the task environment. Chapter 4 discusses internal organizational attributes and how managers need to marshal these resources to operate effectively. From this basis, Chapters 5 through 7 review strategic formation options. Chapter 5 considers how managers develop program-level activities to achieve public benefits. Chapter 6 reviews techniques to analyze the task environment, with particular attention to the nature of cooperation and competition in nonprofits. Chapter 7 introduces corporate strategy that considers decision making from the perspective of organizational leaders and the board of directors. The second half of the text delves into tactics managers can implement to be successful. Chapter 8 reviews program logic models and how this framework helps strengthen service strategies utilized to achieve public benefits. Chapter 9 reviews tactics that are useful to address social and political contexts, which are vital elements in the public benefit domain. Chapter 10 reviews resource development options for nonprofits and key principles of fundraising and relationship management. Chapter 11 reviews the challenges and opportunities of developing interorganizational alliances. Chapter 12 details the strategic leadership challenges inherent in nonprofit organizations.

Discussion Questions

1. There are a number of differences among businesses, governments, and nonprofits. Can you think of examples of where they operate in very similar ways?
2. How would you distill the competing logics that operate in nonprofit organizations? What can managers do to reinforce and support decision making toward particular frames?
3. How do theories of nonprofit organizations impact decisions managers make about services and who receives those services?
4. Compare and contrast the functions of nonprofits to the economic theories about nonprofit organizations.
5. What are the career and managerial implications for such a diverse, growing nonprofit sector?

References

Alexander, J. (2000). Adaptive strategies of nonprofit human service organizations in an era of devolution and new public management. *Nonprofit Management and Leadership, 10*(3), 287–303.

Anheier, H. K. (2005). *Nonprofit organizations: Theory, management, policy*. New York, NY: Routledge.

Bailey, D., & Grochau, K. E. (1993). Aligning leadership needs to the organizational stage of development. *Administration in Social Work, 17*(1), 23–45.

Battilana, J., & Dorado, S. (2010). Building sustainable hybrid organizations: The case of commercial microfinance organizations. *Academy of Management Journal, 53*(6), 1419–1440.

Bernardin, J. C. (1999). Making the case for not-for-profit health care. In *Celebrating the ministry of healing* (pp. 83–93). St. Louis, MO: Catholic Health Association of the United States.

Boris, E. (2006). Nonprofit organizations in a democracy—Roles and responsibilities. In E. Boris & C. E. Steuerle (Eds.), *Nonprofit and government: Collaboration and conflict* (pp. 1–35). Washington, DC: Urban Institute.

Bozeman, B. (2007). *Public values and public interest: Counterbalancing economic individualism.* Washington, DC: Georgetown University Press.

Brickson, S. (2007). Organizational identity orientation: The genesis of the role of the firm and distinct forms of social value. *The Academy of Management Review ARCHIVE, 32*(3), 864–888.

Brody, E. (1996). Agents without principals: The economic convergence of the nonprofit and for-profit organizational forms. *New York Law School Law Review, 40*(3), 457–536.

Bryson, J. M., Crosby, B. C., & Stone, M. M. (2006). The design and implementation of cross-sector collaborations: Propositions from the literature. *Public Administration Review, 66*, 44–55.

Bushouse, B. K. (2011). Governance structures: Using IAD to understand variation in service delivery for club goods with information asymmetry. *Policy Studies Journal, 39*(1), 105–119.

Connelly, B. L., Tihanyi, L., Certo, S. T., & Hitt, M. A. (2010). Marching to the beat of different drummers: Ther influence of institutional owners on competitive actions. *Academy of Management Journal, 53*(4), 723–742.

DiMaggio, P. J. (1991). Constructing an organizational field as a professional project: US art museums, 1920–1940. In W. W. Powell & P. J. DiMaggio (Eds.), The new institutionalism in organizational analysis (pp. 267–292). Chicago, IL: University of Chicago.

Gawande, A. (2009, June 1). The cost conundrum. *The New Yorker*. Retrieved from http://www.newyorker.com/reporting /2009/06/01/090601fa_fact_gawande

Hansmann, H. (1980). The role of the nonprofit enterprise. *Yale Law Journal, 89*, 835–901.

Hasenfeld, Y., & Schmid, H. (1989). The life cycle of human service organizations. In Y. Hasenfeld (Ed.), *Administrative leadership in the social services: The next challenge* (pp. 243). Binghamton, NY: Hawthorne Press.

Hess, C., & Ostrom, E. (2003). Ideas, artifacts, and facilities: Information as a common-pool resource. *Law and Contemporary problems, 66*(111), 111–145.

Internal Revenue Service. (2009, October). Exempt organizations business master file. The Urban Institute, National Center for Charitable Statistics. Retrieved from http://nccsdataweb .urban.org/

Jegers, M. (2008). *Managerial economics of nonprofit organizations*. New York, NY: Routledge.

Kramer, R. M. (1979). Voluntary agencies in the welfare state: An analysis of the vanguard role. *Journal of Social Policy, 8*(04), 473–488.

Kramer, R. M. (1981). *Voluntary agencies in the welfare state*. Los Angeles: University of California Press.

Mintzberg, H. (1978). Patterns in strategy formation. *Management Science, 24*(9), 934–948.

Mullins, D. (2006). Competing institutional logics? Local accountability and scale and efficiency in an expanding non-profit housing sector. *Public Policy and Administration, 21*(3), 6–24.

National taxonomy of exempt entities. National Center for Charitable Statistics. Retrieved from http://nccs.urban.org /classification/NTEE.cfm

Ostrom, E. (2003). How types of goods and property rights jointly affect collective action. *Journal of Theoretical Politics, 15*(3), 239–270.

Place, M. D. (2007). *The importance of not for profit health care*. Unpublished speech presented at the 13th Annual Conference on Catholic Sponsorship. Loyola University, Chicago.

Quinn, R. E., & Cameron, K. (1983). Organizational life cycles and shifting criteria of effectiveness: Some preliminary evidence. *Management Science, 29*(1), 33–51.

Roeger, K. L., Blackwood, A., & Pettijohn, S. L. (2012). *The nonprofit almanac 2012.* Washington, DC: Urban Institute Press.

Salamon, L. M. (1994). The rise of the nonprofit sector. *Foreign Affairs, 73*(4), 109–122.

Schein, E. H. (1995). The role of the founder in creating organizational culture. *Family Business Review, 8*(3), 221–238.

Sirmon, D. G., Hitt, M. A., Ireland, R. D., & Gilbert, B. A. (2011). Resource orchestration to create competitive advantage: Breadth, depth, and life cycle effects. *Journal of Management, 37*(5), 1390–1412.

Smith, K. G., Mitchell, T. R., & Summer, C. E. (1985). Top level management priorities in different stages of organizational life cycle. *Academy of Management Journal, 28*(4), 799–820.

Steinberg, R. (2006). Economic theories of nonprofit organizaions. In W. W. Powell & R. Steinberg (Eds.), *The nonprofit sector: A research handbook* (2nd ed., pp. 117–139). New Haven, CT: Yale University.

Stevens, S. K. (2001). *Nonprofit lifecycles: Stage-based wisdom for nonprofit capacity.* Long Lake, MN: Stagewise Enterprises.

Stone, M. M. (1996). Competing contexts: The evolution of a nonprofit organization's governance system in multiple environments. *Administration & Society, 28*(1), 61.

Strom, S. (2009, December 9). Charities rise, costing U.S. billions in tax breaks. *New York Times,* p. 3.

Thornton, P. H., & Ocasio, W. (2008). Institutional logics. In R. Greenwood, C. Oliver, K. Sahlin, & R. Suddaby (Eds.), *Sage handbook of organizational institutionalism* (pp. 99–129). Thousand Oaks, CA: Sage.

TOMS company overview. Retrieved from http://www.toms.com/corporate-info

Weerawardena, J., McDonald, R. E., & Mort, G. S. (2010). Sustainability of nonprofit organizations: An empirical investigation. *Journal of World Business, 45*(4), 346–356.

Appendix

TABLE 1-6 Public Benefit Industries of the Nonprofit Sector

Broad Categories	Major Groups	Activity Areas
Arts, culture, and humanities	Arts, culture, and humanities	Arts and culture
		Media and communication
		Visual arts
		Museums
		Performing arts
		Humanities
		Historical organizations
Education	Education	Elementary and secondary schools
		Vocational and technical
		Higher education
		Graduate and professional
		Adult education
		Libraries
		Student services
		Educational services
Environment and animals	Environment	Pollution abatement and control
		Natural resources conservation
		Botanical, horticultural
		Environmental beautification
		Environmental education
	Animal related	Animal protection
		Wildlife preservation
		Veterinary services
		Zoos and aquariums
Health	Health care	Hospitals
		Ambulatory and primary care
		Reproductive health care
		Rehabilitative care
		Heath support
		Public health
		Health (general)
		Nursing

Broad Categories	Major Groups	Activity Areas
	Mental health and crisis	Substance abuse dependency and prevention Mental health treatment Hot lines and crisis intervention Counseling
	Diseases, disorders, and medical disciplines	Birth defects and genetic diseases Cancer Diseases of specific organs Nerve, muscle, and bone diseases Digestive diseases Specifically named diseases Medical disciplines
	Medical research	Birth defects and genetic research Cancer research Diseases of specific organs research Nerve, muscle, and bone research Allergy-related research Digestive diseases research Specifically named diseases research Medical disciplines research
Human Services	Crime and legal related	Crime prevention Correctional facilities Rehabilitation services Administration of justice Law enforcement Protection against abuse Legal services
	Employment	Employment preparation Vocational rehabilitation Labor unions
	Food, agriculture, and nutrition	Agriculture programs Food programs Nutrition Home economics

(*continues*)

TABLE 1-6 Public Benefit Industries of the Nonprofit Sector (*continued*)

Broad Categories	Major Groups	Activity Areas
	Housing and shelter	Housing development
		Housing search assistance
		Temporary housing
		Homeowners associations
		Housing support
	Public safety, disaster preparedness, and relief	Disaster preparedness and relief
		Safety education
		Public safety benevolent association
	Recreation and sports	Camps
		Physical fitness and community recreation facilities
		Sports associations and training facilities
		Recreation clubs
		Amateur sports competitions
		Professional athletic leagues
	Youth development	Youth centers and clubs
		Adult and child matching programs
		Scouting organizations
		Youth development programs
	Human services	Human services
		Child and youth services
		Family services
		Personal social services
		Emergency assistance
		Residential care and adult day programs
		Centers to support independence
International, foreign affairs	International, foreign affairs, and national security	Promotion of international understanding
		International development
		International peace and security
		International affairs, foreign policy, and globalization
		International human rights

Broad Categories	Major Groups	Activity Areas
Public, societal benefit	Civil rights	Civil rights Intergroup and race relations Voter education and registration Civil liberties
	Community improvement and capacity building	Community and neighborhood development Economic development Business and industry Nonprofit management Community service clubs
	Philanthropy, voluntarism, and grantmaking foundations	Private grantmaking foundations Public foundation Voluntarism promotion Philanthropy, charity, and voluntarism promotion Federated giving programs
	Science and technology	General science Physical and earth science Engineering and technology Biological and life science
	Social science	Social science Interdisciplinary research
	Public societal benefit	Government and public administration Military and veterans organizations Public transportation systems Telecommunications Financial institutions Leadership development Public utilities Consumer protection
Religion related	Religion relations	Christianity Judaism Islam

(continues)

TABLE 1-6   Public Benefit Industries of the Nonprofit Sector (*continued*)

Broad Categories	Major Groups	Activity Areas
		Buddhism
		Hinduism
		Religious media and communications
		Interfaith coalitions
Mutual/ membership benefit	Mutual and membership benefit	Insurance providers
		Pension and retirement funds
		Fraternal societies
		Cemeteries
Unknown		

Reproduced from National Taxonomy of Exempt Entities, provided by the Urban Institute, National Center for Charitable Statistics.

Framing Strategic Choices

Learning Objectives

- Compare and contrast different aspects of organizational performance
- Identify the phases of the strategic management cycle
- Evaluate the features and importance of mission statements and other guiding statements
- Appreciate the potential conflict between mission purposes and resource opportunities

Strategic management is a blend of management practices that entail interpreting environmental conditions and designing systems to foster success (Miles & Snow, 1978). "The effectiveness of organizational adaptation hinges on the dominant coalition's perceptions of environmental conditions and the decisions it makes concerning how well the organization will cope with these conditions" (p. 21). Effective managers develop coherent practices across all "parts" of the organization, which include operations, fundraising, managing people, and performance assessment.

No organization can drive out all paradoxes, inefficiencies, and contradictions, but strategic management is an attempt to facilitate alignment across various activities to achieve objectives. It is the ability of the dominant coalition—or as we might more commonly refer to it, the leadership of the organization—to interpret environmental opportunities, guide priorities, and control resources to achieve objectives (Mintzberg, 1979). This chapter reviews key principles in strategic management and considers how those principles apply to nonprofit organizations.

This chapter presents the *strategic management cycle*, which frames three decision areas: defining the operating context, creating systems to provide services, and monitoring performance accomplishments. Central to nonprofits and the strategic management cycle is the mission of the organization. This chapter reviews key principles of mission statements and considers how missions frame strategic management activities. Tantamount to this discussion on strategy is the recognition that organizational performance in nonprofits is complex and multifaceted. The lack of a financial bottom line means that managers must consciously define performance priorities and objectives as a fundamental aspect in strategic decision making. This chapter starts with a discussion of organizational performance and how managers must utilize multiple metrics to facilitate success.

Effectiveness in Nonprofits

Some key assumptions in business strategy are potentially problematic in the nonprofit context. As discussed previously, nonprofit organizations have unique features that impact management practices. As is reflected in the statement provided by Miles and Snow (1978), strategic management is intended to guide organizations toward organizational effectiveness. The concept of organizational effectiveness and performance, however, is problematic for nonprofits. In for-profit businesses, the accumulation of surplus funds and the distribution of those profits constitute the most significant measure of success. Now there are many intermediary activities to achieve that objective, such as growing market share, providing good customer service, and retaining high-quality employees, but the universal measure of success is financial. Strategic management is based on the idea of positioning the organization in the environment and building organizational systems to be successful—and yet, if "success" is not clear for many nonprofits, what is a manager to do? What does it mean to be a successful nonprofit? A natural reaction to this question is to believe that fulfillment of the charitable purpose is success. So an organization that exists to eliminate childhood poverty is success- ful when that is achieved. Another way to describe this is the idea of mission accomplishment (Sheehan, 2010). In principle, this is a fine model to guide decision making, but in practice many non- profits have mission statements that are too broad, ambiguous, or difficult to conceptualize as achieving success. Some case could be made that those mission statements should be redesigned to better reflect a realistic conception of what the organization intends or is able to achieve. Some mission statements are nearly impossible to measure. Yet those missions capture values and concepts that reflect the nature and character of the organization and effectively motivate stakeholders to support the organization.

If mission fulfillment is the ideal measure of success, but potentially problematic due to cost or conceptual limitations, are there alternative measures of success? There is extensive literature in the field (Herman & Renz, 1999, 2008; Sowa, Selden, & Sandfort, 2004) and, unfortunately, ambivalent recommenda- tions for nonprofit managers (see **Table 2-1**). Some of the typical areas of consideration include, as was mentioned, focusing on outcomes of program participants and social value (Bagnoli & Megali, 2011; Sowa et al., 2004) or focusing on resources—the ability to secure necessary funds and labor to achieve objectives (Medina-Borja & Triantis, 2007; Moxham, 2009). Both these priorities are significant but also have limitations. An alternative is to recognize that there is implicitly a subjective aspect to non- profit organizations. The ability of organizations to provide value to key stakeholders also turns out to be a reasonable way to focus organizational behavior (Freeman, 1984; Herman & Renz, 1999). Herman and Renz (1999) refer to this idea and proclaim that performance for nonprofits is "socially constructed." That means

TABLE 2-1 Typical Concepts of Effectiveness

Concept	Definition	Examples	Limitations
Mission accomplishment, social value, outcome performance	Fulfill charitable purpose	Ending homelessness, building self-esteem of girls, making children contributing members of society	Difficult and costly to measure, forced quantification may oversimplify or miss key concepts
Resource accumulation	Secure necessary and increasing levels of financial and human capital	Growth in donations from year to year, expanded number of volunteers, employee commitment and retention	Too much focus on inputs can lead to misguided practices
Perceived value and legitimacy from stakeholders	Gain support of key stakeholders	Widespread perceptions of legitimacy, strong support and advocacy by key stakeholders	Can shift purposes of organization to interests of influential stakeholders
Operational efficiency and productivity	Operate according to best practice principles and produce goods and services	Following management guidelines and principles (e.g., transparency), increased volume of services provided (outputs)	Inability to link activities to long-term priorities

if people *think* you are effective, then you are effective. Given the ambiguous nature of much nonprofit work, performance is determined by impressions of stakeholders, and those perceptions of "performance" can affect survival. Or put another way, if a particular stakeholder perceives value in the nonprofit then, for them, the organization is effective. This conception of performance reflects the political or sociological aspects of nonprofit organizations. Many nonprofits fulfill the interests of significant stakeholders and thereby ensure their continued success. Several other propositions are proposed by Herman and Renz (2008), which include the idea that performance in nonprofits is inherently comparative and will typically rely on multiple different dimensions. This reflects the multiple bottom lines of the sector. What is worth reiterating is that as managers, it is tantamount to develop definitions of performance that suit key stakeholders and then use those definitions to guide managerial activities. Without some agreement about what it means to be successful (effective), nonprofits can be awash with conflicting and competing priorities.

Persistence and Growth

Two common indicators of success—persistence and growth—are potentially misleading. Persistence is the idea that longer-lived, older organizations must be more effective than younger organizations or they wouldn't have survived so long. There is indeed research to demonstrate that younger organizations are more likely to disband (Hager, Galaskiewicz, & Larson, 2004), but that does not necessarily mean that older organizations produce more social value. It does typically mean that they are more well-known and potentially more respected than younger organizations, but even that may not be the case. Growth is another example of a socially desirable attribute that might or might not reflect social value performance. Our economy and society thrive on the idea of growth. Growth might not be a useful measure of success for nonprofits that exist to prevent or abolish behaviors and beliefs. Expanded activities and services to reduce negative features in society (e.g., sickness, drug use) might be a good thing, but ultimately success is determined by the eventual demise of the social problem and the opportunity to provide services. The absence of need is potentially more indicative of success. The classic example is the March of Dimes, which was founded to end polio in the United States and achieved that objective with the development and distribution of the polio vaccine ("March of Dimes History," 2010). Subsequently, the organization modified its mission to address premature births and birth defects. So, optimal growth was the increased prevalence of healthy babies and a reduced demand or need for the organization. Increased activity on the part of a nonprofit does not necessarily reflect mission accomplishment. It most likely reflects increased resources (money or labor) that are released on the tasks, which typically is a good thing, but slightly different than performance. So unlike for-profit entities where there is a natural a link between increased market share (i.e., more customers served) and the propensity to secure surplus revenue (success), that is not the case for many nonprofits. For the nonprofit, it might be that serving more people and increasing revenue constitutes success, but as the March of Dimes example illustrates, it is only one aspect of what an entity hopes to achieve. Consider, for example the history and growth of the National Relief Charities (NRC), which is fraught with questionable business practices, bad press, and low ratings from national evaluators, but consistent and persistent revenue growth (see **Exhibit 2-1**). In fact, the only reason the NRC receives anywhere near acceptable ratings (2 out of 4; needs improvement) from a national review system is because of consistent and impressive year over year growth, which constitutes half of the criteria used by Charity Navigator ("Rating of National Relief Charities," 2010).

EXHIBIT 2-1   National Relief Charities (NRC)

The National Relief Charities (NRC) originally formed as the American Indian Relief Council (AIRC). Operating under a number different names (eight are listed on their 2009, 990 tax form), including the Council of Indian Relations (CIR), Navajo Relief Fund (NRF), and Rescue Operation for Animals on the Reservation (ROAR), the NRC has experienced fairly significant growth in revenue during the 10 years of tax returns that were available. According to their annual report, the NRC partners with over 1000 American Indian reservation programs ("Program Partners") to increase the partner's capacity and effectiveness in serving the community. The NRC provides material aid and technical assistance to Program Partners and collaborates with them on programmatic activities and services (National Relief Charities, 2010). Primarily, the NRC raises millions of dollars through telemarketing fundraising and distributes funds to these partner programs. This is not without some questionable practices however. Operating under its affiliate, American Indian Relief Council (AIRC), the NRC was sued by the Pennsylvania Attorney General in 1993 for lying to donors about their practices (amount and percentage of funds distributed to charitable purposes). The then-president agreed to settle and pay the state $350,000 (Rubin, 1996). In 1999, it was estimated that just 30% of revenue was channeled into program activities; the remaining funds were used to pay for fundraising costs and executive salaries (*1999 Return of Organization Exempt Income Tax [Form 990]: National Relief Charities*, 1999). In the latest tax return documents (*2009 Return of Organization Exempt Income Tax [Form 990]: National Relief Charities*, 2009), the NRC raised over $40 million in revenue with a reported fundraising cost of just over $11 million, or about 27% of revenue, earning them two stars out of four (needs improvement) on Charity Navigator ("Rating of National Relief Charities," 2010). The 2009 numbers are not as egregious as those in the past; for instance 2007, when they raised over $25 million and expended 50% on fundraising, earning a single star from Charity Navigator ("Rating of National Relief Charities," 2010). Going back to 1998 they raised $6.4 million in revenue while spending over $4 million on fundraising (over 60%). The pattern seems fairly consistent and outside the bounds of generally accepted practice, but the organization has consistently seen revenue growth and, according to their documents, distributed significant funds to Native American populations (over $28 million in 2009) (National Relief Charities, 2010).

Data from National Relief Charities (2010).

Management Practices and Productivity

The example of National Relief Charities illustrates a fourth concept of performance: adhering to good management practice guidelines can serve as a proxy for performance. The most pervasive principle is that nonprofits should spend the majority of their funds on charitable purposes—program activities as opposed to administrative or fundraising costs. One reason the NRC is problematic is that they spend so much money to raise money.

They appear inefficient and wasteful with donor funds. As a widely accepted guiding principle, nonprofits should spend 75% or more of their expenses on program activities, although this may not necessarily be true in *every* instance. It could be imagined that during initial start-up phases some developmental or administrative costs could be higher. Consider for instance the need to develop information technology infrastructure to manage client relationships. It could take significant resources to develop a system that eventually increases efficiency. Typically, it is very difficult for nonprofits to justify these types of expenses because they appear to misdirect resources away from social needs and charitable purposes. How much should a nonprofit allocate to raising funds? Again, it could be the case that at different times in the organization's expansion additional expenditures on fundraising or management could be justified (Crutchfield & Grant, 2008). The same is true for marketing and promotion. Rarely do nonprofits expend anywhere near the amount of funds for promoting their organization or cause when compared to for-profit corporations (Pallotta, 2008). Nevertheless, the idea that the vast majority of funds should be allocated to program activities at ALL times guides management activities. For many nonprofit managers it is better to emphasize program activities (outputs) then to expend too much on overhead. This principle is in place because of the lack of a clear bottom line that is objective and universal. Most donors want to hear that 95 cents (or some other significant proportion) of every dollar goes to meeting needs and not into administration (fundraising).

The Clarity of Failure

Even in instances when conditions improve as a result of nonprofit initiatives (i.e., meet service beneficiary needs and achieve social benefit outcomes), it might not be enough to ensure survival. It is easy to imagine a nonprofit that provides "good" services but fails to survive. The provision of needed services doesn't unequivocally relate to securing resources. Failure often constitutes an inability to secure sufficient resources. Nonprofits operate in muted markets with inconclusive evidence on performance and rely on third-party constituents to provide resources to augment or underwrite costs. Consequently, perceptions of influential stakeholders can be quite powerful. This is especially true if services are provided in a controversial or political environment. Understanding the power of different stakeholders to impact organizational survival is critical for success. As an illustration, consider the relatively spectacular failure of ACORN (Association for Community Organizations for Reform Now), which provides some insights into the reality of operating a nonprofit. The case reveals that bad exposure can be enough to initiate a landslide of reactions that culminate in the demise of the organization. The lack of resiliency is potentially indicative of poor management, but bad publicity served the final blow, and it was surprising how quickly the events culminated in the organization's demise. ACORN operated in a political context, making them potentially more sensitive to negative publicity, but bad publicity can have a long-standing negative impact in raising resources. For instance, the William Aramony scandal at the United Way had a long-lasting effect on fundraising efforts at regional and national levels (Barman, 2002). In 1995 Aramony was sentenced (along with two other officials) to 7 years in prison for misappropriating $1.2 million in funds (Barrett, 2006). The behavior of executives (or frontline staff) might indeed be indicative of significant and systemic concerns, or it might just be errant behavior of a select number of individuals. The tendency to perceive a problem as either systemic or an issue of "one bad apple" is often based on biases toward or against the organization, which may or may not be formed on objective criteria of success. The ACORN story illustrates that sociopolitical realities can affect perceptions of legitimacy and, ultimately, operations (see **Exhibit 2-2**). The bottom line for many nonprofits is the ability to create value for stakeholders and, as a result, gain their support. The strategic task is to effectively interpret environmental conditions, which includes key stakeholders and opportunities to provide services, while building organizational capabilities to meet those demands.

EXHIBIT 2-2 Association for Community Organizations for Reform Now (ACORN)

Prior to its demise, the Association for Community Organizations for Reform Now (ACORN) appeared to be a fairly successful nonprofit organization. Established in 1970, ACORN served low- and moderate-income families by addressing neighborhood issues such as health care and affordable housing. Over its 40-year history, ACORN could claim many victories in helping low-income individuals. These include increasing the minimum wage and limiting predatory lending practices. It is difficult to know the exact size of the ACORN association as it was a conglomerate of independent organizations that did not file a consolidated financial statement. It is estimated that in 2010 ACORN had over 400,000 members and about 1200 neighborhood chapters in 100 cities across the United States, as well as international offices. Budget estimates range from $25 million to $100 million. The organization was not without controversy or concerns about management capabilities. ACORN was an activist-oriented organization that engaged in voter registration activities and lobbying for policy change, and through its separately organized political action committee, ACORN supported progressive candidates, including Barack Obama in the 2008 presidential campaign. In 2009 a video was circulated that appeared to show ACORN staff members giving business and tax advice to a pimp and prostitute. The video caused a firestorm of reaction from a broad range of stakeholders, including the federal government. Congress enacted legislation that cut funding to ACORN, and several foundations discontinued support. These activities culminated in the parent organization filing bankruptcy and hundreds of neighborhood chapters disassociating themselves from ACORN or closing completely. In November of 2010 ACORN closed or disbanded, bringing to an end a storied history.

Data from Wikipedia contributors. (2013). Association of Community Organizations for Reform Now. Wikipedia, The Free Encyclopedia. Retrieved from http://en.wikipedia.org/w/index.php?title=Association_of_Community_Organizations_for_Reform_Now&oldid=591189079; Where Most Needed. (2008). The Charity Industry Observer Probing the Deeper Links & Linkages. Retrieved from http://www.wheremostneeded.org/2008/10/acorn-wheres-th.html; and Eisenberg, Pablo, (2008). After an Embezzlement, an Advocacy Group Seeks to Regain Trust. Chronicle of Philanthropy, 20(24), p36-42.

Nonprofit Strategic Management Cycle

Strategic management emphasizes positioning the organization in the external environment and formulating internal practices so as to capitalize on the opportunities and overcome the challenges. If managers accurately perceive environmental conditions and actively build capabilities they can improve the likelihood of organizational success. The strategic management cycle provides a framework to consider the strategic choices managers confront (Backman, Grossman, & Rangan, 2000; Chew & Osborne, 2009; Courtney, 2002; Kong, 2008). The model, based on a modified version of the "adaptive cycle" developed by Miles and Snow (1978, p. 24), identifies three "problems" in strategic management (see **Figure 2-1**).

Managers and leaders make decisions about the following questions:

1. What is the organization going to do? What social issues is the organization going to address? What resource opportunities can they utilize?
2. How are they going to do it? What *systems* will be used and what *capacities* does the organization have?
3. How will they judge *performance* and allow *innovation*?

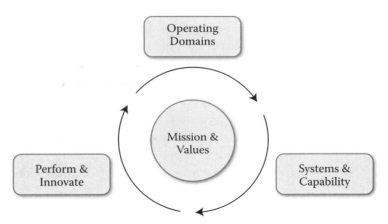

FIGURE 2-1 Strategic Management Cycle

This model is an abstraction of actual decision making in organizations. The three components and the complexities inherent in each are intermixed and interdependent, but if managers can address each of these questions with some consistency they are likely to help the organization perform better. The first question addresses the operational areas of nonprofits. Using for-profit language suggests that nonprofits operate in multiple related but separate "markets." Nonprofits are active in (1) meeting social or community need, and (2) acquiring resources. These domains are external to the organization and operate in contested economic and social space. Other providers are directly or indirectly competing for influence in those domains. Managers interpret the opportunities in these two areas, which then set the course for organizational initiatives. Questions two and three are operational and reflect activities necessary to achieve the objectives specified by answering question one. Question two is primarily concerned with the systems and processes addressing social problems and securing resources. Question three relates to monitoring these practices to determine performance and to understand which activities should be improved, terminated, or expanded. The management tactics included in question three are incredibly important, as they guide adjustments and innovation, which are fundamental weaknesses for many nonprofits. All parts of the nonprofit strategic management cycle work together to constrain choices and facilitate performance (Schiemann, 2009). These questions are a cycle in the sense that modifications and interpretations at each stage are influenced by activities and learning that takes place in other areas. As choices regarding public benefit priorities are considered in phase one, implementation of operational tactics in phase two may reveal additional opportunities or may confront significant barriers that will require some readjustment of how the operating context is defined. Similarly, performance assessment guides operations to continually refine practices to achieve efficiencies, improve quality, and, ultimately, improve outcome benefits.

Operating Domains

Nonprofit organizations confront two fundamental questions regarding operations: What social value do they create and how do they sustain the organization? The first concern is clarifying public benefit purpose. Managers must grapple to define an area of operational activities in relation to perceived social need. A significant aspect of defining the public benefit domain is clarifying the social issue and understanding the beneficiary. Social issues and needs are difficult to define and understand. The idea of an unacceptable social condition is the foundation for action. By understanding social concerns managers articulate the social value that is created by the nonprofit. There are various methods to help define and describe the operating context of nonprofits and how managers must develop answers to basic questions that provide a rationale for the nonprofit's existence. These kinds of issues are often more salient during the founding stages of an organization, but periodic adjustments are appropriate and necessary. Another aspect of the public benefit operating context is a definition of the beneficiary. Who or what benefits as a result of the organization's activities? Again, this is not necessarily an easy question, and the text will explore these ideas in more detail. There are often direct beneficiaries that participate in the services of the organizations, but there are also indirect beneficiaries. Considering the range and type of beneficiaries can also help define the public benefit domain.

Unfortunately, for nonprofit managers, defining the social value proposition and intended beneficiaries is not sufficient. The nature of the public benefit market typically cannot support organizational systems. Social value does not automatically translate into sustainability. Consequently, managers must address the resource domain. Can the nonprofit secure sufficient resources to gain capacity to fulfill public benefit purposes? The elements of the resource market are multifaceted and complex. Four broad resource categories are proposed as reflecting the resource domain: financial capital, physical capital, human capital, and social capital. These reflect key aspects of organizational capacity that nonprofits must secure to remain viable. In strategic decision making, nonprofit managers consider social value concerns and resource sustainability (Bell, Masaoka, & Zimmerman, 2010). Defining the operational domain for resource options is potentially as important as defining the public benefit purpose. The ability to secure resources is contingent on a social value justification, but the ability to capture resources requires a distinct set of operational systems to ensure success. In other words, nonprofit organizations must, almost by design, operate in multiple domain areas and create organizational systems that might or might not utilize similar capabilities. Resource acquisition then is the second element of nonprofit operating context.

These domains are distinct because they often have different targets of activities. In the public benefit market, organizational activities are targeted on changing and improving social conditions. In the resource markets, nonprofits target activities at entities and individuals that can support organizational capacity. There might be overlap in these targeted groups (clients that pay fees), but often there is not. The approach and objectives are different in each domain, and without thoughtful articulation of distinct objectives, design of organizational systems, and monitoring of performance, managers are unlikely to exploit the full potential in each domain. There are also potential synergies between the operational activities in each operational domain, but those linkages must be actively managed to facilitate efficiencies and performance. **Table 2-2** summarizes the two operational domains, typical organizational systems that nonprofits create in these areas, and example performance expectations.

TABLE 2-2 Aspects of the Strategic Management Cycle

Operating Domains	Systems and Capabilities	Performance and Innovation
Public benefit	Services, social capital building, preservation, creative initiatives, advocacy	Social impact, program performance
Resource	Financial, physical, human and social capital	Financial solvency, engagement, participation, organizational legitimacy

Systems and Capabilities

For each operating domain (public benefit and resource), managers need to formulate systems and structures that utilize organizational capabilities to fulfill operating demands. This is *how* the organization fulfills the objectives identified in the first question of the strategic management cycle. What are the methods utilized, and does the organization have effective systems to implement those methods? There is a complex array of responses, but each operating domain requires distinct delivery systems and management tactics. Table 2-2 summarizes example management responses to the different operating domains. The management options are adapted to reflect context requirements, but the table highlights how different systems are focused on different operating domains.

Methods to achieve objectives in the public benefit domain are related to the five functions nonprofits fulfill in society. These functions are listed as the repertoire of operational tactics that managers may utilize to active social value. These functions operate within industries such as health care, education, and human services. Based upon how the social condition is interpreted and defined in phase one of the strategic management cycle, managers may utilize different methods. The most common option and set of activities for nonprofit organizations is related to providing services. Service is defined simply as an act of helpful activity, to help and aid someone ("Service," n.d.). Services are distinct from products or goods (tangible artifacts). While it is difficult to accurately measure, it is reasonable to estimate that roughly 70–80% of the activities carried out by nonprofits are related to providing services. There are countless services provided by nonprofits. Reviewing the National Taxonomy of Exempt Entities provides a thorough classification of industries and services carried out by nonprofits. Services tend to require direct engagement of the beneficiary and the target of activity is clearly focused on the beneficiary.

Social activities entail initiatives that build social capital, address social norms, and raise awareness of public benefit issues. These activities entail both direct and indirect interaction with the intended beneficiary. Preservation activities are those intended to protect sociocultural, environmental, or historical artifacts. Many activities, such as environmental initiatives, do not directly engage beneficiaries in the transformation activities. Creative activities are those that result in the development of innovative ideas and artifacts, such as research and artistic initiatives. Political/advocacy methods are focused on changing institutional systems that affect the condition of intended beneficiaries; consequently beneficiaries are not the target of transformation activities. Advocacy and lobbying initiatives are examples of practices in this method.

In the resource market, managers need to build systems to address financial and human resource capital requirements. This includes the array of fundraising strategies used by development professionals. Human capital refers to labor requirements of non-profits. It includes paid and unpaid participants and the range of activities that must be addressed to engage and coordinate organizational participants. Social capital in the resource context relates to initiatives to build recognition and legitimacy of the organizational entity. Physical capital relates to the segment of organizations that actively secure physical goods as a significant aspect of their operational tactics (e.g., food banks). Systems need to be built that capture and utilize the physical capital.

Performance and Innovation

The third aspect of the strategic management cycle is related to performance, control, and innovation. The key concerns here are related to how managers determine accomplishments and seek opportunities for innovation. How does the nonprofit manager monitor organizational behavior to ensure performance and improvement? Table 2-2 covers some options related to the different market features, and the third column highlights the need to actively construct and monitor performance systems as well as ensure learning and innovation. In relation to services, the typical response is related to program monitoring and evaluation. Putting in place systems to monitor and assess the quality of services allows managers to modify and adjust programs to meet the needs, interests, and preferences of service and program beneficiaries. Again there is a broad range of options and methods that can be utilized to monitor program delivery. In the resource arena, in addition to securing needed resources, performance considerations include attitudes and perceptions of donors, organizational employees, and volunteers. In the sociopolitical operations, performance measurement includes legislative accomplishments and softer attributes related to stakeholder attitudes and opinions. Performance and innovation is a challenge for nonprofits, and this aspect of the strategic management cycle is of particular importance for nonprofit managers. Given the lack of universal bottom-line indicators, creative and aggressive monitoring is very important.

Mission, Vision, and Values

Mission, vision, and values statements articulate important strategic perspectives of the organization. These guiding statements define the purposes of the organization. Why does the organization exist? Missions distill key principles regarding social value objectives and explain the philosophical perspective of the organization. This worldview is a critically important aspect of the organization's strategic position (Checkland, 2000). Vision statements articulate what the organization hopes to accomplish—what is the future state of the community, issue, or field that will result from the nonprofit's work? Values statements explain the key principles that guide operations and can be quite powerful but often lack sufficient credibility to be fully functional (Lencioni, 2002). Yet as values-based organizations, values statements and related management practices may be one of the most important and distinctive elements in nonprofits (Jeavons, 2010). Mission and vision statements are central for several reasons, but fundamentally they are an abbreviated rationale for the nonprofit's existence and provide a cornerstone for subsequent decision making (see **Table 2-3**).

The next section discusses features of mission statements, the inherent challenges of developing and modifying a mission

TABLE 2-3 Features of Guiding Statements: Mission, Vision, and Values

Feature	Description
Distills purpose	Identifies the charitable purposes of the organization
Outcomes or benefits	Explains what the organization hopes to accomplish
Beneficiaries	Describes who or what benefits from organizational activities
Broad	Serves as umbrella of strategic decision making in the organization
Durable	Captures long-standing attributes and purposes
Distinctive	Summarizes the uniqueness of the organization and purpose
Short and memorable	Helps both internal and external audiences remember

statement, and how mission statements can be used in the management of nonprofits. Mission and vision statements are just one aspect of how a nonprofit explains its purpose, but they are used extensively by external stakeholders to ascertain roles and functions of an organization. Those interested in a nonprofit will use these guiding statements to make preliminary judgments regarding the operational domain of the organization. These guiding statements are at the highest level of the strategic management and should capture the "spirit" or heart of the organization. Extended attempts to get it "just right" are not absolutely necessary; rather, taken together these statements and guidelines should be a touchstone that help key decision makers enact the organization's role, purpose, and activities. These guiding statements help mitigate the ambiguous operating contexts (unclear performance indicators, mixed market influences). The mission (and associated statements) should attempt to blend internal beliefs and capabilities with external influences. Table 2-3 lists some the features that should be covered by these statements. The mission statement is the most widely utilized element for nonprofits, but supplementary statements can further define programs, operating domains, and benefits.

Missions should capture the "purpose" of the organization. Why does the nonprofit exist? Typically missions articulate the benefit the organization hopes to achieve and who the organization serves (beneficiaries). It also should be broad enough to serve as an umbrella for the entire organization and to guide decision making for an extended period of time. Furthermore, the mission should be distinctive and somehow differentiate the organization from others. What is unique about this organization, and what does it hope to accomplish? Many recommend that a mission should be captured in a short pithy statement that "fits on a t-shirt." The mission functions as both a guiding philosophy for the management of the organizations (internal) as well as a marketing tool to attract support (external); it is difficult to know exactly how to scope and create the mission to reflect these features and the organization's nature and purpose. Take for example the mission of the Girl Scouts of America, which states, "Girl Scouting builds girls of courage, confidence, and character, who make the world a better place" (Girl Scouts of America, 2010). Such a mission broadly defines the primary customer (girls) and two benefits the organization intends to create. One directed toward the child (creating courage, confidence, and character) and a broader societal benefit (making the world a better place). The organization uses other documents and principles to describe how this is done, through "empowering girls," and then defines a series of activities, which can be used in operational levels. Missions might go so far as to describe the specific customer (girls of a specific age) and service delivery strategy, or it might be more broad and then interpreted though vision and guiding documents that enact the mission in ways that are relevant to the particular division or department (Angelica, 2001). Take for instance the mission of Big Brothers Big Sisters, which states clearly that they will "provide children facing adversity with strong and enduring, professionally supported one-to-one relationships that change their lives for the better, forever" (Big Brothers Big Sisters of America, 2011). Such a mission specifies the primary customer (children facing adversity) and the method of service delivery (professionally supported one-to-one relationships). It goes on to further articulate the benefit (change their lives for the better). To refine this benefit they go on, in separate documents, to identify several elements to which they will be "accountable." They include higher aspirations, avoiding risky behavior, and educational success. Such a mission is very prescriptive and defines many aspects of how the organization is going to operate, while also challenging organizational actors to engage.

How to Use These Statements

The challenge, beyond crafting a set of values and principles that capture what the organization stands for, is putting them into practice. How do the hours of crafting these guiding documents pay off? More than a few individuals have spent painfully long hours in meetings searching for just the right words to capture the true nature of the organization. It may be asking too much of these statements to capture every nuance of an organization's strategic value to all stakeholders. Nevertheless, as guideposts, these statements can be very helpful in a turbulent, uncertain environment. The idea that the mission can be used in management decisions is illustrated in a story told by two different executives. One executive of a child services organization explained that he used the mission as a mechanism to block ideas that were too far afield. "We could do that if you want to change the mission statement," he would say to board members who suggested ideas he felt were outside the organization's purview. In some ways this executive defined the mission as a box to frame and constrain organizational activities. An executive of a drug use prevention organization had just lost a major contract to run drug prevention programs on school campuses. The organization needed to consider how to respond. Some board members thought, "This is it, we were good at what we did and now the sponsor no longer wants our services. Our program is over." Others, in particular the new executive director, felt the organization was about *prevention* and, although they had operated in one way, they needed to consider other ways to provide services to the community at large. The executive used the mission statement much more like a planter from which program ideas "grow." The need for prevention services and drug abuse treatment wasn't going away—if anything drug use and abuse was going up. The sponsor, however, was not interested in paying for those services in the same way they had. The executive pushed forward and developed a new perspective that allowed them to expand their service delivery strategies to provide community-based prevention services to youth while staying true their mission. They might never have been involved in their award-winning community program without the new executive (Brown & Iverson, 2004). Neither one of these frames are necessarily "right" or "wrong" in a generic sense, but they do illustrate the difference between the Girl Scouts mission (much more like a planter) and the mission of Big Brothers Big Sisters (much more like a box or frame), and how these statements can be used as guides for decision making.

In another example, Jonker and Meehan (2008) discuss how program directors use the mission statement to make decisions about including and discontinuing program activities. This includes turning down opportunities to expand programs into new areas. Their case study illustrates the idea of "mission creep" and how these guiding statements can help organizations "stay on track." Instead of following opportunities as they are presented, managers reevaluate activities in light of the original purposes of the organization and ultimately decide to discontinue certain programs in an effort to focus more effectively on certain areas. At what point do new opportunities distract from original purposes and when is it necessary to reconsider the mission and purpose of the organization? The idea that the mission or values statements are sacrosanct may not be in the best interest of the organization or the community. However, chasing resources without guideposts is probably not healthy either. Traditionally there may be some preference to remain "pure" in organizational purpose. Mission attachment, the attraction and commitment of key stakeholders, can be quite powerful. When you consider different stakeholder groups, some may be quite committed to the original purposes and somewhat out of touch with current demands. Consider for example what has happened in the credit union industry. Credit unions gained prominence in the mid-20th century, growing in number until the early 1970s. They were formed on the premise of cooperative banking and the principle of individuals joining together to meet member needs in finance and credit. Many of the board members for these institutions remember when they were formed, their first interaction with the credit union (they gave me a loan to buy my first car), and the sponsoring employer. The original names and constituents were very important and yet the operating context, the credit industry and banking, have changed significantly over the years. So there is, for many of these institutions, a substantial need to adjust operations and reconsider opportunities, and yet many board members are reluctant to shift customers and services. These same board members are often significant depositors in the bank. Shifting, changing, and merging is not the answer for every nonprofit (or credit union), but honestly evaluating original purposes in relation to external demands is a significant challenge for many entities (Brown, 2007).

Mission Attachment

The challenges associated with the mission as guiding beacon or constraining anchor are reflected in the concept of mission attachment. When employees and board members are asked why they work and volunteer for the organization, they invariably discuss the mission and purpose of the organization (Brown, Hillman, & Okun, 2012; Brown & Yoshioka, 2003; Kim & Lee, 2007). They are there because they believe in the mission and purpose of the organization. Employees are willing to accept less pay and volunteers engage more fully because they are attached and committed to the mission and purpose of the organization. They may or may not know the mission word for word, in fact many do not, but they do know core philosophies of the organization and how that relates to them. Board members at a local animal shelter who were in a protracted and rather nasty conflict with the local municipality over payment terms were asked, "Why are you fighting so hard and working these long hours to renegotiate a contract with the city?" The answer was simple: "The dogs (or animals). We are here to help save the dogs." Executives and board members of a child advocacy organization provide a very similar answer to the question, "Why do you work so hard and donate so much time and money?" "The kids." Obviously it is not quite that simple, because in both these examples these organizations were experiencing some pretty impressive results as well. The humane society was securing nearly 50% increases in per-animal payments during very difficult economic times. Accomplishments toward the purpose of the organization were very motivating for these individuals. This is similar to what we heard from youth service employees who ultimately did feel they were underpaid although mission attachment was a significant factor in their overall satisfaction (as were their supervisor and coworkers). Given the power of these core guiding statements, organizations need to consider them carefully and recognize how mission statements signal the *strategic position* of the organization. They frame and define, for stakeholders inside and outside the organization, the public benefit purposes of the nonprofit, which is the cornerstone to guide operations and garner support.

Mission Versus Sustainability

Mission, vision, and values as the heart of the organization are an apt metaphor. It resonates with stakeholders, donors, employees, and volunteers and can guide decision making. However, the chapter starts with a recognition that nonprofits operate in two distinct domains: public benefit and resource. Strategy for nonprofit managers is framed by considering both social value opportunities and resource options that contribute to sustainable organizational systems. While these priorities do not necessarily have to operate in opposition, it is an ongoing tension in many nonprofits. It is one of the more interesting and intriguing challenges present in nonprofit management. **Table 2-4** positions

TABLE 2-4   Creating Social Value and Sustainability

		Social Value	
		High	**Low**
Sustainability	**High**	A sweet spot for organizational participants and community benefits	Potential need to reevaluate exempt purposes
	Low	Must attend to interests of key stakeholders who are dedicated to organizational purpose	Likely struggling and marginalized

social value and sustainability on an axis to create a 2×2 table that reveals four types of organizational activities: those that are highly impactful and garner sufficient resources, those that are impactful but struggle to garner support, those with limited social value and yet capture significant resources, and those that are neither impactful nor sustainable. The table illustrates how managers balance opportunities in the two domains simultaneously and that the sum of organizational activities likely fall across different quadrants. For example, a special event that garners significant financial return and bonds stakeholders to the organization might have low impact but high-resource value. A treatment program that operates in conjunction with a local school district might be both sustainable (strong partnership) and impactful (successful program outcomes). Program activities that struggle to gain support but have high impact require managers to explore how to capture the interest of supporters. Program activities that are neither impactful nor sustainable should be abandoned or modified to achieve more success in one or hopefully both domains.

Conclusion

Strategic management in nonprofit organizations is the ability to understand external opportunities and challenges while weaving together systems to address the multiple stakeholders that are affected by the actions of the organization. Nonprofit managers should guide, strengthen, and modify those practices according to learning that is based on objective, quantifiable information and the guidance and intuition of the dominant coalition. The strategic management cycle frames strategic choices for managers. There are three key "problems": (1) defining operating domains, (2) creating systems that utilize organizational capabilities, and (3) building control and performance management systems that foster learning. The operating domain reflects both the social value proposition and the sustainability dimension. Central to this process is creating and adhering to guiding statements such as mission, vision, and values. These statements reflect philosophical and ideological principles that distill key aspects of the organization and distinguish it from others. Missions do not necessarily operate in opposition to "market" forces, and yet there is a conflict in decision making that must balance philosophical and ideological principles with resource opportunities. The mission is a powerful and useful management tool that attracts supporters and yet can, at times, be disconnected from practical realities of the operating environment. The chapter highlights the challenges managers confront in understanding performance in the sector. The focus on social benefits is mitigated by the influence of legitimacy and perceptions of key stakeholders. This is a central issue in decision making, as performance objectives guide subsequent management decisions including a focus on particular stakeholders and implementation of operational strategies.

Discussion Questions

1. Considering the example of the National Relief Charities, are they indicative of an organization that is ineffective in meeting their charitable purposes? See their website (www.nrcprograms .org) for additional information. What about their management activities do you find problematic? What do you find laudable?

2. Explain how mission statements can function as both a "planter" and a "box" for strategic decisions. What is more of a concern, that an organization might expand organizational purposes (detailed in a mission statement) or miss out on key opportunities to provide services?

3. Can you think of example activities that operate in each quadrant of Table 2-4?

References

1999 Return of Organization Exempt Income Tax (Form 990): National Relief Charities. (1999). Washington, DC: Guidestar.

2009 Return of Organization Exempt Income Tax (Form 990): National Relief Charities. (2009). Washington, DC: Guidestar.

Angelica, E. (2001). *Crafting effective mission and vision statements.* Saint Paul, MN: Wilder Foundation.

Backman, E. B., Grossman, A., & Rangan, V. K. (2000). Introduction to special issue on strategy. *Nonprofit and Voluntary Sector Quarterly, 29*(1(S)), 2–8.

Bagnoli, L., & Megali, C. (2011). Measuring performance in social enterprises. *Nonprofit and Voluntary Sector Quarterly, 40*(1), 149–165.

Barman, E. A. (2002). Asserting difference: Strategic response of nonprofits to competition. *Social Forces, 80*(4), 1191–1222.

Barrett, W. P. (2006, January 16). United Way's New Way. *Forbes.* Retrieved from http://www.forbes.com/2006/01/13/united-way-philanthropy-cz_wb_0117unitedway.html

Bell, J., Masaoka, J., & Zimmerman, S. (2010). *Nonprofit sustainability: Making strategic decisions for financial viability.* San Francisco, CA: Jossey-Bass.

Big Brothers Big Sisters of America. (2011). *Annual report.* Philadelphia, PA: Big Brothers Big Sisters of America.

Brown, W. A. (2007). *The board's role in credit union mergers.* Madison, WI: Filene Research Institute.

Brown, W. A., Hillman, A. J., & Okun, M. A. (2012). Factors that influence monitoring and resource provision among nonprofit board members. *Nonprofit and Voluntary Sector Quarterly, 41*(1), 145–156.

Brown, W. A., & Iverson, J. O. (2004). Exploring strategy and board structure in nonprofit organizations. *Nonprofit and Voluntary Sector Quarterly, 33*(3), 377–400.

Brown, W. A., & Yoshioka, C. F. (2003). Mission attachment and satisfaction as factors in employee retention. *Nonprofit Management & Leadership, 14*(1), 5–18.

Checkland, P. (2000). Soft systems methodology: A thirty year retrospective. *Systems Research and Behavioral Science, 17*(S1), S11.

Chew, C., & Osborne, S. P. (2009). Exploring strategic positioning in the UK charitable sector: Emerging evidence from charitable organizations that provide public services. *British Journal of Management, 20*(1), 90–105.

Courtney, R. (2002). *Strategic management for voluntary non-profit organizations.* New York, NY: Routledge.

Crutchfield, L. R., & Grant, H. M. (2008). *Forces for good: The six practices of high-impact nonprofits.* San Francisco, CA: Jossey-Bass.

Freeman, E. R. (1984). *Strategic management: A stakeholder approach.* Boston, MA: Pitman.

Girl Scouts of America. (2010). *2009 Annual Report.* New York, NY: Girl Scouts of America.

Hager, M. A., Galaskiewicz, J., & Larson, J. A. (2004). Structural embeddedness and the liability of newness among nonprofit organization. *Public Management Review, 6*(2), 159–188.

Herman, R. D., & Renz, D. O. (1999). Theses on nonprofit organizational effectiveness. *Nonprofit and Voluntary Sector Quarterly, 28*(2), 107–126.

Herman, R. D., & Renz, D. O. (2008). Advancing nonprofit organizational effectiveness research and theory: Nine theses. *Nonprofit Management & Leadership, 18*(4), 399–415.

Jeavons, T. (2010). Ethical nonprofit management: Core values and key practices. In D. O. Renz (Ed.), *The Jossey-Bass handbook of nonprofit management* (3rd ed., pp. 178–205). San Francisco, CA: Jossey-Bass.

Jonker, K., & Meehan, W. F. (2008). Curbing mission creep. *Stanford Social Innovation review, 6*(1), 60–65.

Kim, S. E., & Lee, J. W. (2007). Is mission attachment an effective management tool for employee retention? *Review of Public Personnel Administration, 27*(3), 227–248.

Kong, E. (2008). The development of strategic management in the non-profit context: Intellectual capital in social service non-profit organizations. *International Journal of Management Reviews, 10*(3), 281–299.

Lencioni, P. M. (2002, July 1). Making your values mean something. *Harvard Business Review, 6.*

March of Dimes History. (2010). Retrieved from http://www.marchofdimes.com/mission/history.aspx

Medina-Borja, A., & Triantis, K. (2007). A conceptual framework to evaluate performance of non-profit social service organisations. *International Journal of Technology Management, 37*(1/2), 147–161.

Miles, R. E., & Snow, C. C. (1978). *Organizational strategy structure and process.* New York, NY: McGraw-Hill.

Mintzberg, H. (1979). *The structuring of organizations.* Englewood Cliffs, NJ: Prentice Hall.

Moxham, C. (2009). Performance measurement: Examining the applicability of the existing body of knowledge to nonprofit organisations. *International Journal of Operations & Production Management, 29*(7), 740–763.

National Relief Charities. (2010). *2009 annual report: People working together to make a difference.* Sherman, TX: Author.

Pallotta, D. (2008). *Uncharitable: How restraints on nonprofits undermine their potential* Medford, MA: Tufts University.

Rating of national relief charities. (2010). Charity Navigator.

Rubin, P. (1996, December 26). Finances with wolves. *Phoenix New Times.* Retrieved from http://www.phoenixnewtimes.com/1996-12-26/news/finances-with-wolves/

Schiemann, W. A. (2009). Aligning performance with organizational strategy, values and goals. In J. W. Smither & M. London (Eds.), *Performance management* (pp. 45–87). San Francisco, CA: Jossey Bass.

Service. (n.d.). In Dictionary.com. Retrieved from http://dictionary.reference.com/browse/service

Sheehan, R. M. (2010). *Mission impact: Breakthrough strategies for nonprofits.* Hoboken, NJ: John Wiley & Sons.

Sowa, J. E., Selden, S. C., & Sandfort, J. R. (2004). No longer unmeasurable? A multidimensional integrated model of nonprofit organizational effectiveness. *Nonprofit and Voluntary Sector Quarterly, 33*(4), 711–728.

CHAPTER 3

External Environment: Needs, Resources, Community, and Other Providers

Learning Objectives

- Explain the different features of the nonprofit environment
- Introduce techniques to analyze and describe environmental features
- Describe the opportunities and challenges associated with the different aspects of the nonprofit task environment

Understanding the external environment is critical for strategic decision making. The ability to accurately interpret and define the operating context, including the range and capabilities of other providers, makes a significant difference in the potential success or failure of an organization. When compared to for-profit businesses, nonprofits tend to have a different relationship with their service recipients and other providers. In fact, even the idea of a "customer" or "competitor" is at times incongruent to nonprofit decision making. The unpredictable and multifaceted nature of the exchange relationship underlies some of the challenges that nonprofit managers confront when forming strategy. Furthermore, nonprofits must develop operational responses to two distinct and multifaceted contexts: public benefit and resource. The complexities and challenges of the resource environment do not mitigate the need to understand the service recipient, but resource constraints open the door to other factors that influence strategic choices. This chapter will review the basic features of the nonprofit environment and present techniques to explain and interpret the external environment.

The External Environment

A way to categorize the external environment is to think about factors that are closer to the nonprofit (e.g., current funders) or those elements that are more distant (e.g., the overall economic condition). **Figure 3-1** depicts these layers of the external environment with two circles: the one closer to the nonprofit forms the task environment and the second is defined as the general environment, which is more distant but could impact operations over the long term (Hasenfeld, 1983; Rainey, 2003). The advantage to considering two layers of the external environment is that it narrows the number and type of issues that organizations should monitor. The disadvantage is that in a global and interconnected society many more issues that seem distant might affect the nonprofit. The task environment includes elements that could directly impact the organization, such as the volunteer labor pool. This chapter will provide some guidance about which factors might be particularly important for nonprofit organizations. The general environment includes factors that, although not directly impacting the nonprofit, may still be important, such as the demographics of the community. For example, changes in overall demographics may ultimately impact the organization's ability to recruit volunteers (e.g., aging of the population), but currently the nonprofit may have effective mechanisms to secure volunteer labor. By watching the general environment, nonprofits might be able to prepare for changes

FIGURE 3-1 Features of External Environment

that will eventually affect the organization. Before discussing specific features of the general and task environment, it is necessary to review some techniques of understanding and describing environmental features.

Environmental Analysis Techniques

Four basic techniques are related to understanding the external environment (see **Table 3-1**). Organizational participants and strategic decision makers need to have a general awareness of key elements in environment (Hitt, Ireland, & Hoskisson, 2011). This is called *scanning* and entails formal or informal processes to catalog or list key features in the environment. In addition to knowing the primary constituents in the environment there should be some system to *monitor* these elements over time. Regular tracking of changes in the environment is important

TABLE 3-1 Environmental Analysis Techniques

Analysis Technique	Description
Scanning	Identifying elements in the environment
Monitoring	Tracking these elements over time to spot trends and changes
Forecasting	Making estimates about how these factors will change in the future
Assessing	Considering how these elements may impact organizational activities

although difficult, because it entails a system to record and utilize the information. It is not uncommon that "street-level" service providers notice changes in demand for services or the type of requests being made, but there might or might not be a system to truly monitor changes that are critical to organizational success. In addition to knowing the key players and keeping track of how they change, organizations need to make predictions and anticipate changes. This is called *forecasting.* Based upon information in the environment, managers need to anticipate changes to minimize negative influences. For example, a nonprofit that receives funding from the city might monitor local government politics and judge the possibility of significant changes in local government leadership, such as the election of new council members or the appointment of new administrators. The final step is to consider the implications of these changes and the likelihood that they may significantly impact organizational operations. This *assessment* entails judgment and sophisticated knowledge about the environment and the ability to determine the likelihood of significant events affecting the organization. So again considering a local nonprofit that receives funding from the city, what is the likelihood that new city council members will affect current funding practices? Managers make these judgments all the time. These steps reflect a logical series of activities that will improve understanding of the external environment and assessments of its impact.

Characteristics of the Environment

There are some basic descriptive characteristics that can be used to understand the nature of environmental features (Schmid, 2009). These characteristics would be monitored and assessed to determine how and to what degree they change (see **Table 3-2**). These descriptions are helpful when considering the need for organizational planning or response. The first characteristic is the degree to which the environment is *simple versus complex*. A complex environment has many different components or participants. Consider a funding environment that is populated *resources vs public benefit*

TABLE 3-2   Characteristics of the Environment

Characteristic	Description
Simple vs. complex	Range and variety of participants
Homogeneous vs. heterogeneous	Similarity of participants to each other
Turbulence vs. stability	Consistency of participants over time
Rich vs. poor	Actual and perception of wealth and resources
Organized vs. unorganized	Extent of coordination among participants

needs assessment

by many different foundations (family, corporate, and commu-nity) and several different government entities (multiple cities, counties, regional bodies, state, etc.). Compare this to a funding environment that is dominated by a single or few major funding participants (e.g., one large community foundation and a single municipal funder).

Another feature is the degree to which the environmental features are *homogeneous versus heterogeneous.* This attribute considers the extent to which the various funders, for example, are relatively similar to each other (homogeneous) in the amount of grants made, funding preferences, and so on. Alternatively, funders could be very heterogeneous, meaning that there are var-ious sized entities, funding different priorities and requiring dif-ferent processes and procedures for application and evaluation.

A third attribute to consider is the extent to which the envi-ronment is *stable versus turbulent.* This has to do with the extent of change within or among participants and the attributes of those participants. Consider again the nature of a funding envi-ronment that is very stable. Nonprofits could accurately predict and anticipate the number and type of funders from year to year. A turbulent funding environment indicates that the number and type of funders might change from year to year (increasing or decreasing) or funders might change priorities and funding pref-erences, thereby shifting funding from one issue or organization to another. Turbulence suggests increased difficulty in planning and operating because it is difficult to control or understand environmental features over time.

The next characteristic to consider is the extent to which the environmental features are *rich versus poor.* In a resource-poor environment, organizations need to develop more extensive strategies to overcome limited funding. This might include increased competitive or cooperative behavior among other providers.

Finally, elements in the environment can be relatively *organized versus unorganized.* Considering the funding environment, foundations may coordinate with each other, through a regional association of grant makers, developing common applications and discussing regional priorities, or they might operate independently determining their own procedures and priorities more or less independent of other funders. This too has significant implications for how organizations are able to approach and interact with funders.

Managers identify different elements in the distant and task environment to analyze. Managers use the techniques and characteristics just described to make judgments about external threats and opportunities. In the illustration of funding entities just presented, managers are going to utilize different organizational activities in a stable, homogeneous environment than in a turbulent, heterogeneous environment. Managers are principally trying to reduce risk of failure and increase probability of success. The range of organizational actions will be discussed further in the text and includes efforts to build interorganizational relationships or strong partnerships. Understanding *all* environmental forces is impossible, and even understanding something as apparently straightforward as the level of need for services is actually quite complex. Managers do the best they can to describe and understand the different forces operating against the organization and then utilize a broad repertoire of management actions to increase success.

General Environment

Although many nonprofits are modest in size and it may feel overwhelming, it is still necessary to consider general environmental conditions and how they may influence organizational practices, especially in relation to long-term planning.

There are six factors (economic, demographic, social/cultural, political/legal, technological, and ecological) to consider. Overall *economic conditions* can have significant implications for nonprofit organizations. Looking at the most recent financial downturn, nonprofits saw reductions in investment returns and funding contributions from most all sources. Investment returns and endowment funds are thought to be fairly resilient and stable. Most nonprofits anticipated that endowment funds were secure and could be counted on to provide perpetual support to programs and services. Although much of that capital has been restored with a recovering market, many nonprofits had to cut staff and program services because of lost revenue (*2011 State of the Sector*, 2011; Canon, 2011). Beyond a direct impact of lost capital, nonprofits were also affected by shortfalls in donations as many funders felt the effect of lost wealth and curtailed grantmaking and charitable donations (Nonprofit Fundraising Study, 2011). The economy can have a double impact on nonprofits because as resources are constrained, demand for services might increase (Hasenfeld, 1983). During this time many nonprofits saw an unprecedented increase in demand for social services. This double-impact of economic conditions suggests it is necessary to monitor economic conditions not only in reference to investment strategies but also to consider how economic changes might impact the demand for services. An event like the financial crisis is very difficult to predict, and many experts were caught by surprise by the size and wholesale nature of the financial crisis; nevertheless attention to regional and national economic trends will provide insight into potential strategic opportunities and challenges.

The United States continues to experience fairly substantive changes in *demographic* characteristics of the U.S. population. Depending on regional location those changes can be more pronounced or modest. Minority populations continue to grow due to migration and birth rates, whereas aging baby boomers threaten to overwhelm already burdened medical programs with extended life expectancy and higher demand for sophisticated medical care. These baby boomers might also reflect tremendous potential for nonprofits in reference to voluntary labor. Further-more, retiring baby boomers reflect an unprecedented transfer of wealth, which presents new opportunities for nonprofits to con-sider the philanthropic interests of this generation. Monitoring these and other demographic characteristics can provide valuable insight into long-term choices organizations might consider as they build capacity. Similarly, *social and cultural* influences can have a fairly significant impact on nonprofits as values-based organizations. Depending on your perspective, the shift in cul-tural norms might reflect an opportunity or threat to the prin-ciples nonprofits exist to uphold. For example, there appears to be increasing tolerance for gay and lesbian couples and lifestyles in the United States (Dovere, Schultheis, & Summers, 2012). Although by no means universal, these cultural changes might affect an organization's ability to raise funds, expectations of growth or demand, and so on. Alternatively, such a shift might suggest an area where a nonprofit might want to respond, espe-cially if the shifts are counter to the cultural or historical val-ues of the organization. This signifies the nature of nonprofits to capture both progressive and conservative perspectives as well as values-based entities that attend to environmental conditions to either exploit opportunities for growth or counter trends that significant stakeholders believe are important.

Political and legal trends can signal opportunities as well as threats or priorities for different nonprofit organizations. For example, consider how U.S. society has shifted priori-ties toward punishment and incarceration of criminals over rehabilitation. This has caused the prison population to grow (as a percentage of population) and this has implications for not only agencies that directly work with the incarcerated but those associated with social services, prevention, education, and others (Guerino, Harrison, & Sabol, 2011). Furthermore, nonprofits are often positioned to influence political and legal processes. This will be discussed more, but recognizing politi-cal trends can suggest potential struggles or opportunities for the organization. For example, there appears to be a shift in political priorities to address the deficit concerns. It is not clear how that will progress, but it appears the general public is prioritizing this issue. Therefore, politicians will have to move forward some form of federal, state, and local budget cuts, which are likely to affect several areas important to nonprofits (education, health care, social services, and cultural arts) either through reduced funding or shifting demand. For example, reflecting on the prior policies of incarceration over rehabilitation and increasing pressure to cut costs might suggest ways that nonprofits could offer viable alternatives, at less cost, to long prison sentences.

Changes in the *technological* environment influence how individuals communicate and participate in social activities. Consider the use of mobile phone devices in raising funds. Especially in crisis situations, individuals can text donations to an organization in an instant. For example, the Red Cross was able to raise $5 million for the Haiti earthquake relief effort of 2010 in less than 48 hours (Hamblen, 2010). There are numerous other examples of how technology can change the way individuals receive services and organize or participate in philanthropic activities. For example, social media tools have changed the way individuals and organizations can organize political action. The speed and immediacy of action is impressive and changing the landscape of advocacy efforts (Scearce, Kasper, & Grant, 2010).

The last general environmental condition that nonprofits should monitor is *ecological factors*. Understanding how environmental issues are changing is of particular concern for environmental or preservation nonprofits, but as these conditions influence human capabilities, nonprofits should consider how and to what degree environmental conditions influence health and safety issues that might merit attention. That is a long list of potential environmental issues that might influence a particular organization's activities. These factors, however, suggest potential long-term issues for strategic decision making. Organizations should utilize reports and industry associations to help interpret and prioritize how these factors might impact organizational success (Gowdy, Hildebrand, La Piana, & Campos, 2009). The next elements are more proximal and reflect the task environment because they are more directly related to the activities of the organization.

Task Environment

Understanding the task environment is critical to success. Some organizations can operate with modest attention to the distant environmental factors, but all organizations must respond in some way to the task environment. The task environment can be grouped into five areas: social need or demand, funding opportunities, labor/workforce (volunteer and paid), community and political trends, and other providers. These are some of the most salient environmental pressures that nonprofits must address. There are two operating domains (resource and public benefit) and the task environment is the translation of those domains into elements that influence and are influenced by organizational actions. In addition to the two operating domains, nonprofits must attend to sociopolitical influences and these are discussed as part of the task environment. The elements of the task environment are complex, with multiple layers. Choices in one area have implications for actions in another. Fundamentally, it is how managers interpret these features and define the organization's role in relation to environmental opportunities and constraints that is the basis of strategic decision making. There are a few principles that can be useful when trying to define the elements of the task environment. In addition to the descriptive characteristics (e.g., turbulent, stable) already discussed, managers need to consider scope of activities.

There are two types of scope—broad or narrow (Porter, 1998). A broad scope attends to more demands or interests and thereby has an expanded market potential, such as the idea a child development center can serve *all* preschool-age children. This contrasts with a narrow focus that prioritizes a particular type of preschool child, such as those whose families that adhere to a certain religious traditions or to families with special disabilities. There are benefits and challenges to each strategy. A narrow focus allows the organization to specialize and meet the unique needs and preferences of a particular group. Such a strategy can succeed if there is enough demand for that specialization. A broad-based strategy expands the potential number of clients that can receive services from the agency, but some specialized services may not be offered and thereby the organization may not meet the specific interests of certain customers. Scope of activities applies to the resource context as well, such that certain organizations may specialize in securing funding from a particular source, while other organizations may build more broad-based resource strategies that capture funds from multiple and various sources. Scope is a strategic choice that is contingent on organizational capacity and environmental opportunities that managers interpret and define the operating context. Scope is an important aspect of how the dominant coalition has defined and articulated a response to question one from the strategic management cycle: What are we going to do?

Segmentation is the process of categorizing and organizing features of the task environment. Segmentation provides a method to define aspects of the task environment that the organization can or should address. Each of the features discussed in the next section are divided according to standards that are useful for research and operations. Exactly how environmental features are defined and segmented is critical for interpretation. The next section describes features in the task environment that should be considered to effectively answer questions about what the organization is going to do, what social issues it is going to address, and what resources it can utilize. The only way to get a handle on environmental opportunities and challenges is some attempt at segmentation that breaks the operating context into more manageable "bite-size" pieces (Weick, 1984). Segmentation allows leaders to more effectively interpret opportunities and challenges.

Social Need or Demand

By defining a social need or unacceptable social condition nonprofits make a rationale for operations. "A need is a measurable gap between two conditions—'what is' (the current status or state) and 'what should be' (the desired status or state)" (Altschuld & Kumar, 2010, p. 3). Nonprofits address a whole range of "gaps" including spiritual gaps, knowledge gaps, and social/cultural gaps. Definition and articulation of the social condition is fundamentally the public benefit justification that managers utilize to defend their tax-exempt status. How that condition is defined is based on interpretation and world-view (Checkland, 2000). Various actors within the organization engage in defining and describing community needs. At the corporate level, board members and executive leadership define broad categories of social priorities. This is often articulated in the organization's mission. Program managers further define social conditions and prioritize beneficiaries to guide program initiatives.

A needs assessment describes the "problem" and thereby sets the stage to propose the "solution" and the social value that the nonprofit could create. Defining "what is" and "what should be" are not necessarily obvious. Social conditions are complex, and multiple layers function simultaneously to suggest leverage points for improvement. Apparently "objective" definitions of need are influenced by social and cultural norms as well as the philosophical perspective of the nonprofit. Describing the conditions in society could be an objective process, but once that condition is defined as a "need" a worldview has been introduced. Needs suggest potential avenues for intervention; consequently problem definitions are influenced by the nature of solutions offered by the nonprofit.

Types of Needs Assessment

One method to understand the current condition is conducting a needs assessment, which describes social conditions in relation to the desired state so as to identify a gap. Needs assessments can define gaps in any variety of social issues or concerns, such as education, health, housing, culture, and so on. Comparable practices in a for-profit context could be conceptualized as a market analysis (Andreasen & Kotler, 2008), an attempt to understand the features of a customer market in relation to potential profitability. There are two basic types of needs assessments: one that is broad to capture and *describe the social condition* across the community, which is referred to as an extensive assessment (see **Table 3-3**); or one that is deep or intensive to describe the *causes of the problems.* An extensive needs assessment might describe the number and type of individuals that are homeless. This type of assessment can draw on demographic and community statistical information to provide a profile and status of social concerns in a particular community. The features that merit description include the size of the need and the pattern of growth or change over time. The environmental analysis methods discussed earlier (monitoring, forecasting, etc.) are useful in this process to detail and track key attributes that are indicative of the social issue. Nonprofits can utilize demographic statistical data, community surveys, and other community-wide assessments to profile community issues.

An intensive assessment attempts to describe the drivers of the social concern (Altschuld & Witkin, 2000). This often entails an in-depth, case-based approach to explore interrelationships to account for how issues develop. An intensive assessment further defines service options, but it also suggests how advocacy activities might be useful interventions. A needs assessment suggests *how* the organization can intervene to achieve results. This step is important because it facilitates the establishment of goals.

TABLE 3-3   Community Needs Assessment—Key Issues

Concept	Definition
Extensive assessment	Explores the prevalence of social issues and descriptive information regarding the target community
Intensive assessment	Attempts to explain causes of social issues and factors that account for prevalence, depth, and severity of social concerns
Type of need	The nature of need and the extent to which it is detriment to daily functioning
Assets and resources	The range and type of current services and other resource options
Beneficiary	Those associated with the need that gain advantage from organizational actions

Type of Need

Considering the type of need or social concern helps managers prioritize intervention activities that are important to the organization. Using Maslow's hierarchy of needs provides a basis to consider the level of the concern and the extent to which it is reflective of fundamental concerns or higher-level concerns (Maslow, 1943). Base-level *physiological needs* of food and water are described as a primary motivation for human behavior. While developed societies work to minimize these needs in the general population, disasters and emergency conditions can raise basic survival concerns. Similarly, *safety needs* are described as those related to housing, shelter, and so on that provides the basis for daily life and the ability to achieve higher-level needs. Next are *love needs* and those related to social relations. This includes the need to have positive social relationships that facilitate development, growth, and comfort. *Esteem needs* relate to psychological aspects of confidence and respect. The highest level of need is *self-actualization*, where individuals achieve moral and philosophical fulfillment. Societies build systems to address and facilitate human concerns across these needs. Nonprofits consider the extent to which they address more fundamental, base-level issues or higher-order needs. Nonprofits also build, develop, and sustain the systems that facilitate fulfillment. Given the complexity of social systems it can be difficult to ascertain how systems interwork to create societies that allow for all aspects of human development. Facilitating factors can at times be difficult to understand. What is the role of open space in civilized society, and how does that reflect cultural and norms and interests? Each nonprofit considers how they are part of the social systems that facilitate and support human development to create social value for a healthy society.

Assets and Resources

The definition of social conditions operate in conjunction with resources and sociopolitical factors, because by the very definition *needs* suggest a deficit in resource attributes or at the very least a gap in the systems that implement remediation. It is through the implementation of assets and capabilities that social conditions are improved (Kaufman, 2000). Nonprofits are the in the "business" of facilitating that process. In whatever way the gap is conceptualized (knowledge, economic, cultural, spiritual), nonprofits function to improve those conditions through the utilization of resources and sociopolitical forces. Sociopolitical forces include social norms and capital as well as the political systems that undergird society. Understanding the nature of community assets and capabilities provides a basis to build and structure interventions. There are a range of assets and systems that merit consideration and would include institutions and cultural relations. Knowledge of community assets informs how interventions can be designed or modified. Also, by exploring asset elements, nonprofits can identify a gap in service networks, thereby identifying service opportunities.

Beneficiary

Many nonprofits fulfill public benefit purposes through the delivery of services to particular service recipients. These beneficiaries or customers help define the public benefit market that the organization intends to influence. The process of selecting and prioritizing target beneficiaries is challenging. One way that businesses respond to selecting and prioritizing customers is through exchange relationships that generate profit. Nonprofits do not necessarily respond in this fashion (Shoham, Ruvio, Vigoda-Gadot, & Schwabsky, 2006; Zaleski & Esposto, 2007). After all, nonprofits often operate in a "failed" market (Steinberg, 2006). For instance, wait lists are much more common in nonprofits as opposed to for-profit organizations. Waiting lists signify a demand for services that is not met by current services. There are also examples of nonprofits that stay in service areas long after the need for services have shifted or changed. Nonprofits may not expand capacity to meet the full scale of needs, or they may be slow to adjust practices to changing needs.

In two different studies (Lynk, 1995; Starkweather, 1994) researchers found that some nonprofit hospitals don't take advantage of market dominance in the same way as for-profit entities. If a provider is the "only game in town," normally there would be some price inflation because competition tends to drive prices down. It appears nonprofits may not always do that. They may expand services or take on more difficult cases; in other words they use surplus market power to extend their charitable purposes. This doesn't happen in every instance, and there are plenty of examples of nonprofits that seem to abandon their charitable purposes (Keeler, Melnick, & Zwanziger, 1999; Starkweather, 1994). Confusion with market forces, and in particular beneficiaries, is not all that surprising because nonprofits do not operate exclusively on the exchange basis (i.e., customers = revenue).

This lack of market sensitivity might indeed be a good thing, because it potentially allows nonprofits to remain focused on their charitable purposes. However, given the potential for power differentials between service recipients and the nonprofit, some scholars recognize that nonprofits may not attend to the needs of beneficiaries in the way they should (Bruce, 1995; Twersky, Buchanan, & Threlfall, 2013). The literature identifies "market orientation," a concept entailing the extent to which organizations attend to market factors such as customer preferences (Pavicic, Alfirevic, & Mihanovic, 2009). In general, research suggests that organizations oriented toward customers (beneficiaries in this instance) are more effective. Nonprofits are morally accountable to beneficiaries but not financially accountable, and the ambiguity and power differential can be difficult to negotiate.

Financial Resources

Nonprofits secure funding from a variety of sources that include donors, government entities, corporations, individuals, and private foundations (Foster, 2007; Froelich, 1999; Jennings, 2004). Nonprofits utilize a variety of strategies to secure financial resources. The range of strategies to secure donations includes annual funds, major gifts, planned giving, and grants. Nonprofits also earn money through exchange relationships with paying clients and third-party contractors (insurance and government contract). Earned income, also referred to as fee income, is fundamentally different from gift or donated income. Fee income is provided with the expectation of receiving services, benefits, or rights that are commensurate with the amount of funds provided. Donations or gifts are provided without an expectation or legal right to receive services, rights, or benefits that are commensurate with the donation value (see **Table 3-4**). The ability to earn revenue through fees versus the ability to secure donations is invariably related to the types of services provided (Moulton & Eckerd, 2012).

TABLE 3-4   Financial Resource Options for Nonprofits

Type	Source	Description
Earned		
	Fees	Payment in exchange for services
	Private	Funds from personal resources
	Third party	Funds from third party
	Public	Government (federal, state, local) contract to provide services
Donated		
	Individuals	Gifts and donations through a variety of mechanisms
	Size	Gift size as determined by recipient
	Frequency	Gift frequency and reliability
	Private	Charitable foundations For-profit companies donations, sponsorships
	In-kind	New or used materials and supplies; professional and commercial services provided at no or low cost
Other		
	Investments	Return from invested capital
	Enterprise	"Business" activities to generate revenue

An important consideration is the extent to which nonprofits provide services that create private benefits or more public-type benefits. Defining nonprofit activities as primarily "public" or "private" is not simple (Fischer, Wilsker, & Young, 2011). The distinction reflects the tendency of benefits to reside with individuals or with the community. Education is an example of services that can reflect individual as well as public benefits. An educated population is critical for society and can be characterized as having broad social benefits. Consequently, many societies have decided that a certain level of education is available to everyone. Being educated also creates private benefits in the sense that higher levels of education are related to higher rates of pay. So as an individual you are motivated to gain an education because it improves your ability to earn an income. Services provided for a fee sets a criteria of eligibility that may dissuade those with less financial means, and nonprofits are potentially in a position to mitigate the influence of market-type factors such as ability to pay (Eikenberry, 2009). Providing services that meet private benefits facilities an organization's ability to charge fees, but it might diverge from the public benefit purposes of the organization.

Earned

Fees

The largest category of revenue for nonprofit organizations comes from fees paid for services or membership. According to the Urban Institute, nonprofits in the United States secured roughly 75% of their funds from fees (Roeger, Blackwood, & Pettijohn, 2011). The main source of fee income is related to payment for services. These fees come from private sources (individuals pay from their own means), or the fees come from other sources that include public sources (Medicaid) and third-party payment systems (insurance companies). Different industries rely on fees to different degrees. For instance, institutions of higher education rely heavily on fees through tuition to support their initiatives. Health care also relies heavily on fees and the funds come from multiple sources, which include individuals, insurance companies, and the government. The distinction is important because involvement of third-party entities influences the autonomy that individuals can exert in selecting services. Private sources foster individual autonomy whereas third-party sources might constrain the choice of services or providers. Similarly, the cost of services might be negotiated by the third-party source. One way to think about fee revenue (either private or public source) is that the funds are "earned" through the provision of service. The fee or price is linked to the level of service, and the recipient of the service has some control over the type of services desired. In many ways this appears similar to a commercial exchange.

Another source of fee income is from members. Many nonprofits have members, and these members pay a fee to gain certain rights. Member benefit organizations, for instance, charge a membership fee, which allows members to participate in a range of services and meetings (often for additional cost). Another example is the "Y" (formally the YMCA) that charges members a fee to access facilities and programs. Some nonprofits might subsidize certain membership categories if they perceive a public or private benefit in offering lower-cost membership to some. Often, however, membership fees are reflective of costs and market forces that influence pricing.

Part of what nonprofit managers need to understand is how their services are similar to commercial services and the extent to which the exchange relationship limits access to services and operates in competitive market forces. Fee-based revenue requires attention to customers in a way that is reflective of commercial services. If services are primarily offered to beneficiaries on the basis of ability to pay, nonprofit managers may be tempted to position or modify service-delivery options so as to capture paying customers. This has significant strategic and social implications. *creaming?*

Public Entities

Public entities include local, state, and federal governments. Contained within these broad categories are numerous departments and divisions that manage resource allocation to nonprofits. Public entities have historically been a fairly reliable source of funds for nonprofits. These funds used to be primarily granted to nonprofits to fulfill predetermined public purposes.

In 2009 government entities provided grants to nonprofits that accounted for about 9% of the aggregate revenue of the sector. As was discussed, governments also pay for services through fees. In 2009 these fees paid by government entailed 23% of the revenue reported by nonprofits. Either through fees or grants, government funds come with a number of restrictions. For example, there are guidelines regarding faith-based groups. Religious entities can receive funds from governments, but they are restricted in how they can expend those funds. They are not allowed to expend public funds on worship or proselytizing activities. There have been a number of initiatives to remove barriers from faith-based organizations so that they can provide public benefit services while retaining private priorities. There are a number of criteria required by public funders that some nonprofits may find constraining.

Public funds tend to come with high accountability demands (Smith & Lipsky, 1995). This is particularly true for grant funds. Given the nature of public funds, administrators need to document how the funds were used. These accountability demands can be quite burdensome. The requirements tend to reflect documentation regarding who was served, the type of services provided, and the outcomes achieved. As was noted, governments tend to be shifting toward fee-based support, often empowering the beneficiary to utilize authorized services that are then paid by the government to nonprofits. Medicare is the most significant provider of these types of funds. Public funds have traditionally been a reliable source of revenue, but with the shift to fee-based funding and cuts to state and local governments, many nonprofits are challenged to operate under the current regime. For instance, fee or voucher programs require nonprofits to negotiate the consumer market in ways that they may not be prepared for. The other challenge with public funds is that the funds are typically provided *after* the services are provided. This reflects the accountability demands of public entities. They need to clearly define and control how funds are used. Providing funds through reimbursements allows public entities significant control to deny or limit certain expenses, but this places significant cash flow pressure on nonprofits (Boris, de Leon, Roeger, & Nikolova, 2010).

Donated

In 2012 nonprofits raised a total of $316.23 billion (Giving USA 2013, 2013). Individuals provide the bulk of those funds. In 2012 individuals provided $227.7 billion (72%) in donated income. Individual bequests (gifts given after death) accounted for another $28.5 billion (9%). About a third of those gifts went to religious institutions. Educational entities secured 13% of those funds, as did human service organizations. These gifts are given or donated with limited or no expectation of directly receiving something of comparable value in exchange. Donated or philanthropic gifts are fundamentally different in that the donor receives no direct benefit for the provision of funds. That does not mean there might not be expectations for particular actions on the part of the nonprofit. The nature and character of those expectations have significant implications for managers and donors. There are two basic features of the gift that guide decision making for managers. The first is the size of the gift and second is frequency (current or anticipated). The development manager tries to increase the size and frequency of gifts, consequently the third criteria is the potential capacity of the giver.

Size of the gift is a basic method to analyze donations. Size is determined by the recipient. That is, the nonprofit makes a judgment of what constitutes a "major" gift. For small nonprofits that might be as little as a $1000, and for institutions of higher education it could be $10,000 or more before they perceive the gift as significant. Depending on the size of the gift, nonprofits will enact different practices to secure and manage the gift. With larger gifts nonprofits are willing to relinquish some autonomy and to expend more resources.

Frequency of the gift is also a consideration for nonprofit managers. Small gifts are often managed through development campaigns that seek to secure regular gifts that are provided at least once a year but hopefully more often. Consider houses of worship that secure the bulk of individual donations typically obtained through regular, small contributions that are collected and managed on an ongoing basis. Conversely, major gifts are typically conceived as one-time gifts.

capacity of giver

Assessing and determining the capacity of the giver is the crux of fundraising. Determining prospects for giving is complex as the features that merit analysis are not all objective. Rather, attachment and commitment influences the donor's willingness to give as much as objective factors related to wealth. This reflects the need of development officers to monitor current fundraising successes as well as making judgments about potential givers.

Private Entities

Private foundations granted over $45 billion in 2012. While this is a significant amount of money, it reflects just 3% of the gross revenue for nonprofits and just 15% of the charitable giving. There are a number of different types of foundations (private, corporate, community, etc.), and the funds are disbursed in a number of different forms. The most common are formalized grants, with clear, deliverable expectations, but foundations also provided funds in a way that is similar to major gifts from individuals. The level of formality often relates to the strength of prior relationships and the priorities of the foundation. Private foundations reflect two stages of funding arrangements. Initially, funding is fairly formal, and over time the arrangements can evolve to be more informal and less contractual (Grønbjerg, Martell, & Paarlberg, 2000).

In-Kind Donations

Beyond cash, some nonprofits are active in receiving in-kind gifts and services. In-kind gifts are products (new or used) that are given to the nonprofit to either use or sell. These can come from individuals or organizations. For instance, food banks receive millions of dollars in food products that they then distribute to the needy. Many nonprofits gather used clothing or household items and then either sell those items on the secondary market or within their own thrift store (see the following section on enterprise activities).

It is not uncommon for municipalities to provide in-kind support to nonprofits through low-cost use of facilities. This is a mutually beneficial arrangement that locates services in a desirable location for the municipality. Other organizations may support the nonprofit through professional services or access to technical assistance. In-kind gifts can be very valuable and reflect another "kind" of gift that requires the nonprofit to extract the value either for their own use (e.g., pro bono accounting services) or for the benefit of the service recipients (e.g., food given to the needy). The translation of in-kind gifts into valuable assets can be fairly straightforward, as the two examples reflect, or the translation can be more complex. Consider for instance, when someone donates an old car to the local PBS radio station. The nonprofit has to have a system to extract any remaining value in that item, which is completely outside of their skill sets. In-kind gifts can require the development of competencies that are unique to the gift, and at times those competencies can be complex and expensive. In the example of an old car donated for scrap or the wholesale market, there can be relatively limited value in the item and significant cost to process paperwork, transport, and disposal of the vehicle. Thus, in-kind gifts can be valuable, but they also reflect a need to be flexible so the nonprofit can use the items or develop a system that translates these items into value.

Other Sources of Funds

In addition to the resources just described, nonprofits can also look to other avenues to secure funds. Although these methods account for just a fraction of the total revenue for nonprofits nationally, for some nonprofits these alternative sources can be quite significant. Two alternative sources of funds are discussed. Enterprise activities are increasingly appealing and reflect the efforts of nonprofits to engage in business activities that net profits that are then provided to the nonprofit. Investment income is highly desirable, but it is difficult to build a large capital base that generates significant revenue.

Investment Income

Income from investments is a desirable source of funds because they are historically quite reliable. The fundamental challenge is, of course, to have enough money to invest. It takes a significant corpus of capital to generate substantial revenue. While returns generated from investments varies with the market, 5% returns have been the rule-of-thumb that nonprofits anticipate being able to spend annually. That amount typically preserves the capital base, pays for administrative costs, and may even build the corpus overtime. Most private charitable foundations have significant capital invested and spend only the proceeds of those funds. The challenge is securing the capital. The most common practice is to solicit major gifts that are then deposited and invested. These are also called endowments, and institutions of higher education are quite adept at securing these types of funds. The specific purposes of these funds are influenced by the donor preferences, but nonprofits can have some latitude in how these proceeds are expended. In those instances when nonprofits can preserve capital earned through other sources, they are able to use the investment income to meet basic operating costs or for any purpose they see fit. There is some controversy regarding whether nonprofits should hold large sums of money while only expending modest amounts. Could those funds be put to better use if the money were made available for programs and services? The alternative argument is that holding assets secures the work of the nonprofit for the long haul. The ability to hold and manage significant assets has significant implications for management and sustainability (Bowman, Tuckman, & Young, 2012).

Enterprise Activities

Some nonprofits engage in business activities that generate revenue. This can include renting facilities or operating a business activity that transfers profits to the nonprofit. These "enterprise" activities can be difficult to operate. There are competitive forces that are distinct from the core mission purpose. There are business activities that more aligned with the purposes of the organization, such as operating a coffee shop to provide skills training to developmentally disabled clients or having a museum gift shop. Some nonprofits operate activities that are not directly related but capitalize on their name recognition. Big Brothers Big Sisters (BBBS) of Central Arizona raises millions of dollars every year through donated clothing and household items. They operate an entire fleet of trucks and a processing center that evaluates and sorts the items. They net on average $1 million dollars a year, and although the operations have been challenged by other nonprofits conducting similar operations, it has been a surprisingly stable source of funds. Some case could be made that it is too disconnected from the purposes of the organization and the competencies required to operate the program are too difficult, but BBBS of Central Arizona has nurtured and managed this operation for over 20 years. Furthermore, they rely on these funds and have not been able to develop an alternative source of funds that is as reliable, autonomous, and significant. Once BBBS has these funds they are able to use them for a whole range of administrative and operational costs. If these businesses can be operated at a profit, it can provide a reliable and independent source of funds. The challenge is creating a viable business "on the side" or determining if a business enterprise can be created that extends the existing service activities into commercial activities. The philosophy of enterprise activities is that if nonprofits can access commercial sales they might be able to tap into significant market opportunities.

Summary of Financial Resources

These revenue sources are complex and require specialized capabilities and sophisticated relationship management techniques. Consequently, organizations must prioritize revenue-generation practices while vigilantly monitoring changes in the funding environment. Nonprofits have two basic problems in relation to revenues. First is the degree to which the funds are *restricted* by the funder. That means the funder controls how the money can be spent. Many government contracts and foundation grants have very specific guidelines about how the money can be spent and allocated. On the other hand, fees generated through services and, to some degree, individual donations (although major gifts are notable exceptions) are less restrictive and allow nonprofits to allocate funds according to needs. The second concern is related to stability or *reliability* over time. Few income streams can be guaranteed forever. Investment income is probably the most stable, but as the recent financial downturn demonstrated, even that source of revenue can be unreliable. So the challenge is to find revenue that is unrestricted and reliable. The prevalent management advice is to diversify revenue streams so as to minimize the effect of any one revenue source. If grants from foundations are down, then government contracts might be able to hold the agency over, and so on. This, however, requires building capabilities in various resource development and fundraising methods, which might be very difficult to accomplish. An alternative is to focus revenue generation on a select few entities or sources and become very adept at those sources. Of course, viability is contingent on that revenue source. Research suggests that some of the largest nonprofits tend to rely on just a few sources of revenue (e.g., fees, government grants) (Foster, 2007).

Labor

The heterogeneity of the sector makes it difficult to generalize too much about the nonprofit workforce, but some characteristics are worth noting. First, nonprofits benefit from utilizing two types of labor: paid and unpaid (volunteers). There are fundamental differences in working with paid and unpaid workers that have implications for organizational structures and capabilities (Anheier & Kendall, 2002). There is a vast literature in human resource management that details practices of recruitment, selection, job design, evaluation, compensation, and separation for paid employees (Schneider, 2009). These practices are primarily based on research and learning from for-profit businesses or public entities. There is an increasing level of research looking specifically at nonprofits, but the field is relatively limited (Coffe & Geys, 2007; Weisinger & Black, 2006). Some features to consider about the nonprofit workforce include the tendency to have highly specialized workers, the work tends to be values based, and individuals often engage to meet expressive needs. These factors can be prevalent for both paid and unpaid workers. For many nonprofits, the workforce is specialized and highly educated. For example, doctors practice in hospitals, faculty teach in institutions of higher education, scientists work in research centers, and artists and musicians perform in cultural and arts organizations. This type of workforce has high demands for autonomy and creativity. Nonprofit work also tends to be values based, and many individuals have a high commitment to the cause as much as or more than to the organization. For these individuals the work is highly expressive (Cornforth, 2001) and participating in the organization is based upon intrinsic value. Not exclusively, but the influence of mission and purpose is a significant element in retaining and attracting the nonprofit workforce (Brown & Yoshioka, 2003). Many volunteers as well engage and participate in the work of nonprofits because they believe in the mission of the organization. Volunteers may serve for social or professional development reasons, but volunteers that are committed to the purpose of the organization are likely to work harder and stay longer (Brown, Hillman, & Okun, 2012; Preston & Brown, 2004). In addition, there are staff members that operate and carry out services with some attachment to the cause or organization while also being dependent on the entity for their livelihood. Part of the challenge for all organizations is to balance and capitalize on intrinsic and expressive benefits while meeting instrumental needs. For nonprofits, compensation is typically under market value, although numerous factors influence compensation in the sector. Furthermore, nonprofits are in a unique position to help individuals fulfill expressive interests. For instance, one demographic trend is the impending retirement of the baby boomer generation, who have a strong civic interest (Gowdy et al., 2009). How will nonprofits capitalize on this potential workforce? This is just one more example of the complex workforce that nonprofits can utilize.

Sociopolitical Interests

Of the five elements of the nonprofit task environment, social and political interests are probably the most ambiguous. It reflects the mix of nonmarket factors (Henisz & Zelner, 2012) such as social capital, cultural norms, political power, and legal structures. Nonprofits are dependent on the attribution of legitimacy ascribed by significant stakeholders, and operating to influence attitudes, rules, and structures in the sociopolitical domain has potential organizational and social benefits (see **Table 3-5**). Nonprofits focus their activities toward sociopolitical entities as a method to achieve mission and charitable purpose and to sustain organizational operations. Nonprofits need to develop a political strategy (Bigelow, Stone, & Arndt, 1996), which is the combination of efforts to manage perceptions of legitimacy and influence social structures.

develop political strategy

Legitimacy

There are three types of legitimacy: legal/regulatory, normative, and cognitive (Schmid, 2009) (see Table 3-5).

specific

The *legal/regulatory* aspect reflects the formal rules and laws that organizations and groups must comply with. This includes such things as filing paperwork for recognition as a nonprofit and annual reporting expectations that track and monitor nonprofit organizations. Regulatory compliance reflects adherence to principles and rules associated with industry standards. For instance, the inability of childcare centers to get licensed can limit their ability to function and operate. In some ways these are rather benign and fundamental aspects of operating an organization and are not all that distinctive to the sector, although some

TABLE 3-5 Types of Legitimacy and Potential Organizational Response

Type	Definition	Example Activities
Legal and regulatory	Legal rules and laws that guide organizations	Compliance with laws, participation in accreditation practices, and advocacy to influence and change rules and laws
Normative	Values of dominant stakeholders	Alignment with values system and tactics to alter social values
Cognitive	Thoughts and perceptions of significant stakeholders	Education, marketing, and public relations

nonprofits do have special exemptions for government oversight (e.g., religious institutions). Government and regulatory bodies are the primary granters of legal legitimacy.

Normative legitimacy is associated with understanding the values basis of significant stakeholders and attending to those interests. This shifts the source of legitimacy from specific legal or government entities to a broader idea of "community." To be [*broad*] clear, nonprofits often exist to promote minority interests, so primary stakeholders in this context might be a disenfranchised group. The extent to which nonprofits hope to influence constituencies is partially dependent on the way they define and articulate core values and beliefs. One significant source of legitimacy [*source*] is the extent to which the entity is perceived to operate fairly (Tyler, 2006). This reflects the need for organizations to operate openly and transparently so as to demonstrate their honest and fair practices. Stakeholders look to see if the organizations operate according to reasonable practices that demonstrate fairness. Tapping into norms and beliefs that reflect interests of key stakeholders is central to attaining normative legitimacy.

Cognitive legitimacy reflects the perceptions of key stakeholders and how they understand the organization. Many nonprofits complain that many individuals just don't understand [*reputation*] what they do. This is probably true in many instances. Part of what a nonprofit has to consider is the extent to which they can educate, influence, and change perceptions. Widespread recognition may not be a viable option for many nonprofits, but understanding and influencing perceptions of key groups is a fundamental and critical task. This, in some ways, is similar to building a "brand" with generally positive perceptions. Cognitive legitimacy is related to the concept of reputation. Positive reputation recognizes that the nonprofit is able to build a brand image that is legitimate and salient to key stakeholders.

Targets of Sociopolitical Activities

To frame the range and type of activities utilized in this area it is useful to consider three broad segments of the sociopolitical domain: community members, public entities, and private entities (see **Table 3-6**). Activities targeted at community members

TABLE 3-6 Targets and Objectives of Advocacy

Target	Objectives: What Is Intended to Change?
Community members, general public, and key stakeholders	Knowledge, awareness, attitudes, social capital, social norms, behavior, and engagement
Public entities	Election results, resource allocation, law creation, policy implementation, regulatory action, and enforcement behavior
Private entities	Organizational practices related to product development, labor, distribution, and so on; support for social policies; industry standards

have several objectives including raising awareness about a social problem or issues, shifting perceptions about appropriate behavior, and trying to unite and mobilize constituents into action to influence other targets (government or corporations). Public entities can be the focus of political action. This is a common focus of many advocacy and lobbying activities and includes all levels of public entities: local governments, oversight boards, county government, state government, and federal government. The objectives in this area relate to influencing all phases of the legislative and governing processes, which includes attempts to influence election results, shift allocation practices, and guide the creation and implementation of laws and policies. There are also advocacy-type activities targeted at private institutions. Private institutions are the target of advocacy activities when their activities may negatively impact priorities of the nonprofit. This includes environmental practices, consumer rights, and labor issues. The next section explores these targets and the intended objectives nonprofits might try to achieve.

Community Members

The public serves as a target for sociopolitical activities in several ways. First, many nonprofits seek to bring together community members as a coalition of concerned individuals. Grassroots organizing is the historical basis of how nonprofits identify issues and garner sufficient power to achieve political and social objectives. A related objective is to build social networks and connections among community members. An organized and socially connected community is significantly more powerful and serves as a basis to engage community members in action. Broader objectives in this area include a desire to raise awareness and knowledge about the issue. This includes educating community members about the range, size, and scope of the issue as well as information about how to overcome the challenges posed by the issue. Public education campaigns are a common practice utilized to educate and inform constituents about issues. Aggregating individual awareness into shared social norms is also an objective when working with community members. The norms regarding smoking in public are an example of how these shifts become the dominant philosophy guiding behavior in society. The ability to create dominant social norms is an incredibly powerful social influence mechanism, but these norms are not easily developed. Community organizing and educational initiatives are based on fundamental principles of shifting and changing human behavior.

Public Entities

A range of public entities can be the focus of advocacy activities. This includes local government entities and boards to state-level politicians and federal bureaucracies. There are numerous methods to influence the policy discussion. These activities are typically conceptualized as lobbying, and they entail a broad range of tactics that involve direct engagement in policy decision making as well as information and research activities that form the backbone of knowledge that guides advocacy activities. One way to organize these activities is to think about the political, legislative, and regulatory process from the beginning to the end. The beginning of the process relates to elections or appointing policy decision makers. Organizations work to ensure the *right* individual is charged with decision making. Elections are the focus of massive financial and political pressure. The middle steps are associated with creating laws, policies, and rules that will be enacted either through administrative or legislative action. A particular focus of lobbying activities is to influence how government funds are dispersed and allocated in all the various formats, contracting, budgeting, tax-incentives, earmarks that set aside funds for particular initiatives, and entitlement disbursements through social security and Medicare. During policy making, an initial stage is advocating for an issue to be discussed. There are lots of competing pressures, and not all social issues receive the same amount of discussion and attention. Garnering attention to social concerns requires significant effort to elevate issues to policy makers' attention. Once an issue is under consideration, lobbying activities inform and guide decision makers about priorities and policy options. Nonprofits try to help policy makers understand the issue and options. The "end" of the process entails implementation of these policies and the tedious work of creating and interpreting how the rules will be carried out. Once a law is authorized there are a number leverage points related to how the law is implemented and enforced. Nonprofit "watchdog" groups focus on how the government acts to fulfill the objectives detailed in the law. Furthermore, through court action, nonprofits can force government entities to defend and explain practices related to laws and regulations. Watchdog groups allocate significant resources to evaluate the effectiveness of policy decisions. They provide long-term tracking of the effect of the policy decision. The creation or enactment of laws is the first phase; monitoring and tracking implementation and, ultimately, outcomes of policy decisions is a critical role for nonprofit advocacy groups. It is not quite that simple, but the three areas provide a framework to consider nonprofit advocacy activities.

Private Entities

There are a number of private entities that can be the focus of advocacy activities; this includes businesses and corporations, trade and professional associations, and other nonprofit entities that have activities related to the issues under consideration. Fundamentally, these initiatives are intended to change organizational practices so as to align or comply with the philosophical objectives of the nonprofit. Consumer rights organizations have become widely recognized as instrumental actors. The pioneering work of Ralph Nader compiled a litany of concerns against automobile manufactures (Nader, 1965) and raised public awareness about these issues. Ultimately, manufactures had to adjust the quality and type of automobiles produced. In addition to concerns regarding products and services, private entities can be the target of advocacy activities to force them to comply with production and manufacturing standards to ensure appropriate use of resources, labor practices, and pollution concerns. For example, Greenpeace engaged in an advocacy campaign against Kimberly-Clark and brought about changes in the production of paper products. In 2004, Greenpeace targeted Kimberly-Clark because of their sourcing practices. According to Greenpeace, Kimberly-Clark received nearly a quarter of its tissue paper from Canadian boreal forests and 200-year-old trees. Greenpeace waged an aggressive campaign with YouTube videos, blockades, and protests. General media picked up on the campaign, and Kimberly-Clark began to worry about the negative publicity. By 2008 Kimberly-Clark and Greenpeace met to discuss a future relationship and sustainability goals. Kimberly-Clark set goals to increase product recycling and stopped sourcing noncertified wood. They continue to meet biannually with Greenpeace to discuss initiatives and goals. Greenpeace advocated, set goals to change sourcing requirements, and effectively educated Kimberly-Clark (Schwartz, 2011). This case provides a nice summary of the activities in this area because it demonstrates that some activities are conflict based while other efforts are cooperative. The blending of attack-type activities and cooperative activities seems critical to success in these areas.

Other Providers

The final element of the nonprofit task environment is other "providers." Other providers entail the variety of entities that operate in similar task environments. One set of other providers are those that are offering similar services to similar beneficiaries. There are also those entities that provide similar services but focus on different beneficiaries. Nonprofits must be aware of other entities that are providing similar services or are concerned and involved in similar public benefit purposes. In addition to considering other providers exclusively in relation to service beneficiaries, nonprofits must also consider entities that might compete for similar resources or funding streams (Lange, Lee, & Dai, 2011). Although a social service agency may partner and collaborate with another provider to meet the needs of a particular client or to expand services to another region, they may be less inclined to share information about major donors. Furthermore, donors may be active across multiple domains (homeless services, education, etc.). This tendency of funders to operate across multiple industries expands the number and type of entities nonprofits might be competing with in a resource environment. For example, a community foundation may be active in multiple funding areas: children and family, health, neighborhood revitalization, and so on. Allocations in one area may impact funding in other areas. This could be a strategic choice of the funder or it could be a unique opportunity revealed as applications are reviewed and prioritized. Consequently, a child services organization may lose out on funding because more funds were allocated to an innovative alcohol and drug abuse prevention program. There may not be much the nonprofit can do to thwart the activities of the drug and alcohol prevention program (nor would they necessarily want to). The nonprofit can, however, attend to the funder to help manage that relationship so that they do not lose necessary resources. Nonprofits attend to funder interests to understand which other entities are potentially threatening revenue. Each of the areas discussed in the task environment may involve a similar cast of other providers or a different set of entities that can affect the nonprofit's success, and it is tantamount to know about those entities, their purposes, and their motivations.

Conclusion

The external environment is a critical factor in the success and failure of nonprofit organizations. The chapter describes several key aspects of the nonprofit environment and proposed two realms of environmental factors: one that is more distant and the second that is more likely to directly affect the operating activities of the organization. Understanding the range and depth of key elements in the environment helps the organization succeed. Basic techniques to scan and monitor key elements in the general and task environment are critical ongoing activities. These elements in the environment exhibit various characteristics, some relatively simple (just a few dominant funders) and others more complex (a broad range of funders and resource opportunities). It is critical to understand how these characteristics are exhibited in the various aspects of the environment. Describing the task environment of a nonprofit can be challenging for many organizations that tend to operate with indeterminate purposes to achieve ambitious objectives. The fundamental advantage of strategic management decision making is the explicit definitions of domain focus. Alternative language discusses industries and markets. Industries are broad categories that encompass a full range of issues, participants, and concerns within markets. The specification of the domain, in reference to public or member benefit, is the first priority for nonprofits, but that focus is influenced by the resource opportunities available. So not only do nonprofits consider entities and issues relevant to their specific public benefit purpose, they must also understand how resource opportunities function and how other providers interact and utilize those resources. Nonprofits have to frame and understand their operating context, which includes their public benefit purpose, the resource opportunities available, and the political or community context.

Discussion Questions

1. Explain the different features of the nonprofit task environment. Which of these are *most* important to a nonprofit and why?
2. Do you think most nonprofits are more oriented toward service beneficiaries or funding opportunities? Why do you think that is the case? How can nonprofits balance the influence of these two forces?
3. Compare and contrast the different revenue sources in relation to control and stability.

References

2011 State of the Sector. (2011). New York, NY: Nonprofit Finance Fund.

Altschuld, J. W., & Kumar, D. D. (2010). *Needs assessment: An overview.* Los Angeles, CA: Sage.

Altschuld, J. W., & Witkin, B. R. (2000). *From needs assessment to action.* Thousand Oaks, CA: Sage.

Andreasen, A. R., & Kotler, P. (2008). *Strategic marketing for nonprofit organizations* (7th ed.). Upper Saddle Rover, NJ: Pearson, Prentice Hall.

Anheier, H., & Kendall, J. (2002). Interpersonal trust and voluntary associations: Examining three approaches. *The British Journal of Sociology, 53*(3), 343–362.

Bigelow, B., Stone, M. M., & Arndt, M. (1996). Corporate political strategy: A framework for understanding nonprofit strategy. *Nonprofit Management and Leadership, 7*(1), 29–43.

Boris, E. T., de Leon, E., Roeger, K. L., & Nikolova, M. (2010). *Human service nonprofits and government collboration: Findings from the 2010 national survey.* Washington, DC: Urban Institute.

Bowman, W., Tuckman, H. P., & Young, D. R. (2012). Issues in nonprofit finance research. *Nonprofit and Voluntary Sector Quarterly, 41*(4), 560–579.

Brown, W. A., Hillman, A. J., & Okun, M. A. (2012). Factors that influence monitoring and resource provision among nonprofit board members. *Nonprofit and Voluntary Sector Quarterly, 41*(1), 145–156.

Brown, W. A., & Yoshioka, C. F. (2003). Mission attachment and satisfaction as factors in employee retention. *Nonprofit Management & Leadership, 14*(1), 5–18.

Bruce, I. (1995). Do not-for-profits value their customers and their needs? *International Marketing Review, 12*(4), 77–84.

Canon, G. (2011). Economic recession continues to hit nonprofits hard. *Huffington Post.* Retrieved from http://www.huffingtonpost.com/2011/03/22/nonprofits-continue-to-fe_n_838855.html

Checkland, P. (2000). Soft systems methodology: A thirty year retrospective. *Systems Research and Behavioral Science, 17*(S1), S11.

Coffe, H., & Geys, B. (2007). Toward an empirical characterization of bridging and bonding social capital. *Nonprofit and Voluntary Sector Quarterly, 36*(1), 121–139.

Cornforth, C. (2001). What makes board effective? An examination of the relationships between board inputs, structures, processes and effectiveness in non-profit organizations. *Corporate Governance, 9*(3), 217–229.

Crutchfield, L. R., & Grant, H. M. (2008). *Forces for good: The six practices of high-impact nonprofits.* San Francisco, CA: Jossey-Bass.

Davis, L. (2005). 25 years of saving lives. *Driven,* (Fall ed., pp. 8–17): Mothers Against Drunk Driving.

Dovere, E. I., Schultheis, E., & Summers, J. (2012). Gay marriage takes next steps. *Politico.* Retrieved from http://www.politico .com/news/stories/1112/84064.html

Eikenberry, A. M. (2009). Refusing the market: A democratic discorse for voluntary and nonprofit organizations. *Nonprofit and Voluntary Sector Quarterly, 38*(4), 582–596.

Fischer, R. L., Wilsker, A., & Young, D. R. (2011). Exploring the revenue mix of nonprofit organizations: Does it relate to publicness? *Nonprofit and Voluntary Sector Quarterly, 40*(4), 662–681.

Foster, W. (2007, Spring). How nonprofits get really big. *Stanford Social Innovation review,* 46–55.

Froelich, K. A. (1999). Diversification of revenue strategies: Evolving resource dependence in nonprofit organizations. *Nonprofit and Voluntary Sector Quarterly, 28*(3), 246–268.

Giving USA 2013. (2013). Indianapolis, IN: Center on Philanthropy.

Gowdy, H., Hildebrand, A., La Piana, D., & Campos, M. M. (2009). *Convergence: How five trends will reshape the social sector.* San Francisco, CA: James Irvine Foundation.

Grønbjerg, K. A., Martell, L., & Paarlberg, L. (2000). Philanthropic funding of human services: Solving ambiguity through the two-stage competitive process. *Nonprofit and Voluntary Sector Quarterly, 29*(suppl 1), 9–40.

Guerino, P., Harrison, P. M, & Sabol, W. J. (2011). *Prisoners in 2010.* Washington, DC: U.S. Department of Justice.

Hamblen, M. (2010, January 15). Text donations for Haiti earthquake overwhelm Red Cross. *Computerworld.* Retrieved from http://www.computerworld.com/s/article/9145398/Text_donations_for_Haiti_earthquake_overwhelm_Red_Cross_?pageNumber=1

Hasenfeld, Y. (1983). *Human service organizations.* Englewood Cliffs, NJ: Prentice Hall.

Henisz, W. J., & Zelner, B. A. (2012). Strategy and competition in the market and nonmarket arenas. *The Academy of Management Perspectives, 26*(3), 40–51.

Hitt, M. A., Ireland, D. R., & Hoskisson, R. E. (2011). *Strategic management competitiveness and globalization* (9th ed.). Mason, OH: South-Western Cengage.

Jennings, N. K. (2004). Which came first, the project or the fundraising? *The Bottom Line: Managing Library Finances, 17*(3), 108–110.

Kaufman, R. (2000). *Mega planning: Practical tools for organizational success.* Thousand Oaks, CA: Sage.

Keeler, E. B., Melnick, G., & Zwanziger, J. (1999). The changing effects of competition on non-profit and for-profit hospital pricing behavior. *Journal of Health Economics, 18*(1), 69–86.

Lange, D., Lee, P. M., & Dai, Y. (2011). Organizational reputation: A review. *Journal of Management, 37*(1), 153–184.

Lynk, W. J. (1995). Nonprofit hospital mergers and the exercise of market power. *Journal of Law and Economics, 38*(2), 437–461.

Maslow, A. H. (1943). A theory of human motivation. *Psychological Review, 50*(4), 370–396.

Moulton, S., & Eckerd, A. (2012). Preserving the publicness of the nonprofit sector. *Nonprofit and Voluntary Sector Quarterly, 41*(4), 656–685.

Nader, R. (1965). *Unsafe at any speed.* New York, NY: Grossman.

Nonprofit Fundraising Study. (2011). Nonprofit Research Collaborative.

Pavicic, J., Alfirevic, N., & Mihanovic, Z. (2009). Market orientation in managing relatoinships with multiple constituencies of Croatian higher education. *Higher Education, 57*, 191–207.

Porter, M. E. (1998). *Competitive strategy: Techniques for analyzing industries and competitors* (2nd ed.). New York, NY: Free Press.

Preston, J. B., & Brown, W. A. (2004). Commitment and performance of nonprofit board members. *Nonprofit Management & Leadership, 15*(2), 221–238.

Rainey, H. G. (2003). *Understanding and managing public organizations* (3rd ed.). San Francisco, CA: Wiley Imprint.

Roeger, K. L., Blackwood, A., & Pettijohn, S. L. (2011). *The nonprofit sector in brief.* Washington, DC: Urban Institute.

Scearce, D., Kasper, G., & Grant, H. M. (2010, Summer). Working wikily. *Stanford Social Innovation Review,* 31–37.

Schmid, H. (2009). Agency-environmental relations: Understanding external and natural environments. In R. J. Patti (Ed.), *The handbook of human services management* (pp. 411–434). Thousand Oaks, CA: Sage.

Schneider, J. A. (2009). Organizational social capital and nonprofits. *Nonprofit and Voluntary Sector Quarterly, 38*(4), 643–662.

Schwartz, A. (2011, January 18). How Kimberly-Clark ditched its forest-destroying reputation and embraced Greenpeace. *Fast Company.* Retrieved from http://www.fastcompany.com/1718476/exclusive-how-kimberly-clark-ditched-its-forest-destroying-reputation-and-embraced-greenpeac

Shoham, A., Ruvio, A., Vigoda-Gadot, E., & Schwabsky, N. (2006). Market orientations in the nonprofit and voluntary sector: A meta-analysis of their relationships with organizational performance. *Nonprofit and Voluntary Sector Quarterly, 35*(3), 453–476.

Smith, S. R., & Lipsky, M. (1995). *Nonprofits for hire: The welfare state in the age of contracting.* Boston, MA: Harvard University Press.

Starkweather, D. B. (1994). Profit making by nonprofit hospitals. In D. Hammack & D. R. Young (Eds.), *Nonprofit organizations in a market economy* (pp. 105–137). San Francisco, CA: Jossey Bass.

Steinberg, R. (2006). Economic theories of nonprofit organizaions. In W. W. Powell & R. Steinberg (Eds.), *The nonprofit sector: A research handbook* (2nd ed., pp. 117–139). New Haven, CT: Yale University.

Twersky, F., Buchanan, P., & Threlfall, V. (2013). Listening to those who matter most, the beneficiaries. *Stanford Social Innovation Review, 6*(Spring), 40–45.

Tyler, T. R. (2006). Psychological perspectives on legitimacy and legitimation. *Annual Review of Psychology, 57*, 375–400.

Weick, K. E. (1984). Small wins: Redefining the scale of social problems. *American Psychologist, 39*(1), 40–49.

Weisinger, J. Y., & Black, J. A. (2006). Strategic resources and social capital. *Irish Journal of Management, 27*(Special Issue), 145–170.

Zaleski, P., & Esposto, A. (2007). The response to market power: Non-profit hospitals versus for-profit hospitals. *Atlantic Economic Journal, 35*(3), 315–325.

CHAPTER 4

Internal Capabilities

Learning Objectives

- Explain the rationale for creating a comparative advantage
- Understand the aspects of the nonprofit value framework
- Describe attributes of the nonprofit resource portfolio
- Summarize key management functions

Understanding the external environment is only part of the formula for effective strategic management. The ability of the organization to *respond* and create value for stakeholders is the other half of the equation. This chapter will review some of the attributes of nonprofit organizations that facilitate their ability to achieve public benefits. Using a resource-based view of the organization (Hitt, Ireland, & Hoskisson, 2011), the chapter presents a model to explain how nonprofits can structure and build organizational capabilities. Capabilities entail the use of organizational systems and resources to achieve objectives. Defining operating domains recognizes that there are multiple and at times competing demands for nonprofits. We expect that nonprofits will utilize capabilities to achieve public benefit or social impact. We know as well that nonprofits build capabilities to secure resources. Nonprofits also build capabilities to increase their influence in the sociopolitical domain. These objectives are guided by the public benefit mission of the organization. Part of how nonprofits fulfill priorities is by providing value to significant stakeholders including beneficiaries and donors. Nonprofit managers must determine the extent to which they can meet those objectives in unique and distinctive ways. There is no long-term advantage to meeting stakeholder interests in ways that can be easily provided by others. Effective utilization of resource capabilities and focusing on select core competencies is difficult. The chapter presents the nonprofit value framework, which depicts the resource portfolio, management functions, and program activities working together to achieve public benefit outcomes.

Nonprofit Value Framework

There are three parts to the nonprofit value framework (NVF): resource portfolio, management functions, and program activities (see **Figure 4-1**). These parts represent the internal attributes of a nonprofit organization, which are structured to achieve public benefit. This chapter will review features of the *resource portfolio*, including tangible assets (e.g., cash) and intangible assets (e.g., donor relations). Next, *management functions* (Mintzberg, 1980) that exploit resource attributes to support *public benefit activities* are reviewed. Public benefit activities include a variety of

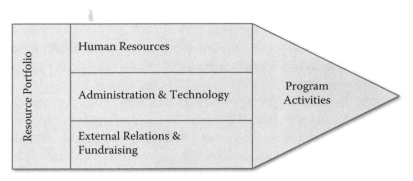

FIGURE 4-1   Nonprofit Value Framework

program areas such social services and advocacy-type activities that are utilized to produce social benefit. Before reviewing the resource portfolio it is necessary to discuss some key principles of comparative advantage, or as conceptualized in the corporate strategy, "competitive advantage."

Comparative Advantage

The idea of competitive advantage can be somewhat controversial in a nonprofit context, as the sector was founded on concepts of cooperation and collaboration. Nevertheless, organizations need to be clear on what they bring to a collaborative relationship and how their contribution is unique and supplementary to existing services. So even if the intent isn't to "drive out" other providers, the idea that each nonprofit should contribute unique qualities and resources is irrefutable. Goold (1997, pg. 292) defines *institutional advantage* as "when a not-for-profit . . . performs its tasks more effectively than comparable organizations." Perhaps a more appropriate term is *comparative advantage* as *institution* is used in numerous ways in the organizational behavior literature. Furthermore, comparative advantage defines an organization's capabilities in relation to other providers, which is an important distinction. The ability to create a comparative advantage is based on unique resources and functions under the control of an organization (Billis & Glennerster, 1998; Hunt & Morgan, 1995). For example, it can be as simple as providing services in a location that is accessible to key service recipients but difficult for other providers to replicate. So a youth development organization that has program space in a housing complex or at a school may have an advantage over an organization that provides services in a neighborhood church that requires participants to take a bus or van. Access to participants is facilitated by offering the program at a school or housing complex. Acquiring, integrating, and leveraging resources to build a comparative advantage is central to organizational sustainability.

The next section presents the resource portfolio, which details the range and type of resources nonprofit managers can acquire. There are several features that make resources strategically viable. The *value* of a resource is determined by the ability to exploit the asset for strategic advantage. Two ideas are of particular concern: Can the nonprofit easily use the resource to support strategic priorities and is the resource/asset unique? To answer the first, consider, for example, an asset such as a dilapidated building in a poor location for services. The building is indeed an asset but it has little relevance to the purposes of the nonprofit. If the nonprofit can sell the building, then the cash can be quickly utilized in various ways to achieve objectives. In reference to the second question (degree of uniqueness), there are several attributes that suggest whether an attribute may provide a *comparative* advantage. To add comparative advantage the resource should be considered in relation to other providers. Managers should consider such things as the extent to which the resources are *rare* (few others possess similar assets), *costly to imitate* (complex and interconnected), and *substitutable* (other assets or capabilities can work in similar function). Resources that exhibit these attributes build a potential comparative advantage. The utilization or integration of resources is considered a *capability*. Capabilities tend to be unique to an organization and reflect the utilization of resources for comparative advantage.

The ability to define which organizational resource or combination of assets form an advantage is often difficult to ascertain. Nonprofit managers need to understand how they create public benefits. What is the causal explanation for how benefits are created (Brest, 2010)? Considering the nonprofit value framework, managers need to first coordinate organizational features (resources and management functions) to produce programs activities. Second, those program outcomes need to produce social value (public benefits). Third, those public benefits must be valued by influential stakeholders (e.g., donors and community members). Identifying and building core competencies that create such value is a critical task. One way to do this is to create *core competencies* that are a mix of resources, management functions, and public benefit activities. It is the integration of multiple components to produce unique services more efficiently. These core competencies are difficult for others to replicate. The management literature suggests (Hitt et al., 2011) that an organization can build and maintain only a select number of core competencies (three to five). These core competencies are the critical attributes that help achieve objectives and build value for stakeholders. The next section describes key resource attributes and then introduces four management functions. These functions utilize resource elements to undergird program activities.

Resource Portfolio

A few resources are fairly tangible and easily identified, such as financial assets, physical assets, and human capital (see **Table 4-1**). Even the idea of human capital, however, can become more ambiguous as we consider concepts of commitment or attachment, which are very important when considering the "value" of a workforce (paid or unpaid). Beyond these relatively tangible resources are assets that are important but less concrete, such as reputation, external relationships, and capacity to innovate. These resources are more difficult to quantify but in many ways are more important than tangible assets because often they are more difficult to replicate. Table 4-1 lists some typical resources available to nonprofit organizations.

TABLE 4-1   Resource Portfolio

Type	Features Indicative of Strategic Value
Human capital	Number and quality of staff
	Number and quality of volunteers
	Attitudes and perceptions (commitment) of organization members
Financial assets	Cash, investments, and endowment
	Reliable revenue trends and forecasts
Physical assets	Facilities and equipment
	Historical or cultural artifacts

(continues)

TABLE 4-1 Resource Portfolio (*continued*)

Type	Features Indicative of Strategic Value
Information and innovation	Database of contacts
	Scientific or creative capabilities
Relationships	Funders and donors
	Community
	Other providers
Reputation	Recognition
	Perceptions of quality
	Values and ideology

Human Capital

Human capital is the sum of individuals engaged in the work of the organization, which includes paid staff, volunteers, and leaders (paid and unpaid). It goes almost without saying that human capabilities are often one of the most significant resources in nonprofits. A typical nonprofit with paid staff will often allocate 70–80% of the budget to compensation. Capable, committed, and coordinated staff (paid or unpaid) are the lifeblood of performance and effectiveness. Nonprofits are fortunate to have both paid and unpaid participants. Nonprofit organizations can accomplish significant objectives though the donated labor of volunteers. In 2010, it is estimated 62.8 million individuals donated a median of 52 hours (U.S. Bureau of Labor Statistics, 2011). This is valued at over $1000 per person, or nearly 70 trillion dollars in donated time (Independent Sector, 2011). The vast majority of this "work" is accomplished though the coordinated activities of nonprofits. The degree to which these human capital characteristics are rare depends on the unique skill sets and capabilities of organizational participants, but perhaps even more important is the degree to which the organization is able to utilize these capabilities. Volunteer labor possesses significant potential but hinges on the systems that facilitate participation. Value emerges from the commitment these individuals feel toward the nonprofit. Commitment builds from various sources and includes the extent to which organizational participants can achieve their interests independent of the organizational system. Can volunteers or paid labor easily move to another organizational system to gain similar benefits? For example, St. Vincent de Paul relies on thousands of volunteers to provide services to low-income families. Volunteers perform numerous tasks including preparing meals, organizing clothes, and staffing the thrift shop. The extent to which these volunteers feel that St. Vincent de Paul is the "best" place to fulfill their volunteer service is an aspect of what it takes to count these volunteers as a reliable human resource. If, however, volunteers feel that several other entities (e.g., a local church pantry) fulfill their needs even better, then they might be likely to shift their engagement to another organization. It is the ability to promote satisfaction and commitment in organizational participants that can be a distinctive advantage.

Leadership is another key concept of human capital. Does the organization have capable and talented individuals to guide the organization? Also does the organization have a system to ensure succession for new leaders and development systems to build the next leadership cohort? Leadership includes senior executives and volunteer leadership. Leadership is part vision, part message, and part influence (Bass & Bass, 2008). A great deal of effort has been put forward to define the traits, behaviors, and styles of effective leaders. Leadership is widely recognized as critical to organizational performance and success (Yukl, 2012). The responsibility for strategic leadership in nonprofits is shared among the senior staff, the governing board, and occasionally other significant stakeholders (e.g., funders). The exact composition of the "dominant coalition" (Miles & Snow, 1978) is unique to the organizational context. The point here is that leadership is a critical aspect of the human capital asset.

Financial Assets

Financial assets are a fundamental aspect of operational success for most all organizations. Even all-volunteer organizations realize that the ability to achieve objectives is constrained by access to cash. Financial assets may not be required to form a nonprofit and nonprofits can function entirely with volunteers, but at some point expansion and sustainability require financial capital.

Three aspects of financial assets merit discussion. First is the amount of money held by the organization, second is the ability to acquire capital, and third is reliability of revenue streams. Nonprofits often function as repositories of philanthropic capital. Endowments are a special kind of capital that is built through the donated gifts of individuals or foundations. This capital is invested and only the proceeds are used to fund program activities. This preserves the capital and allows it to grow though reinvestment. A bigger endowment generates more funds that are available for program expenditures. Endowments and capital reserves are difficult to build, but once established they provide long-term stability for programs. If managed effectively, endowments can grow while still providing operational funds. Endowments are most commonly held by foundations and institutions of higher education, although larger and older nonprofits in the social services and arts do develop and build large investment portfolios. Endowments are particularly difficult to build because donors transfer wealth to the nonprofit with the realization that just a fraction of those funds will go toward direct provision of services in exchange for long-term viability of the organization or the program. There is debate about the wisdom of investing capital instead of spending down investments to increase the amount of funds available for programs (Fremont-Smith, n.d.; Ramirez, 2011). Federal law requires that foundations give away 5% of their market value. Operating foundations (foundations established for particular research or educational purposes) tend to follow similar 5% guidelines, although organizations vary significantly on how they manage and use invested assets. Maintaining a large endowment provides high overall value because it provides stability for organizational programs as they retain control of both the capital and proceeds that are gained, thereby increasing flexibility and stability. It is costly for others to build endowments as it is difficult to attract major donors who have the capacity to invest substantial wealth.

Related to endowment is the ability to raise sufficient capital for growth or expansion. Nonprofits are constrained in their ability to raise capital through the investment market. They cannot offer stock for sale and typically cannot offer corporate bonds (seek funds from investors through the bond market) because the economic principles of the sector rely on donated funds. If a non-profit can raise capital it can be a significant advantage. This can come in the form of capital campaigns that seek donated funds or secured loans through associated entities. For example, a church may wish to open a new facility in a growing area of the city, but if the church cannot raise sufficient capital to purchase the land and build a building they are unable to take advantage of the new growth opportunity. Affiliation with an umbrella organiza-tion can facilitate growth because those larger, more established national organizations may have the necessary capital to invest in subsidiary growth. Access to capital has significant overall value because the ability to grow strategically at opportune times can be critical. It is difficult to replicate and most organizations are significantly constrained by the number and type of large capital campaigns that they can undertake, as donors are only willing to respond to so many large requests.

The third aspect of the financial asset portfolio is the nature or character of the revenue streams, in particular the reliability and consistency of revenue over time. Evaluating and assessing rev-enue streams for continued viability is of significant importance. For example, some faith-based organizations have long-standing relationships with houses of worship, and these long-term rela-tionships may demonstrate a more stable revenue stream than a comparable nonprofit without such relationships. A broad and longstanding membership base can also be a fairly reliable and stable revenue source for nonprofits and can be very difficult for others to replicate. Relationship management and commitment are discussed later, but this section highlights the strategic benefit of a particular revenue stream and how difficult it is for others to build similar sources of income. Financial assets are critical to the strategic success of a nonprofit and reflect a significant distinc-tive advantage to move into new service areas and to maintain stability over time.

Physical Assets

Physical assets entail the range of tangible objects owned and controlled by a nonprofit. This includes things such as buildings, land, equipment, and other artifacts of value. Similar to endowments, some nonprofits serve as a repository for semipublic assets such as historical, cultural, and artistic pieces. These assets typically are rare and unique. However, just because something is rare or old does not mean that it has strategic value. Sometimes these artifacts can be of tremendous strategic advantage, while in other instances the assets may entail significant cost to maintain and preserve (e.g., historical buildings). For small- to medium-size nonprofits it is not uncommon that a significant percentage of their wealth (if they have any) is locked into their physical assets, typically a building or land. This can be an advantage, as it may keep costs low if the facilities were purchased in favorable economic circumstances, but physical assets tend to be illiquid, meaning that they might lock up significant funds with limited ability to shift those assets to other purposes. For example, houses of worship may hold significant physical assets, but if the building is located in communities with changing demographics that no longer have the interest or ability to support the church it can be difficult to divest from those assets. There can be both economic and philosophical barriers that limit the flexibility of these assets ("Editorial: O'Malley's Decision," 2011). The Catholic Church has experienced some challenges in divesting from certain assets that serve a limited population and cost more than an objective criteria might justify (e.g., parochial schools in urban areas). However, these places hold significant attraction to certain constituents and can cause some public relations challenges. Although the future direction or capital needs of the organization might suggest that it is necessary to divest from particular holdings, cultural, historical, or spiritual conditions might limit the ability of the organization to sell the property, regardless of economic conditions, which might affect the value of the asset.

Strategic acquisition of assets can be of significant value as long as they are readily useful, they retain some liquidity, and/or the cost to maintain is modest. For example, a local animal shelter was renegotiating contract arrangements with a local municipality (they served three municipal partners). The shelter determined that the municipality was underpaying for the cost of services. Unfortunately for the shelter, they were also operating in a facility provided by the municipality, which might have limited their ability to negotiate aggressively. Previously, however, a donor had provided some land in a different location. The land was ideal in many ways but required significant improvements before it was suitable for the shelter. Through the process of renegotiating the contract it became clear that the municipality did not want to pay a higher price. The shelter was able to mount a public relations campaign that simultaneously resulted in additional donations to improve the new location. This significantly improved their position because they had an alternative site to house the animals and could stick to their position and more or less require that the municipality pay more of their share. The municipality did not have the capacity to run a shelter on their own. In the end, the shelter was able to improve the land for use as a new facility and gain increased payment from the municipality. Without the backdoor option to "move out," the shelter might not have been able to gain the increased support from the city.

Information and Innovation

In technology firms, innovation is the lifeblood of success. The products and services are constantly changing and the ability to create new products and innovate is critical to success and survival. Consider what happens in the smartphone market, where Apple introduced the iPhone and quickly challenged dominant providers. Apple and other technology providers actively guard these innovations to ensure that they remain proprietary. Owning patents and regularly updating products makes it more difficult for others to copy these innovations and retain the benefits. Creating and producing innovative products is costly and risky. Nonprofits too can be a source of innovation. For example, Aprovecho Research Center (ARC) has been working for over 30 years to develop and create small clean-burning stoves that can be used by millions of families in developing countries (Aprovecho Research Center, n.d.). Through this time, ARC has created significant innovations and improvements in the way these stoves work, increasing efficiency and reducing waste, for example (Kaste, 2011). ARC has also been particularly noncompetitive in developing these stoves and innovations. They work to share their innovations so others who are working on creating and distributing these stoves in developing countries can benefit from these innovations. They are inherently open and collaborative in sharing their knowledge and innovations. Recently, they developed a "not just for profit" subsidiary to sell and distribute the stove more aggressively (StoveTec, n.d.). All the proceeds from this entity are returned to ARC.

Many nonprofits are involved in knowledge creation, innovation, and development. Research centers and educational nonprofits are developed with this specific purpose in mind. It is an interesting quandary. If a social service nonprofit has created an innovative method to treat drug addicts should they actively work to share those innovations with other drug abuse providers? To what extent should the nonprofit look to sell the innovative curriculum versus promote and share with other providers? There is an inherent cultural philosophy or institutional logic within the sector that reinforces the desire for collective and cooperative action that shares innovations and knowledge to address common social issues. For example, the Exploratorium in San Francisco was one of the first hands-on science museums, and they have been active in sharing their methods and strategies for creating and maintaining this type of museum (Crutchfield & Grant, 2008). They have been instrumental in the development of numerous other museums and yet they often receive limited compensation for these activities. Expanding and developing learning opportunities in the sciences is part of what they hoped to accomplish. It became a part of their management philosophy to share information and strategies. This strategy was important in the development of these types of museums. The Exploratorium has significant impact on the industry and the ability to expand these opportunities. Yet, as the example with the stoves reminds us, there are also market or resource opportunities. Considering how innovations are proprietary or collective is an interesting challenge for nonprofit managers, and it illustrates how economic concerns influence social priorities.

An interesting contradiction is that many nonprofits are actually not very good at maintaining knowledge and information on best practices. As processes are developed in one part of the organization it is not uncommon that there are few systematic methods to share these practices within the organization or within their network (Milway & Saxton, 2011). Part of the challenge is innovations are not always recognized as such. What amounts to significant innovation or improvement? Many nonprofits are loosely coupled organizations (Weick, 1979) that benefit from creative activity embedded in the local context. However, the inability to capture and share practices that can improve efficiencies and effectiveness is a significant concern. The ability to build systems that maintain knowledge creation and retention are critical to success. As was discussed, these organizations are often dependent on the contributions and commitment of individuals, and the ability to facilitate their effectiveness is critical to improving satisfaction and creating consistency of services. As cited by Milway and Saxton (2011), KIPP Academy (Knowledge is Power Program, with 99 charter schools and 1900 teachers) found that many teachers were creating their own materials instead of using a standardized curriculum or collaborating to refine existing resources. KIPP administrators worked to create methods to help teachers collaborate and share materials more easily. These knowledge management practices entail technological solutions and operational practices that foster opportunities for learning and sharing. Innovations are pervasive elements at an organization like KIPP, and they have worked aggressively to build and expand on successful ideas (KIPP Foundation, 2010).

In addition to capitalizing on innovations and best practices, nonprofits need to maintain information about stakeholders. Nonprofits have a complex network of constituents, from donors to volunteers to community partners, and a key resource for many nonprofits is the ability to maintain accurate information about these individuals. The concept here is the ability to systematize practices and build methods to maintain accurate and accessible information. The information technology requirements can be significant and costly, and at times are prohibitive to smaller organizations. Nevertheless, maintaining the information can add significant value for the nonprofit. In addition to the technology requirements there is cost in information management practices, such as how the information is captured and cleaned. Related is the need to maintain information about services and beneficiaries. Many nonprofits have significant information management demands associated with evaluation and performance assessment. This too is a cumbersome task that can appear bureaucratic and time-consuming, but accurate information about how services are provided and the benefits of those services is key to gaining support. Effective evaluation is built on a reliable and accurate information management system.

Information and innovation management practices are a key resource for many nonprofits. If maintained effectively, a database of contacts is an extremely valuable asset that is not easily replicated. Similarly, the ability to accurately describe the range and type of services provided as well as the benefits produced is an incredibility valuable asset. Nonprofits are a source of innovation, and philosophical principles of cooperation and collaboration encourage nonprofits to share these innovations. There are costs and benefits to sharing information, and nonprofits must balance the need to maintain proprietary information while building active and viable networks that operate more effectively and capitalize on these innovations.

Relationships

This section highlights how it is necessary to create real and substantive relationships with key stakeholders. Knowledge and awareness facilitate the ability to nurture relationships, but in practice, relationship management goes beyond accurate record keeping. Individuals and organizations maintain various types of relationships. Individuals across various levels of the organization (leaders, staff, and volunteers) maintain and develop relationships; furthermore, organizational entities can nurture and maintain relationships in and through interactions that exist independent of individuals (Schneider, 2009). That is, they can continue beyond the departure of individual actors. Nonprofits are particularly sensitive to the social context because of resource and sociopolitical factors. Nonprofits operate in economic and social markets. Relationships are instrumental to managing these nonfinancial systems (Akingbola, 2006). Relationship management becomes a reoccurring theme throughout the text and highlights the importance of attending to each of the stake-holder groups (e.g., service beneficiaries, funders). These groups and individuals require different tactics and result in different benefits. This section covers the general nature of these relation-ships and their potential value to the organization.

Managing and developing relationships creates social capi-tal. Social capital recognizes the inherent value of relationships (King, 2004; Putnam, 2000). Similar to financial capital (money) and human capital (people), social capital is an attempt to rec-ognize the value of interpersonal and interorganizational rela-tionships. Social capital is an ambiguous concept that takes an investment of resources and provides benefits that can be difficult to quantify (Nahapiet & Ghoshal, 1998). Social capital theorists recognize various types of social relationships and the concept is complex, so this section introduces just a few basic ideas. Two types of social capital are *bonding* relationships, which tend to be deeper and more socially homogeneous (coworkers), and *bridging* relationships, which extend to more distant actors and include more heterogeneous groups and individuals (clients or donors) (Putnam, 2000). These types operate within the organi-zation as well as with external stakeholders. Both types of social capital can be of value for a nonprofit organization. Bridging relationships tend to bring access to resources. Bonding relation-ships facilitate sharing, integration, and utilization of resources (Coffe & Geys, 2007).

There is a large amount of research that explores the bene-fits of interpersonal relationships. This extends to communities, groups, or organizations. It is generally recognized that these interpersonal benefits transfer to organizations such that effec-tive relationships can expand access to resources, ease the process of creating partnerships, and increase legitimacy and improved reputation. Within the organization, healthy relationships facil-itate information sharing and learning. For individuals, social capital is associated with higher levels of trust, which is in turn related to increased attachment and commitment. Relationships are the foundation of effective communication and information sharing (Whetten & Cameron, 2007). The range and type of rela-tionships include coworker and peer connections (horizontal) that operate more or less within particular divisions or program areas as well as relationships that extend across the organization and involve interdepartmental connections. Hierarchically, supervisory/subordinate relationships are enhanced when those involved trust and respect each other. Similarly, synergy between the board and top management team allows for strategic change (Castro, De La Concha Dominguez, Gavel, & Perinan, 2009) and more effective strategic decision making. Organizational cultures and norms are enacted, created, and shared through effective relationships throughout the organization. Furthermore, effective control and monitoring practices are facilitated by organizational relationships.

Extending connections outside of the organization also has significant benefits. External connections tend to reflect bridging relationships that can result in increased access to resources and ease partnerships. How individuals at different levels in the organization facilitate these relationships has implications for the benefits and costs that are realized. Social capital is instrumental in recruiting organizational participants, employees (Adler & Kwon, 2002), volunteers (Hartenian & Lilly, 2009; Weisinger & Black, 2006), and board members (King, 2004). Social capital supports funding relationships and building interorganizational partnerships (Zaheer, McEvily, & Perrone, 1989). There is a fair amount of research that recognizes the importance of board members building and maintaining external relationships (Brown, 2005). Some of the benefits include more successful fundraising initiatives and more effective strategic decision making. In general, stakeholder relationships are related to improved perceptions of performance for nonprofit organizations (Balser & McClusky, 2005).

It is difficult to assess the level of social capital that exists in an organization. Assessment typically entails looking at the nature and character of relationships across various stakeholder groups. It is possible to assess the sense of trust among organizational participants or the level of awareness of different stakeholder groups in the community. Social capital is also interconnected with human capital features (Hillman & Dalziel,

2003). Relationship or stakeholder management then becomes a core function to create social capital. However, the success of these activities is not always apparent because social capital reflects a social construct that is valuable but difficult, if not impossible, to quantify. Consequently, management functions must balance costs of relationship management with more obvious costs (e.g., payroll, program). High levels of social capital both within and external to the organization are of value. How valuable these high levels of social capital are is difficult to ascertain, and how much managers should invest in developing the relationships that form the basis of social capital is difficult to judge. In principle, healthy relationships, rich in social capital, are difficult to replicate and thereby can provide tremendous strategic advantage.

Reputation

Reputation is another "soft" asset that is difficult to quantify and create, but it offers significant benefits. High name recognition and a positive reputation are of significant value for nonprofits. The indeterminate nature of nonprofit work (it's difficult to prove public benefit) makes it critical for key stakeholders and the broader community to have awareness and positive perceptions of the nonprofit. Reputation, like social capital, is a fairly complex idea but in principle it entails three components: name recognition (awareness), an overall impression of the organization, and, for some stakeholders, there is knowledge of what the organization does and *judgments* on how it does that (e.g., high-quality services for the elderly) (Lange, Lee, & Dai, 2011). Reputation is a perception held by stakeholders. This perception is often socially created through interaction and shared knowledge. Perceptions and thereby reputation can be idiosyncratic to different individuals or stakeholder groups. This complicates the idea that an organization can "own" its reputation. Rather, reputation is created through the actions and history of the organization and how that is *perceived* by stakeholders. General management guidance suggests that positive reputations take a long time to develop and can be lost much more quickly.

The idea of name recognition or "being known" is similar in many ways to brand recognition or awareness. Forbes conducts an annual ranking of the "World's Most Admired Companies," and in 2011, Apple and Google topped the list (Forbes, 2011). Similar rankings exist for nonprofit organizations. For example, the Harris Poll found that St. Jude's Research Hospital and Susan G. Komen for the Cure are among the "most trusted" nonprofits (Hall, 2010). A similar study by marketing firms Cone and Intangible Business found that the YMCA and the Salvation Army topped the list of most valuable brands (Cone, 2009; Preston & Wallace, 2009). Most recognized organizations tend to be national in scope, have long histories of providing services, and tend to have extensive networks of local affiliates (Oster, 1995). Beyond awareness is the idea that stakeholders evaluate the nonprofit in regards to the activities and services that are of most interest to them. Being known for something is reflective of a stakeholder's impression of the organization's ability to meet their preferences (Rindova, Williamson, Petkova, & Sever, 2005). Organizations should have a sense of what stakeholders expect from them and what they value, because this can be an issue if expectations are too high. Organizations need to understand which attributes different stakeholder groups value (e.g., trustworthiness, quality services) so as to manage messaging.

Research suggests that reputation is positively associated with a number of desirable outcomes, such as improved financial performance, the tendency to give the benefit of the doubt when bad news develops, and the ability to attract a workforce, donors, and potential service beneficiaries. Increased recognition and awareness also might lead to high expectations and potentially increased scrutiny from interested stakeholders. Reputation is rooted in perception of organizational action and historical patterns of behavior. An affiliation with other high recognition entities also tends to increase recognition, as do basic demographic details such as size and age (Lange et al., 2011).

Reputation is an asset insofar as organizations can benefit from positive impressions. Organizations also have a responsibility to actively monitor and to manage those impressions. This broad set of management tasks might fall under the rubric of public relations, marketing, and communications. It is also important to remember that many stakeholders look beyond these messages and make informed judgments about actual performance. Reputation is socially constructed among individuals and groups. This means that people talk about their experiences with organizations and modify their impressions of an organization based upon the attitudes of others. During an extensive analysis of the Mayo Clinic, Leonard Berry observed that quality care tended to be at the root of many of the positive impressions about the organization (Berry & Seltman, 2008). As a result, the management process entails monitoring and tracking attitudes and perceptions of stakeholders, communicating and articulating the benefits and qualities of the organization, and also ensuring that the rhetoric is substantiated by real performance and practice. As stakeholders learn about the organization and what it does they build expectations, and the organization must consider its capacity to support the impressions of stakeholders. These reputations are built over time and often based on fulfillment of routine management functions. Furthermore, these impressions are based on the strategic position and orientation of the organization (Fombrun & Shanley, 1990). Strategic decision making and action in relation to other providers, supplies, and so on also form a basis for the impressions of stakeholders. How does this organization compare to others in a similar industry or organizational field? Obviously, entirely controlling an organization's reputation across all stakeholders is impossible, as some groups form impressions based on incomplete and inaccurate information. Furthermore, certain groups attend to different aspects of the organization. Consequently, consistency in organizational practices is very critical to reputation management as it simplifies the "message" of what the organization does and how it acts.

Management Functions

Management functions entail the range of activities and responsibilities enacted by organizational participants to achieve objectives. This includes reporting structures, planning and control systems, and functional activities such as accounting and fundraising. These organizational systems exploit the resource portfolio to fulfill public benefit functions (i.e., provide services). It is important to support competency in management functions, and these systems must coordinate and collaborate toward organizational objectives. For example, fundraising managers monitor donor interests and develop communication practices to external constituents. To be instrumental, development staff must match donor interests with program services. The external work of prospecting and nurturing donor relationships must be linked into the internal features and capabilities of the organization. How and to what extent the interplay is enacted is a critical and significant organizational advantage.

Another example is the use of volunteers. There are several aspects of attracting, selecting, and supervising volunteers, each of which can be conceptualized as a management function. An organization can attract potential volunteers, but volunteers need to be placed, supervised, and monitored to ensure their engagement. It is the ability to utilize volunteers in rewarding opportunities that bond them to the organization; effectiveness in some areas with deficiencies in others leads to challenges and frustrations for volunteers. Creating a coherent system to attract and utilize volunteer labor is how comparative advantage is created. Teach for America (see **Exhibit 4-1**) demonstrates a masterful compilation of organizational capabilities, not only recruiting and selecting but also training and placing potential members in such a way that they were incredibly appealing to the highly skilled and capable participants. The systems of support and partner relationships with school districts further enriched the experience for participants. The creation of complex organizational systems that provide value for stakeholders is often difficult for other providers to replicate. Managers focus activities to build these systems over time. Accurately interpreting which areas add value is not easy. An abundance of particular assets does not necessarily translate into benefits for stakeholders; rather it is the utilization and administration of those assets that creates a highly effective organization.

EXHIBIT 4-1 Teach for America

Teach for America (TFA) placed their first 500 corps members in 1990 (Teach for America, n.d.). Teach for America has experienced significant growth over the 20-year history of the organization. TFA has always been a highly selective placement opportunity for graduates from prestigious institutions. How is TFA able to compete for highly educated college graduates and often be the preferred placement destination? The organization has a significant training and preparation requirement that quickly gets corps members ready for their teaching experience. They maintain active partnerships with school districts that are reliant on TFA to provide skilled teachers. Placing upwards of 5000 teachers a year is an impressive accomplishment. Part of the system requires understanding the interests and preferences of potential recruits. These recent graduates have prosocial interests but also expect professional recruitment systems. No other nonprofit has capitalized on these interests, treating the recruits as young professionals to the scale of TFA. The system has evolved over the years, and in 2009 TFA was listed in the top 10 best places to launch a career by business week ("Best Place," 2009). They are on the list with the likes of Deloitte, Ernst & Young, and IBM. It is quite an accomplishment and reflects the benefits of an integrated system.

Management Framework

Using the competing values framework, management functions can be clustered into four general areas (Quinn & Rohrbaugh, 1983). This framework has been applied to numerous organizational contexts including human service organizations (Austin, 1989), corporations, and government. The model recognizes the paradoxical nature of management activities. The framework organizes tasks by considering four diametrically opposed features: internal versus external orientations and control versus flexibility structures (see **Figure 4-2**). Internal orientations reflect the needs of coordinating elements inside the organization, whereas external orientations reflect the interface between the organization and the external environment. The control

Flexible Structures

1 Human Relations Tasks Supporting engagement, cooperation, communication and commitment	**2** Open Systems Tasks External relations, fundraising, and marketing
3 Internal Process Tasks Administration, information technology, and monitoring	**4** Goal and Production Tasks Planning, coordination, program activities

Internal Orientation — External Orientation

Control Structures

FIGURE 4-2 Management Functions as Competing Priorities

Data from Quinn, R. E., & Rohrbaugh, J. (1983). A spatial model of effectiveness criteria: Towards a competing values approach to organizational analysis. *Management Science, 29*(3), 363–377.

versus flexibility perspective balances the need to be responsive to individuals and opportunities while building consistency and stability. This model does not address all the challenges of understanding what managers do because some tasks overlap or are utilized in multiple contexts, such as negotiation and conflict resolution. However, it is useful to consider how organizations build competencies in the four functional areas (human relations, open systems, internal processes, and production) (Edwards, Austin, & Altpeter, 1998).

Managers emphasize different aspects of these roles and functions based upon their responsibilities in the organization. Finance managers, for instance, may attend to internal processes, while program directors attend to coordination and service delivery. Human resource issues confront all managers. Coordinated and capable staff, utilized in the right way, are recognized as one of the most salient competencies that organizations can utilize (Akingbola, 2013; Cappelli & Crocker-Hefter, 1996). Organizational life stage and strategic choices also guide priorities. For example, managers trying to professionalize the organization are concerned with formalizing behaviors and building policies (internal process tasks) that can communicate practices to a broadening workforce and often increasingly complex finances and service initiatives, while younger organizations might be more concerned with building program delivery systems (goal and production tasks).

The four functional areas are related to the nonprofit value framework (see Figure 4-1) in that human resource tasks, open systems tasks, and internal process tasks are conceptualized as management support functions and depicted in the middle section of the diagram. Production tasks are depicted in the point of the diagram (e.g., program activities). Production tasks are conceptualized as the operational method to achieve public benefits and management support functions are conceptualized as the capacity for production. As with every abstraction of complex systems it is more dynamic than that, but the NVF facilitates identification of key internal components that must be coordinated to achieve objectives. The competing values framework recognizes the multiple management functions operating in the organization. The next section summarizes each of these functional areas.

Human relations tasks include all of what it takes to manage people in the organization. This quadrant is a mix between internally oriented activities such as facilitating communication among organizational members and flexible structures to respond to the needs and talents of organizational participants. Managing people is a mix of structural systems that facilitate coordination while also developing relationships that support professional development and engagement. The measures of performance include concepts of engagement, commitment, and satisfaction. Are there sufficient human resources and do they put forward significant effort to achieve objectives?

Internal process tasks are those activities that are more internal and control oriented to monitor performance and ensure quality. This includes aspects of the information technology infrastructure, but also accounting procedures and the like. These activities encompass the administrative aspects of the organization and are often concerned with efficiency and, perhaps even more importantly, accuracy or quality. Effective administration is seamless to organizational functioning and enhances performance and engagement.

Open systems tasks reflect an orientation toward the external environment and tend to require more flexible structures that facilitate learning and innovation. Specific tasks include fundraising as well as public relations activities that work to manage significant stakeholder relationships. This might entail initiatives to improve awareness of the organization and the issues it is trying to address. It is also about interpreting the external environment of the organization so as to guide the strategic direction. Success in this area relates to commitment from key stakeholders, positive perceptions of the organization, and sufficient access to resources. This quadrant reflects the organization's ability to capture assets in the resource environment.

Goal and production tasks are those activities focused on the service beneficiary and attending to meeting the public benefit goals of the organization. In the value framework these activities are depicted in the "point" and entail a range of services and advocacy activities. Given the complexity of the nonprofit sector, it is difficult to easily distill practices. The chapter on public benefit strategies reviews the public benefit functions utilized by nonprofits, which include social services, community building, and political advocacy. This quadrant considers the extent to which the nonprofit can produce activities that relate to public benefit objectives. Considerations include the number and type of initiatives carried out as well as the social value of those activities.

Conclusion

Resource attributes such as financial capital and a committed workforce are instrumental for organizational sustainability and the creation of comparative advantage. Management functions attend to building organizational stability and the use of resource attributes to create social value. Organizational leadership provides guidance to foster the coordination and compilation of organizational assets and management functions to create organizational competencies. These systems operate in functional areas (e.g., accounting, fundraising, program services) as well cross-functional initiatives (e.g., human resources, public relations). Ultimately, managers try to define a limited set of core systems that are strategically optimal. That is, managers nurture organizational systems that provide distinctive value to stakeholders. Some systems provide functional value that improves efficiency thereby allowing the organization to deliver programs cost effectively. Some systems create programs that are desired by stakeholders. Of critical concern is the extent to which public benefit activities create social value that is appreciated by key stakeholders.

Discussion Questions

Reflecting on a nonprofit you are familiar with, answer the following questions:

1. What assets do they control? What is their resource portfolio?
2. How capable are their management activities in the four functional areas?
3. Do they appear to have organizational systems that operate effectively, blending assets and management functions?
4. Do those systems provide value to key stakeholders?

References

Adler, P. S., & Kwon, S. W. (2002). Social capital: Prospects for a new concept. *The Academy of Management Review, 27*(1), 17–40.

Akingbola, K. (2006). Strategic choices and change in non-profit organizations. *Strategic Change, 15*(6), 265–281.

Akingbola, K. (2013). A model of strategic nonprofit human resource management. *Voluntas: International Journal of Voluntary and Nonprofit Organizations, 24*(1), 214–240.

Aprovecho Research Center. (n.d.). ARC's mission. Retrieved from http://www.aprovecho.org/lab/aboutarclist/mission

Austin, D. M. (1989). The human service executive. In Y. Hasenfeld (Ed.), *Administrative leadership in social services* (pp. 13–36). Binghampton, NY: Hawthorn Press.

Balser, D., & McClusky, J. (2005). Managing stakeholder relationships and nonprofit organization effectiveness. *Nonprofit Management & Leadership, 15*(3), 295–315.

Bass, B. M., & Bass, R. (2008). *The Bass handbook of leadership: Theory, research and managerial applications.* New York, NY: Free Press.

Berry, L. L., & Seltman, K. D. (2008). *Management lessons from the Mayo Clinic.* New York, NY: McGraw-Hill.

Billis, D., & Glennerster, H. (1998). Human services and the voluntary sector: Towards a theory of comparative advantage. *Journal of Social Policy, 27*(01), 79–98.

Best place to launch a career in 2009. (2009). *Bloomberg Businessweek.* Retrieved from http://www.businessweek.com/interactive_reports/career_launch_2009.html

Editorial: O'Malley's decision should end dispute over closing parishes [Editorial]. (July 23, 2011). *Boston Globe.* Retrieved from http://www.boston.com/bostonglobe/editorial_opinion/editorials/articles/2011/07/23/omalleys_decision_should_end_dispute_over_closing_parishes/

Brest, P. (2010, Spring). The power of theories of change. *Stanford Social Innovation Review,* 47–51.

Brown, W. A. (2005). Exploring the association between board and organizational performance in nonprofit organizations. *Nonprofit Management & Leadership, 15*(3), 317–339.

Cappelli, P., & Crocker-Hefter, A. (1996). Distinctive human resources are firms' core competencies. *Organizational Dynamics, 24*(3), 7–22.

Castro, C. B., De La Concha Dominguez, M., Gavel, J. V., & Perinan, V. (2009). Does team leverage the board's decisions. *Corporate Governance, 17*(6), 744–761.

Coffe, H., & Geys, B. (2007). Toward an empirical characterization of bridging and bonding social capital. *Nonprofit and Voluntary Sector Quarterly, 36*(1), 121–139.

Cone. (2009). The Cone Nonprofit Power Brand 100. Retrieved from http://www.conecomm.com/the-cone-nonprofit-power-brand-100

Crutchfield, L. R., & Grant, H. M. (2008). *Forces for good: The six practices of high-impact nonprofits.* San Francisco, CA: Jossey-Bass.

Edwards, R. L, Austin, D. M., & Altpeter, M. A. (1998). Managing effectively in an environment of competing values. In R. L. Edwards, J. A. Yankey, & M. A. Altpeter (Eds.), *Skills for effective management of nonprofit organizations* (p. 585). Washington, DC: National Association of Social Workers Press.

Fombrun, C., & Shanley, M. (1990). What's in a name? Reputation building and corporate strategy. *The Academy of Management Journal, 33*(2), 233–258.

Forbes. (2011). World's most admired companies. CNN Money. Retrieved from http://money.cnn.com/magazines/fortune /mostadmired/2011/index.html

Fremont-Smith, M. R. (n.d.). *Accumulations of wealth by nonprofits.* Washington, DC: The Urban Institute, Center on Nonprofits and Philanthropy.

Goold, M. (1997). Institutional advantage: A way into strategic managment in not-for-profit organizations. *Long Range Planning, 30*(2), 291–293.

Hall, A. (2010). *Harris Poll finds: St. Jude's Research Hospital and Susan G. Komen for the Cure are among most trusted nonprofits* [Press release]. Harris Interactive. Retrieved from http:// www.harrisinteractive.com/NewsRoom/PressReleases/tabid /446/mid/1506/articleId/52/ctl/ReadCustom%20Default /Default.aspx

Hartenian, L. S., & Lilly, B. (2009). Egoism and commitment: A multidimensional approach to understanding sustained volunteering. *Journal of Managerial Issues, 21*(1), 97–119.

Hillman, A. J., & Dalziel, T. (2003). Boards of directors and firm performance: Integrating agency and resource dependence perspectives. *Academy of Management Review, 28*(3), 383–396.

Hitt, M. A., Ireland, R. D., & Hoskisson, R. E. (2011). *Strategic management competitiveness and globalization* (9th ed.). Mason, OH: South-Western Cengage.

Hunt, S. D., & Morgan, R. M. (1995). The comparative advantage theory of competition. *Journal of Marketing, 59*(2), 1–15.

Independent Sector. (2011). *Value of volunteer time.* Retrieved from http://independentsector.org/volunteer_time

Kaste, M. (2011). Engineers hone clean-energy stoves for the world. *All Things Considered.* Retrieved from http://www.npr.org/2011/02/09/133598036/engineers-hone-clean-energy-stoves-for-the-world

King, N. K. (2004). Social capital and nonprofit leaders. *Nonprofit Management & Leadership, 14*(4), 471–486.

KIPP Foundation. (2010, December). $50 million federal i3 grant makes deep impact across Kipp network. *KIPP Newsletter.* Retrieved from http://www.kipp.org/kippnews/1012/01.htm

Lange, D., Lee, P. M., & Dai, Y. (2011). Organizational reputation: A review. *Journal of Management, 37*(1), 153–184.

Miles, R. E., & Snow, C. C. (1978). *Organizational strategy structure and process.* New York, NY: McGraw-Hill.

Milway, K., & Saxton, A. (2011, Summer). The challenge of organizational learning. *Stanford Social Innovation review,* 44–49.

Mintzberg, H. (1980). *The nature of magagerial work.* Englewood Cliffs, NJ: Prentice-Hall.

Nahapiet, J., & Ghoshal, S. (1998). Social capital, intellectual capital, and the organizational advantage. *Academy of Management Review, 23*(2), 242–266.

Oster, S. M. (1995). *Strategic management for nonprofit organizations.* New York, NY: Oxford University Press.

Preston, C., & Wallace, N. (2009). YMCA tops list of 100 most-valuable brands in the nonprofit world. *Chronicle of Philanthropy, 21*(18), 13.

Putnam, R. D. (2000). *Bowling alone.* New York, NY: Simon & Schuster.

Quinn, R. E., & Rohrbaugh, J. (1983). A spatial model of effectiveness criteria: Towards a competing values approach to organizational analysis. *Management Science, 29*(3), 363–377.

Ramirez, A. (2011). Nonprofit cash holdings: Determinants and implications. *Public Finance Review, 39*(5), 653–681.

Rindova, V. P., Williamson, I. O., Petkova, A. P., & Sever, J. M. (2005). Being good or being known: An empirical examination of the dimensions, antecedents, and consequences of organizational reputation. *The Academy of Management Journal, 48*(6), 1033–1049.

Schneider, J. A. (2009). Organizational social capital and non-profits. *Nonprofit and Voluntary Sector Quarterly, 38*(4), 643–662.

StoveTec. (n.d.). About us. Retrieved from http://stovetec.net/us /stove-information/about-us/about-stovetec

Teach for America. (n.d.). History. Retrieved from http://www .teachforamerica.org/our-organization/history

U.S. Bureau of Labor Statistics. (2011). Volunteering in the United States, 2010. Retrieved from http://www.bls.gov/news .release/archives/volun_01262011.pdf

Weick, K. E. (1979). *The social psychology of organizing* (2nd ed.). New York, NY: Random House.

Weisinger, J. Y., & Black, J. A. (2006). Strategic resources and social capital. *Irish Journal of Management, 27*(Special Issue), 145–170.

Whetten, D. A., & Cameron, K. S. (2007). *Devloping management skills* (7th ed.). Upper Saddle River, NJ: Prentice Hall.

Yukl, G. (2012). Effective leadership behavior: What we know and what questions need more attention. *The Academy of Management Perspectives, 26*(4), 66–85.

Zaheer, A., McEvily, B., & Perrone, V. (1989). Does trust matter? Exploring the effects of interorganizational and interpersonal trust on performance. *Organization Science, 9*(2), 141–159.

Program Strategies

Learning Objectives

- Define and explain five common public benefit methods
- Distill key elements of public benefit methods using an input-process-output model
- Recognize the different "customers" nonprofits serve
- Introduce strategy formation practices
- Review criteria and analysis techniques to evaluate the selection of program activities

This chapter introduces factors that managers consider when developing programs and activities to fulfill public benefit objectives. How do managers create the right mix of activities that constitute the "point" of the nonprofit value framework? What exactly will the nonprofit do to produce public value? In the for-profit language, these issues are conceptualized as business strategy (Hitt, Ireland, & Hoskisson, 2011). The term *program* will be used instead of business, but business strategy principles inform program strategizing by nonprofit leaders. Making choices about program activities blends environmental influences with internal capabilities to address stakeholder interests. A salient stakeholder in business-level strategy is the customer. Understanding what the customer wants and providing products and services that address customers' desires are key features of business-level strategy. For nonprofits, the definition of the customer is convoluted, and consequently program choices are influenced by numerous factors. This includes resource opportunities, perceptions of needs, as well as philosophical and ideological perspectives of nonprofit leaders (Checkland, 2000).

Inherent in activities that create public benefit is the sense of need, gap, or inequality. The social "problem" to be addressed is assumed to be the source of action for public benefit organizations. The nature of the concern and the definition of the gap are socially constructed. The worldview or philosophical perspective of the actor (Checkland & Poulter, 2010) influences how social issues are defined and interpreted. These frames are important because they inform operations and suggest salience of organizational activities. How the problem is framed and how the organization defines its purpose then become a significant justification for activities (see **Exhibit 5-1**). How a nonprofit creates value is by addressing social concerns. The definition of the social concern becomes a space where the organization acts. Nonprofits advocate and work to help shift how society perceives social problems. The ability to frame how issues are discussed and interpreted provides a context to suggest interventions. This then is a significant aspect of a nonprofit's positioning. The definition of the social concern facilitates articulation of the solution and furthers the nonprofit's objectives.

EXHIBIT 5-1   The Boys and Girls Clubs of America

The Boys and Girls Clubs of America (BGCA) provides an illustration of how a nonprofit may shift or modify their target beneficiary. The BGCA initially identified their target beneficiary as boys from disadvantaged communities. As is often the case, founding members of the organization (three women in this case) identified "the need" by observing the behavior of boys hanging out on the streets of Hartford, Connecticut, in 1860 (Boys and Girls Clubs of America, n.d.). These founders believed the boys needed a safe place to learn, grow, and have fun during nonschool hours. Two key principles guided program development and expansion: recreation and education. The clubs grew in size and expanded to municipalities across the country. A network of independent clubs was formed, while guiding principles were developed centrally about programming and service recipients. The boys always paid a very nominal fee to join the club, and often they were located in areas where there were few other recreational options. Although similar types of programs existed (e.g., the YMCA, city services, Jewish Family Services), the BGCA often coordinated their services to limit overlap. The purposes of the club included helping boys become more productive members of society. Thus, there were individual and society benefits. Similar services were not as widely available to girls. Some chapters of the BGCA provided services to girls, while in other municipalities there were independent "girls clubs" operated by other providers. Over time the disparity became more apparent, but the clubs operated for over 50 years primarily serving boys. Beginning in the 1950s, more and more regional clubs were open to girls as facilities and policies recognized the need for high-quality services for girls and a social benefit case was developed. These conversations culminated in a decision by the BGCA in the mid-1980s to change its name and mission to reflect the expanded target population. These decisions were not without controversy within and outside the clubs. Some chapter members felt the historical and primary purpose of the organizations was to serve boys and expanding to other populations would dilute and threaten current services. Some other providers, who already served girls, felt the BGCA would push them out of the market because the BGCA had more resources. This indeed happened in many areas. Where appropriate, the "boys" clubs merged and acquired existing "girls clubs" or opened new branches to serve a broader population. Throughout this time, the BGCA's primary target has always been economically disadvantaged children. They have modest outreach and programs for families and parents, which reflects a narrow scope of service that broadened to include girls as the demand became more apparent.

Boys and Girls Club of America (n.d.). Our history. Retrieved from http://www.bgca.org/whoweare/Pages/History.aspx

Techniques to Form Program Strategies

Confluent with an understanding of social issues is the identification of solutions. Social problems are complex and multifaceted. An organization's ability to identify intermediary and partial remediation is often how interventions develop (Heimovics, Herman, & Jurkiewicz, 1995; Weick, 1984). This is how resources and capabilities influence action (Eisenhardt & Zbaracki, 1992). Managers consider the scope of opportunities concurrent with options for intervention. Framing on each (social concern and resource capabilities) is bounded by experience and information (Etzioni, 1967). Feasibility and viability of intervention activities then is a crucial consideration for nonprofit managers (Alexander, 2000; Bell, Masaoka, & Zimmerman, 2010). This is not intended to suggest that all actions are opportunistic but rather to recognize the influence of resources in defining problems. **Table 5-1** summarizes some prominent techniques to develop program strategies.

TABLE 5-1   Strategy Formation Techniques

Technique	Characteristics
Planned and logical	This method suggests that rationale choice, systematic processes, and analysis of internal and external elements can result in the development of goals and objectives that are operationalized through organizational systems.
Resource based	Based on framing program initiatives and comparative advantage through the lens of resource elements. This includes internal systems and external resources that can be captured by the organization.
Incremental	Based on trial-and-error methods to build and refine activities over time. Learning is a key element in that managers attend to successes and challenges and adjust program activities according to existing practices.
Systems of intervention (theory of change)	This is based on cognitive mapping. A prominent example is a theory of change model that attends to outcomes and a mix of interventions to achieve objectives.
Inspirational and intuitive	Reliance on vision and mission perspectives to inspire and motivate action. Often based on inspirational leaders.

Literature on strategic formation identifies multiple techniques to develop program strategies (Mintzberg & Lampel, 1999). These techniques provide different perspectives on a complex and, at times, ambiguous process. These perspectives range from thorough, logical, planned initiatives to more intuitive and entrepreneurial methods that draw on insights of talented leaders. Each of these techniques can be viable in different contexts. Considerations include the life stage of the organization, the nature of the operating context, and the historical pattern of operations. Planning perspectives are pervasive in the strategic management literature (Bryson, 1995). Planning perspectives recognize a series of steps that, if followed, can facilitate decision making. The planning process is thorough and can engage participants within and outside the organization. It is a complex process that can at times operate disconnected from realities of fast-paced organizations. There are volumes of studies on the planning process and how it can be instrumental in facilitating decision making (Gruber, 2007).

Resource-based perspectives recognize organizational capabilities as influential in guiding strategic options (Barney, Ketchen, & Wright, 2011). The ability to develop and design interventions is contingent on the resource capabilities within or accessible to the nonprofit. Resources constraints are salient for nonprofit managers who often perceive significant opportunities (i.e., need) in the environment but realize limitations on what interventions can be sustained. This is true for nonprofits because they operate with limited exchange relationships. Movement into expanded program delivery is not necessarily associated with increased income. Incremental perspectives are proposed as a realistic and descriptive process of what happens in many organizations (Quinn, 1989). Managers make modest and partial commitments that are evaluated and refined over time. Tactics are incorporated or abandoned based on various criteria of performance, sustainability, growth, and so on. A system of intervention proposes that managers conceptualize the theory or rationalization of how activities build to create long-term objectives (March & Simon, 1958). The discussion on institutional logic recognized that managers have mental models about how the organization operates, and these models inform and guide program choices. An example in the social sector is *a theory of change*. These models guide action and provide structure to the range and type of activities implemented (Brest, 2010). In many ways a theory of change is an expanded logic model that incorporates all intervention activities so as to justify and explain current and proposed activity. A visionary perspective utilizes inspirational tactics to help organizational participants understand why their engagement and participation is important (Angelica, 2001; Jayakody, 2008). Often, although not always, contingent on an inspirational leader, these perspectives can also be conceptualized as entrepreneurial in that the leader perceives and articulates opportunities and objectives that are not commonly recognized.

What these perspectives highlight is that strategic formation is complex. Each technique is valid and potentially useful for managers and leaders. Mintzberg and Lampel (1999) conclude (after summarizing 10 different perspectives) that theorists and practitioners are often focused on different parts of the strategic process or on different conditions. Some techniques are more general and applicable than others, but different approaches are instructive to the complexities of designing program strategies. Two other issues to consider include an appreciation that power plays a significant role in strategic decision making. Some stakeholders simply have more influence and power in the process and thereby have more ability to determine the activities of the organization (Pfeffer & Salancik, 1978). Another consideration is that decision making takes place at different levels of the organization. Frontline providers to board members play a role in formation and implementation of strategic objectives (Hart, 1992). There are guidelines and perspectives that suggest optimal or desirable roles and techniques but, ultimately, managers and leaders have to come to terms with who informs strategic decisions and how they do so.

Public Benefit Methods

This chapter focuses on program activities. What activities are nonprofits going to carry out to produce public value?

Understanding how these activities are implemented and the potential for value creation is central to designing programs. The text proposes five categories of program activities, which are called public benefit methods. Public benefit methods are related to the functions that nonprofits fulfill in society (Boris, 2006; Hansmann, 1980; Kramer, 1981) (see **Table 5-2**). *Service methods* entail a broad range of activities that involve a direct interaction with the target beneficiary to "help and assist." Common activities in this area include human services, education, and health care. *Social methods* entail initiatives that build social capital, address social norms, and seek to raise awareness of public benefit issues. These activities entail both direct and indirect interaction with the intended beneficiary. *Political methods* are focused on changing institutional systems that affect the condition of intended beneficiaries; consequently, beneficiaries are not the target of activities. Advocacy and lobbying initiatives are examples of practices in this method. *Preservation methods* are those intended to protect sociocultural, environmental, and/or historical artifacts. Many nonprofits work in areas such as environmental conservation that do not directly engage beneficiaries in transformation activities but seek the preservation of significant natural features, which indirectly benefits society. Through preservation of social, cultural, or environmental artifacts, conditions are improved, thereby benefiting society. *Creative methods* are those that result in the development of innovative ideas and artifacts, such as research and artistic initiatives. This is not an exhaustive summary of public benefit methods utilized by nonprofits but reflects dominant methods that explain much of the work carried out by nonprofits. There remains significant variability within each methodological category, and nonprofits can blend or combine these activities in innovative ways. The next section reviews the input-process-output model to explain the nature of production for each of these methods.

Systems of Intervention

A systems perspective, which is based on the simple input-process-output model, is useful to understand how nonprofits

TABLE 5-2 Dimensions of Public Benefit Methods

	Service	Social	Political	Preservation	Creative
Example activities	Health care, education, counseling	Community building, public education	Direct lobbying	Historical or cultural conservation	Research or artistic activities
Nature of activities	Service methods	Information and relationship	Advocacy methods	Curating and maintaining	Intellectual and artistic
Target	Service recipient	Individual and community	Political or economic entities	Preservation artifact	Creative work
Beneficiary engagement	Direct	Direct and indirect	Indirect	Indirect	Indirect
Input	Labor	Community	Social influence	Artifact	Creativity
Output	Amount and quality of service	Number engaged	Number of issues addressed	Number of elements preserved	Number of elements created
Public benefit outcomes	Improved condition	Social capital and norms	Influence social structures	Heritage	Innovation

implement these activities. Furthermore, these dimensions provide leverage points of interaction with the external environment. The dimensions of public benefit methods provide a framework to consider how organizations operate. These dimensions are points of action that provide the context for cooperation or competition with other actors. *Inputs* are the utilization of resources or engagement of intended targets. *Process* is the activities carried out by the organization. *Outputs* are the tangible result of production. Outputs should contribute to outcomes that produce social value. Understanding public benefit methods facilitates analysis and interpretation of the operating context. The soft systems model (Checkland, 2000; Reavill, 1991) and the salient operational dimensions identified by Porac, Thomas, Wilson, Paton, and Kanfer (1995) are useful for considering the nature of production. A key consideration that can distinguish the public benefit methods listed in Table 5-2 is the target of activity. What is enacted upon to achieve change? In a classic production model, raw materials are utilized to develop a product. Drucker (1990) and others (Hasenfeld, 1983) utilize this thinking to identify the target of human service activities as the person that receives services (e.g., child in classroom). This relatively self-evident conclusion (service activities tend to be enacted on or with those they are designed to help) becomes more instrumental in defining the targets for other methods. For instance, the target in political/advocacy initiatives is the institutional entity (e.g., legislative body) that controls policy making. Even in service activities, the link between target and beneficiary can be tenuous, or at the very least, secondary beneficiaries can be a concern (e.g., parents of a child).

Beneficiaries are an important constituency of a nonprofit. Nonprofits have both direct and indirect beneficiaries (La Piana & Hayes, 2004). In service activities, the target is almost universally a key beneficiary. Indirect beneficiaries are defined as individuals, groups, or entities that gain benefit from organizational activities but are distant enough from the organization that they are not aware of how the benefits were created. Thinking about political work that targets government institutions, the beneficiary is not the government institution, but rather some distal constituency that will eventually gain advantage through the results of the political activity. Direct beneficiaries are likely to gain advantage through *output* production. That is, the more activities produced by the nonprofit, the more likely that the beneficiary is to secure advantage (e.g., classroom instruction). Indirect beneficiaries do not attain advantage simply through increased production. Indirect beneficiaries gain advantage through the *outcome* of organizational activities ("Proposed Approach," n.d.). Outcomes are the result of production. The nature of outcomes and the nature of public goods suggest that at times it is very difficult to prove the value of activities. This distance and ambiguity of beneficiaries can cause all kinds of challenges for managers as they seek to understand and connect with beneficiaries to gain support for activities. Consequently, defining the beneficiary is critical to understanding the social value created by the nonprofit.

Beneficiaries' Influence on Program Strategies

Managing direct and indirect beneficiaries is a challenge for nonprofits. Service activities tend to have direct beneficiaries, and advocacy activities tend to have indirect beneficiaries, but there is significant variability depending on the specific activity. Sometimes it is useful to conceptualize beneficiaries as customers. **Table 5-3** summarizes six issues that challenge managers in reference to service beneficiaries. These challenges are not present in every interaction but reflect some patterns of nonprofit service engagement. The first three are reflective of beneficiary characteristics and their ability (or inability) to make choices about service providers. The last three are related to the challenges nonprofits and managers impose as they define and conceptualize their public benefit purpose. These six features are aspects of a service delivery system that has limitations on how managers respond to the interests of beneficiaries.

Limited Exchange Relationship

In many instances, service beneficiaries pay only a fraction of the cost associated with the service or product received. So the

TABLE 5-3 Issues in Service Beneficiary Power

Challenge	Definition
1. Limited exchange relationship	Customers or service beneficiaries often pay only a fraction of the actual cost of the product or service.
2. Few competitors	Given the limited exchange relationship, often there are few other organizations providing a similar service.
3. Information asymmetry	Difficult for customers to know the quality of services and thereby make choices about different services.
4. Professional ethos	Service providers believe they know best for client population.
5. Broader society priorities	There are societal priorities that supersede client interests or preferences.
6. Mission/historical preferences	Similar to professional ethos is the philosophical preference of the nonprofit that wants to move forward a social, cultural, or political agenda.

one-on-one (customer-to-business) exchange relationship exhibited in a typical market arrangement is muted by a third party, thereby diluting the influence of users. This has numerous implications for management and industry structure.

Few Competing Providers

In many cases (although not always) the nonprofit is the only service provider, and beneficiaries don't have an alternative. How many museums of fine arts does a community need or can it support? This idea of "other providers" will be discussed further, but at this point a basis of the competitive market is formed on consumer choice, which is often limited in the nonprofit context. Even if there are other providers, the need or demand for services often outstrips the capabilities of all providers, so providers coordinate to do what they can and are cognizant of the excessive demand.

Information Asymmetry

For many of the services provided by nonprofits (e.g., health care, education), it can be very difficult to determine quality, and it can be difficult to select alternatives based on reliable criteria. Consequently, the customer has to base the exchange of services on trust. Consider the purchase of a pizza from a local restaurant. As a consumer you can determine the quality of the pizza fairly quickly by tasting the product. If you like it, you will continue to buy the product; if not, you'll try other providers until you find one you like. Conversely, consider visiting the doctor for a pain or ailment. The visit is pleasant but the diagnosis was indeterminate. Was that a high-quality visit? Would another doctor do a better job? Did you get accurate value for your fee? It is hard to know—right? Many nonprofit services exhibit that same characteristic called information asymmetry, which means that the provider tends to know quite a bit more about the product or service than the consumer, making it very difficult for recipients to make effective choices. In fact, one of the reasons nonprofits operate in these areas is exactly because of information and quality challenges. By operating a nonprofit, the provider is encouraged not to take advantage of the consumer's ignorance by charging higher prices or decreasing quality.

Professional Ethos

There are also aspects of the nonprofit culture and ethos that, at times, may bias or minimize customer preferences. Some service beneficiaries have limited (cognitive) abilities and the nonprofit providers, as professionals and experts in the field, serve as an authority to provide guidance, thereby directing client behavior. The potential for providers to assume a professional or even moral justification to control services because they "know what is best" might marginalize beneficiary preferences.

Broader Social Priorities

Many nonprofits exist to achieve society-wide benefits that supersede interests of any particular "customer." The very definition of tax-exempt entities requires that they exist for public purposes. These broader society objectives might also mute client preferences.

Mission and Historical Precedence

This is often captured in the mission of the organization, which articulates society benefits in addition to individual benefits. Consider a nature conservancy that is founded to preserve land. Many consumers might want to ride off-road vehicles on the land or take part in other activities that do not match with the intent of the agency. The nonprofit isn't going to offer the land to off-road users merely because they are willing to pay for it, but instead it will adhere to its preservation principles and work to find individuals who are willing to support that purpose. This also illustrates an interesting issue that many nonprofits confront as they consider the opportunity to sell some services in a way that could bring funds while potentially being contrary to the organization's mission.

Segmentation—Who Is Our Customer?

Decisions regarding program strategies are influenced by how stakeholders might perceive the value of those activities (Boenigk, Helmig, Bruhn, Hadwich, & Batt, 2012; Sirmon, Hitt, & Ireland, 2007). Borrowing from business strategy, a salient stakeholder is the customer. For nonprofits there are potentially several customers. In a classic sense, customers are those individuals or entities who pay. They are engaged in an exchange relationship. Beneficiaries are a customer, but as was just discussed even direct beneficiaries can be challenged in their ability to influence program practices. Indirect beneficiaries are more distant, often difficult to define, and at times uninformed of key activities— consequently, they are unable to significantly influence practices without some shift in their relationship with the nonprofit (e.g., coordinating or organizing among themselves might be one way to do that). A key issue has to do with power to influence organizational activities. The admonition by Drucker for nonprofits to define their primary and secondary customer is relevant for this discussion (Drucker, 1990). If beneficiaries reflect the customer in the public benefic domain, then resource providers are the customer in the resource domain (see **Table 5-4**). This includes funders, significant labor issues, and stakeholders, all of which can influence legitimacy receptions of the nonprofit (Bruce, 1995). Each of these constituencies influence directly or indirectly what programs are offered and how those programs are implemented.

Nonprofit managers confront several challenges to prioritize and segment customers or influential stakeholders to determine for whom and how to provide value. The strategy formation processes just discussed provide viable methods to consider some of

TABLE 5-4   Potential Customers for Nonprofits

Customers	Key Characteristics	Generic Interests
Direct beneficiary	Participant of program activities or sufficiently aware of program features intended to generate benefits.	Private benefits, quality, efficiency, effectiveness
Indirect beneficiary	Limited awareness of program features and limited ability to determine quality of activities.	Social value, outcomes
Funding entities	Various methods to support activities, some of which are closely linked to program activities, others that are not linked to specific activities, but intended to support the nonprofit. Limited engagement in activities, but interested in program elements.	Production outputs, efficiencies, quality, innovations, impact performance, stability
Labor concerns	Varying degrees of instrumentality in production capacity, but potentially central to quality and production.	Instrumental, expressive, and social benefits
Legitimacy providers	Limited engagement in activities, but interest in benefits and alliances that build social capital.	Statue and influence, stability

these issues, as do stakeholder analysis techniques (Ackermann & Eden, 2011; Balser & McClusky, 2005). Segmentation is the process of categorizing and organizing customers (this term will be used to refer to the stakeholder for whom nonprofit activities are intended to provide value) according to a system that facilitates defining the current and potential customer (Harvey, 1990). Managers can also prioritize customers to determine primary and secondary customers. The nature of the operating domain and industry inform the type of categorizations and prioritizations that are the most useful for managers. Segmentation allows managers to explore the range and type of individuals and institutions they serve and the size and scope of potential customers. This allows managers to make judgments about the growth potential of markets as well as the competitive nature of particular segments. Defining the customer is a simple question that is surprisingly difficult for nonprofit managers.

Reach and Richness

Reach and richness in a customer relationship reflect the range and depth of services provided to customers (Hitt et al., 2011). Cable companies do this when they "bundle services" (telephone, cable, and internet) so as to expand the service reach. They intend to provide more to the customers they already have. In the nonprofit context, the YMCA is an organization that tries to extend its reach and range of services provided to family members. Many YMCAs target the fitness and recreation needs of families. If the YMCA provides fitness services to moms and supporting services for other members of the family, such as childcare or team sports, the YMCA can extend the reach and richness of services provided to the family unit. A deeper relationship tends to reflect strength of association and thereby limits the tendency of users to shift providers (Berry, 1995; Grönroos, 2004). It is one thing if an individual (mom) wants to change fitness facilities, but if your children attend the day care, your daughter plays sports in a club, and your teenager is on the swim team, it becomes even more difficult to change providers. These principles (segmentation, type of beneficiary, and reach of activities) provide additional guidance regarding the type of services and activities an organization might carry out.

What Value to Provide and How to Provide Value

In principle, organizations should provide something of value. Organizations need to understand and anticipate how the different stakeholders perceive the value of activities and how that might change over time. Anticipating interests and needs of the various stakeholder groups is critical to the success for nonprofit entities and will influence what nonprofits provide. The next section reviews two "generic" approaches to provide value. Managers must decide if the nonprofit is going to perform *different activities* than other providers or if the nonprofit is going to perform *similar activities differently* (Hitt et al., 2011). Either strategy requires that the organization understands the current range of services offered within a particular operating context and tailors their activities to ensure that they are different from those already offered.

Generic Business Strategies

Program-level strategies are intended to help nonprofit managers position the organization in such a way as to differentiate services and activities from others. This facilitates survival as well as coordination of services to meet community needs. This discussion focuses on service activities in the public benefit market and development activities in the resource market. Understanding the service beneficiaries and resource markets helps nonprofit managers select strategies that fulfill public purposes while supporting organizational sustainability.

One method to categorize program-level strategies is to consider how certain types of activities provide a comparative advantage. Classic strategic management literature considers two basic methods to provide value to customers. Organizations can provide services or products that are low cost (e.g., Walmart). Alternatively, organizations can provide services or products that are unique (e.g., Starbucks) (see **Table 5-5**). Organizations can try to accomplish both (low cost and unique) simultaneously, but the discussion differentiates these two types so as to distill the strategic advantage inherent in each type. In addition to considering the strategic approach to creating organizational advantage, managers can provide these products or services to a broad-based market or they can be more focused. Scope of activities considers whether the organization is focused on a niche market or the broad overall market. This creates four generic strategies. Public benefit *and* resource markets are discussed in reference to the features, strengths, and challenges of the different generic approaches.

Cost Efficiency Strategies

Cost efficiency strategies are intended to provide services at a lower cost when compared to other providers. Walmart is the classic broad-scope cost leader. Walmart built efficiencies into every stage of the supply chain to provide lower-cost items to customers. This method has been very successful to gain dominance in the retail consumer market. In the nonprofit context, low-cost strategies relate to the ability to provide services at a low user price and compliance with efficiency measures that suggest a certain percentage of expenses should be spent on programs (typically 70–80% or more) as opposed to management

TABLE 5-5   Generic Business Strategies

		Advantage	
		Cost efficiency	Unique
Scope	**Broad target**	Cost leadership	Differentiation
	Focused target	Focused cost	Focused differentiation

or fundraising costs. Frumkin and Andre-Clark (2000) analyze competition among human service nonprofits and for-profits and recognize some limitations for nonprofits due to limited financial resources, and the mission-based culture, which might mute pure efficiency initiatives. The next section reviews some market forces (Porter, 1979) and how they are enacted in a cost-sensitive market or industry.

Bargaining Power of Customers

Powerful customers can force providers to seek efficiencies to keep costs low. In the social service context, government entities that contract with nonprofit providers invoke various methods to share or transfer costs and risks to social service providers. Governments limit reimbursement practices and delay payments, which require providers to cover costs while waiting for payment. These practices require nonprofits to secure supplemental funds. While difficult to comply with, nonprofits that operate with government contracts can rarely replace that funding and are often required to comply with reimbursement protocols that detail services qualities and beneficiaries, while constraining reimbursements (Smith & Lipsky, 1995; Van Slyke, 2007).

Donors as well are often concerned about the efficient use of resources. The general rule of thumb for operating costs suggests that nonprofits should spend no more than 25% of expenses on management and fundraising. The philanthropic guideline is widely used by some of the largest donor advocacy groups, such as Charity Navigator and the United Way. It is not exactly clear how much the average donor might use this metric, but the United Way and employee charitable campaigns rely on the 25% mark as the primary marker for efficiency. It is not uncommon that nonprofits will promote the efficient use of donated funds, suggesting that a significant percentage of donated funds (90–95%) go directly to program activities. This can be an important method to distinguish a nonprofit from other providers.

Bargaining Power of Suppliers

The labor markets in cost-sensitive services can be a critical resource to help mitigate expenses. The ability to use unpaid

human capital

labor (volunteers) to supplement services may keep costs low, while providing personalized services (Simmons & Emanuele, 2010). Consequently, managers consider what volunteers are willing to support and the reliability of that workforce. At times a volunteer labor pool may be deep and very stable, but there are also limitations about what volunteers are willing to do in exchange for participating in the social service activities (Cnaan & Cascio, 1999). In principle, volunteers want some expressive benefit in their engagement (Mason, 1996). It can be difficult to secure enough volunteers on a consistent and reliable basis; consequently, organizations that build and maintain the range of systems necessary to recruit, train, place, and supervise volunteers might be in a particular advantage. Volunteers or low-cost labor are a fundamental part of cost efficiency strategies.

Potential Entrants

Cost-leader strategies are susceptible to new service providers if new entrants can demonstrate an ability to provide comparable services at lower cost. In human service markets, national for-profit providers can extract efficiencies that localized and independent nonprofits might find very difficult to replicate (Frumkin & Andre-Clark, 2000). Once an organization has developed efficient service delivery systems, it can be difficult for other entities to compete. This is because these systems typically require a complex mix of paid and unpaid labor, plus technology systems and *weakness* specialized competencies to comply with accountability requirements that can be onerous.

Product Substitutes

Programs based on cost efficiency may be particularly susceptible to substitutes. In senior nutrition services (meals-on-wheels), there are a number of efforts to reduce costs and increase efficiencies. Some programs utilize frozen meals as that can reduce the number of visits while providing nutritiously suitable meals. These meals can be delivered easily and often at less cost than a prepared meal. Although the program may compromise some of the visitation priorities, the frozen meals provide nutrition to a larger number of individuals while utilizing fewer resources.

Third-party contractors who want to provide expanded benefits (nutrition) for reduced cost find the instrumental benefit appealing. These frozen meals have replaced some traditional meal delivery services that provide prepared meals to homebound seniors.

Differentiation Strategies

Organizations that use differentiation strategies seek to gain an advantage by providing services and activities in a way that is substantively different from others. They don't compete by providing services at a lower cost or more efficiently, but rather seek to provide services that are unique. For nonprofits, that distinction might be philosophical/ideological or a differentiation on the type of services provided. An arts example might be in order. It is not uncommon in large metropolitan areas that there are a number of different arts organizations, and in very large markets, providers only display subtle distinctions. They tend to differentiate themselves by providing different kinds of cultural services. They seek to monopolize certain niche areas (Seaman, 2004). This can be accomplished because of high cost barriers that reward differentiation and limited market potential. In the museum industry, it is common practice to coordinate and share resources while trying build unique collections that draw and attract particular stakeholders. This attempt to differentiate and cooperate culminates with a very real competition for audience and donors (Freedman, 1986). Arts organizations use differentiation to ensure survival and to gain support from key stakeholders without having to prioritize cost or efficiency measures. Rather they provide something of *distinctive* value. This is an essential program strategy for many nonprofits that relies on strong attachment and affinity by stakeholder groups.

Bargaining Power of Customers

Given the niche-market focus that might be common for nonprofits, users can organize to influence services and programs. In many ways this might be a perfectly reasonable response from a core stakeholder group, as nonprofits utilizing this strategy rely on strong stakeholder relationships to attend to interests and preferences. Nonprofit managers would want to balance the preferences from several groups. This can get contentious if some users find that their preferences are overshadowed by other constituencies. Factions can form, which causes conflict among the leadership. Depending on constituency power, size, and motivations, these subgroups either can try to influence services or they will eventually remove themselves from the organization if they believe their preferences are not attended to. Whether a faith community or a member association, strong interest groups can have significant influence in the type and range of services offered. Consequently, managers need to develop systems that support specialized interests and preferences while building a unifying theme (or brand) to keep disparate interests intact. The term *brand* reflects some of the management literature concerning consumer attachments toward particular products and services (Sargeant, Hudson, & West, 2008). An ability to gain strong attachments among key stakeholders is a critical dimension to this strategy.

Donors obviously have choices as to when and how they provide funds, but if they have a particular interest in a nonprofit's service initiatives or beneficiaries they may have difficulty finding other comparable organizations (Boenigk & Helmig, 2013). Donors can form an independent entity that addresses their interests, although, unless they are fundamentally disenfranchised, donors may try to use their influence to guide and modify programs and activities to reflect their preferences. The extent to which donors organize and coordinate is not widely understood. Similar to users, donors may form alliances with other funders, and, as a result, can exert more influence over the nonprofit. Managers need to monitor donor attitudes and ensure that donors understand the organization's distinctive portfolio and how those distinctions relate to the donors interests. Major donor pressure on nonprofit managers is not new (Cannon, 2012). Donors seek to fulfill their interests through the activities of the nonprofit. This strategy suggests that managers seek to position the organization as a unique provider with distinctive qualities, which attract and retain donors.

Bargaining Power of Suppliers

Organizations that try to differentiate services or activities can have challenging labor requirements, especially when you consider how specialized talents can have significant benefits for an organization's ability to meet interests and preferences of members. There are a variety of nonprofit-dominated fields (arts, research, higher education, and health care) that require specialized labor to fulfill services and in particular to differentiate services. Talented labor can be instrumental in organizational positioning, and therefore employees exert some influence over resource allocation and practices. For example, specialized doctors can be instrumental in recruiting other specialists as well as providing unique services. Additionally, artists, musicians, researchers, and the like expect some creative liberties to design and create according to their interests and thereby exert some influence over strategic options.

Potential Entrants

One of the challenges of a differentiation strategy is to maintain strong bonds with stakeholder groups. These attachments, when utilized appropriately, can make it difficult for other providers to enter into the user or resource market because these stakeholders have an affinity with the organization, which might be very resilient.

Product Substitutes

The differentiation strategy survives on the principle that the organization is irreplaceable because of what it is and the services it provides. Managers must consider how new or alternative ventures might replace current practices. Concerning donor markets, there are potentially a number of alternative choices for donors in relation to how they distribute funds. If donors become disenfranchised with a particular organization, they may decide to shift priorities to a different entity. Even though there isn't another provider in a particular niche, there are alternative venues for them to fulfill their philanthropic interests. Donor fatigue occurs when donors grow tired of a particular interest area and seek to move into other areas. Volunteers as well may shift interests and attachments. Some of the variances may be driven by practices of the agency, but it is also reflective of the philanthropic market that interests do change and modify and, as a result, any one organization has limitations on how donors or volunteers might connect.

Conclusion

These program-level strategies are informed by understanding the customer; whether that is a donor or a service recipient, these generic models summarize the tactics managers can use to grow program-delivery options. Managers use these strategies to expand services to new customers within a market segment or to deepen the services provided to existing customers. Inevitably, organizations find themselves operating in cost-sensitive markets with stakeholders that also have interest in unique attributes. Especially when considering the mix of resource and public benefit markets, there are likely to be dimensions within each arena that are attuned to different features. Nonprofits can't effectively compete on all levels in all markets, so some choices about scope and generic strategy are likely to be optimal. Crittenden (2000) summarized the strategic choices of an exemplar nonprofit organization. The organization understood the logic of social value creation and the core competencies that facilitated their success. The set of program offerings (the point of the nonprofit value framework) were strongly interrelated. There was coherence among program offerings and an effort to extend services to existing program participants as opposed to seeking new markets and new customers. Managers in these organizations attend to the resource market and diversified funding options sufficiently to minimize risk but not beyond the capabilities necessary to manage the funding streams. They targeted donors and funders to establish strong relationships, which further stabilized their funding. These choices were relevant to their operating context and reflect "effectiveness" in a particular operating environment. The remaining chapters in the text seek to provide additional guidance regarding program strategies. The final chapter on leadership revisits some concepts of corporate strategy and the role of the board of directors as providing guidance to organizational activities.

Discussion Questions

1. Reflect on your organizational experiences. How have strategic choices been enacted in those organizations? What influenced the level and quality of programs offered?
2. Which of the strategy formation processes described seems the best for organizations you have worked with? Why do you believe the process is best?
3. What customers *should* be the most important in for nonprofit managers?
4. Summarizing the generic business strategies, in what operating contexts would cost leadership strategy be best? What about differentiation strategies? Are there aspects of the operating environment that might suggest likely success in one strategy or another?

References

Ackermann, F., & Eden, C. (2011). Strategic management of stakeholders: Theory and practice. *Long Range Planning, 44,* 179–196.

Alexander, J. (2000). Adaptive strategies of nonprofit human service organizations in an era of devolution and new public management. *Nonprofit Management and Leadership, 10*(3), 287–303.

Angelica, E. (2001). *Crafting effective mission and vision statements.* Saint Paul, MN: Wilder Foundation.

Balser, D., & McClusky, J. (2005). Managing stakeholder relationships and nonprofit organization effectiveness. *Nonprofit Management & Leadership, 15*(3), 295–315.

Barney, J. B., Ketchen, D. J., & Wright, M. (2011). The future of resource-based theory: Revitalization or decline? *Journal of Management, 37*(5), 1299–1315.

Bell, J., Masaoka, J., & Zimmerman, S. (2010). *Nonprofit sustainability: Making strategic decisions for financial viability.* San Francisco, CA: Jossey-Bass.

Berry, L. (1995). Relationship marketing of services—Growing interest, emerging perspectives. *Journal of the Academy of Marketing Science, 23*(4), 236–245.

Boenigk, S., & Helmig, B. (2013). Why do donors donate? Examining the effects of organizational identification and identity salience on the relationships among satisfaction, loyalty, and donation behavior. *Journal of Service Research, 16*(4), 533–548.

Boenigk, S., Helmig, B., Bruhn, M., Hadwich, K., & Batt, V. (2012). An empirical investigation of experiences and the link between a service-dominant logic mindset, competitive advantage, and performance of nonprofit organizations. In M. Bruhn & K. Hadwich (Eds.), *Customer experience* (pp. 469–500). Wiesbaden, Germany: Gabler Verlag.

Boris, E. (2006). Nonprofit organizations in a democracy—Roles and responsibilities. In E. Boris & C. E. Steuerle (Eds.), *Nonprofit and government: Collaboration and conflict* (pp. 1–35). Washington, DC: Urban Institute.

Boys and Girls Club of America (n.d.). Our history. Retrieved from http://www.bgca.org/whoweare/Pages/History.aspx

Brest, P. (2010, Spring). The power of theories of change. *Stanford Social Innovation Review,* 47–51.

Bruce, I. (1995). Do not-for-profits value their customers and their needs? *International Marketing Review, 12*(4), 77–84.

Bryson, J. M. (1995). *Strategic planning for public and nonprofit organizations* (Revised ed.). San Francisco, CA: Jossey-Bass.

Cannon, H. B. (2012). U.Va. to launch contemplative sciences center. Retrieved from http://www.uvatibetcenter.org/?page_id=5760

Checkland, P. (2000). Soft systems methodology: A thirty year retrospective. *Systems Research and Behavioral Science, 17*(S1), S11.

Checkland, P., & Poulter, J. (2010). Soft systems methodology. In M. Reynolds & S. Holwell (Eds.), *Systems approaches to managing change: A practical guide* (pp. 191–242). London, UK: Springer-Verlag.

Cnaan, R. A., & Cascio, T. (1999). Performance and commitment: Issues in management of volunteers in human service organizations. *Journal of Social Service Research, 24*(3/4), 1–37.

Crittenden, W. (2000). Spinning straw into gold: The tenous strategy, funding, and financial performance linkage. *Nonprofit and Voluntary Sector Quarterly, 29,* 164–182.

Drucker, P. F. (1990). *Managing the nonprofit organization.* New York, NY: Harper Collins.

Eisenhardt, K. M., & Zbaracki, M. J. (1992). Strategic decision making. *Strategic Management Journal, 13*(S2), 17–37.

Etzioni, A. (1967). Mixed-scanning: A "third" approach to decision-making. *Public Administration Review, 27*(5), 385–392.

Freedman, M. R. (1986). The elusive promise of management cooperation in the performing arts. In P. J. DiMaggio (Ed.), *Nonprofit enterprises in the arts: Studies in mission and constraint.* New York, NY: Oxford University.

Frumkin, P., & Andre-Clark, A. (2000). When missions, markets, and politics collide: Values and strategy in the nonprofit human services. *Nonprofit and Voluntary Sector Quarterly, 29*(Suppl. 1), 141–163.

Grönroos, C. (2004). The relationship marketing process: Communication, interaction, dialogue, value. *The Journal of Business & Industrial Marketing, 19*(2), 99–113.

Gruber, M. (2007). Uncovering the value of planning in new venture creation: A process and contingency perspective. *Journal of Business Venturing, 22*(6), 782–807.

Hansmann, H. (1980). The role of the nonprofit enterprise. *Yale Law Journal, 89,* 835–901.

Hart, S. L. (1992). An integrative framework for strategy-making processes. *The Academy of Management Review, 17*(2), 327–351.

Harvey, J. W. (1990). Benefit segmentation for fund raisers. *Journal of the Academy of Marketing Science, 18*(1), 77–86.

Hasenfeld, Y. (1983). *Human service organizations.* Englewood Cliffs, NJ: Prentice Hall.

Heimovics, R. D., Herman, R. D., & Jurkiewicz, C. L. (1995). The political dimension of effective nonprofit executive leadership. *Nonprofit Management & Leadership, 5*(3), 233–248.

Hitt, M. A., Ireland, R. D, & Hoskisson, R. E. (2011). *Strategic management competitiveness and globalization* (9th ed.). Mason, OH: South-Western Cengage.

Jayakody, J. A. S. K. (2008). Charismatic leadership in Sri Lankan business organizations. *The Journal of Management Development, 27*(5), 480–498.

Kramer, R. M. (1981). *Voluntary agencies in the welfare state.* Los Angeles: University of California Press.

La Piana, D., & Hayes, M. (2004). *Play to win: The nonprofit guide to competitive strategy.* San Francisco, CA: Jossey-Bass.

March, J. G., & Simon, H. A. (1958). *Organizations.* Oxford, England: Wiley.

Mason, D. E. (1996). *Leading and managing the expressive dimension: Harnessing the hidden power source of the nonprofit sector.* San Francisco, CA: Jossey Bass.

Mintzberg, H., & Lampel, J. (1999). Reflecting on the strategy process. *Sloan Management Review, 40*(3), 21–30.

Pfeffer, J., & Salancik, G. R. (1978). *The external control of organizations: A resource dependance perspective.* New York, NY: Harper & Row.

Porac, J. F., Thomas, H., Wilson, F., Paton, D., & Kanfer, A. (1995). Rivalry and the industry model of Scottish knitwear producers. *Administrative Science Quarterly, 40*(2), 203–227.

Porter, M. E. (1979). How competitive forces shape strategy. *Harvard Business Review*, 2008, 24–40.

Proposed Approach for Identifying Beneficiaries for DFID's Civil Society Challenge Fund. (2012). United Kingdom AID. http://www.dfid.gov.uk/Documents/funding/cscf/background-beneficiary-approach.doc

Quinn, J. B. (1989). Strategic shange: 'Logical incrementalism.' *Sloan Management Review, 30*(4), 45–60.

Reavill, L. R. P. (1991). Quality assessment, total quality management and the stakeholders in the UK higher education system. *Managing Service Quality, 8*(1), 55–63.

Sargeant, A., Hudson, J., & West, D. C. (2008). Conceptualizing brand values in the charity sector: The relationship between sector, cause and organization. *Service Industries Journal, 28*(5), 615–632.

Seaman, B. A. (2004). Competition and the non-profit arts: The lost industrial organization agenda. *Journal of Cultural Economics, 28*(3), 167–193.

Simmons, W. O., & Emanuele, R. (2010). Are volunteers substitute for paid labor in nonprofit organizations? *Journal of Economics and Business, 62*(1), 65–77.

Sirmon, D. G., Hitt, M. A., & Ireland, R. (2007). Managing firm resources in dynamic environments to create value: Looking inside the black box. *The Academy of Management Review ARCHIVE, 32*(1), 273–292.

Smith, S. R., & Lipsky, M. (1995). *Nonprofits for hire: The welfare state in the age of contracting.* Boston, MA: Harvard University Press.

Van Slyke, D. M. (2007). Agents or stewards: Using theory to understand the government-nonprofit social service contracting relationship. *Journal of Public Administration Research and Theory, 17*(2), 157–187.

Weick, K. E. (1984). Small wins: Redefining the scale of social problems. *American Psychologist, 39*(1), 40–49.

CHAPTER 6

Analysis of the Task Environment: Understanding Pressures for Competition and Cooperation

Learning Objectives

- Gain techniques to analyze the nonprofit task environment
- Recognize some of the factors that may foster cooperative or competitive behavior among nonprofit organizations
- Understand the fundamentals of stakeholder analysis
- Interpret and apply competitive analysis techniques to the nonprofit sector

The task environment reflects key elements of the organization's operating domain. The operating domain is the claim an organization makes to address particular social concerns with certain intervention activities. The operating domain sets boundaries on the forces and influences in the task environment (Hasenfeld, 1983). The ability to define the operating context helps nonprofit managers understand those entities that are likely to influence performance or success. Appropriate definitions of operating domains are critical because definitions that are too narrow are likely to miss the influence of entities that could impact performance. Conversely, definitions that are too broad suggest responses that are not viable given capabilities.

Operating domains are not necessarily self-evident and are dependent on how an organization perceives itself in relation to others. Consider for instance a natural history museum. Is it most appropriate to consider their scope of work as the preservation of historic artifacts, or are they concerned about education, or are they primarily engaged in entertainment? How the dominant coalition defines the scope of work has implications for the program activities and the resources they seek (Eggers & Kaplan, 2013). Mission statements and other guiding principles provide a perspective on how the organization defines itself. Nonprofits operate in two domains (public benefit and resource) and it is necessary to conceptualize operating focus in each area.

The chapter starts with a discussion of cooperative and competitive dynamics and how managers can interpret and understand the operating domain. Two analytic methods are reviewed. Stakeholder analysis techniques (Freeman, 1984) are discussed as a practical strategy to analyze key actors in the operating context. The chapter concludes with competitive analysis techniques (Porter, 1998) that help managers understand industry factors that influence the tendency of organizations to cooperate or compete.

Competitive and Cooperative Dynamics in Nonprofits

Understanding the nature of cooperative and competitive dynamics in the nonprofit sector is challenging. The discussion of program-level strategy introduced a system model that conceptualized the inputs, processes, and outputs of production. Each dimension outlined in that model is a potential leverage point for cooperative or competitive behavior. In addition, the philosophical values perspective of the organization could instigate cooperative or competitive tendencies among other providers. The commonality of the public benefit purpose and the tendency to utilize similar resources will drive relations with others (Lange,

Lee, & Dai, 2011). So organizations serving similar clients (e.g., at-risk youth) to achieve similar objectives (e.g., college readiness) and/or organizations that utilize similar resources (e.g., volunteer labor pool, charitable donations) are going to either compete or cooperate at some point. Sometimes the engagement is purposeful whereas at other times a nonprofit might operate within the sphere of influence of others (soliciting similar donors) without being aware of the potential for conflict.

The theoretical literature on nonprofit strategy is developing, and the heterogeneity of the sector further complicates understanding. Much of the theory on competitive dynamics is framed by the for-profit business literature and so must be adapted to reflect the nature of nonprofits. The theory of awareness, motivation, capacity (AMC) (Chen & Miller, 2012) provides a framework to understand the behavior of organizations. *Awareness* reflects the tendency of organizational actors to understand the dynamics of the operating context. Awareness is constrained by how organizations define their operating environment. Key factors to consider include significant stakeholders (e.g., funders, other providers, and legitimacy elements) (Sosin, 2012) and interpreting their interests, especially to gain insight into how those interests align or diverge from organizational objectives. *Motivation* addresses the perspective of organizational actors both as enactors and responders to competitive and cooperative opportunities. To understand organizational action the perceptions and orientation of organizational leadership is critical. *Capacity* reflects the ability of organizations to enact behaviors. Managers need to have sufficient awareness of potential collaborators or competitors to instigate action. Clarity regarding the motivations and interests of those actors will signal the tendency to cooperate or potentially compete. Finally, organizations must have sufficient capacity to enact strategic choices.

Research on social interactions in society (Loch, Galunic, & Schneider, 2006) identifies motivations that provide insight into competitive and cooperative behavior. Competitive behavior is likely to be revealed when actors are seeking resources and/or status (Chew, 2009; Hitt, Ireland, & Hoskisson, 2011). The tendency of nonprofits to seek capacity through increased capital (financial, human, physical, or social) is more likely to instigate a competitive response in others that are striving for similar capacity elements. Cooperative behavior is likely to be exhibited through a desire for relational or reciprocal ties. Organizations are less likely to compete when they share a common bond. This is built through reciprocal relationships or the sense of shared purpose toward social or community objectives. It gets complicated when social impact goals are linked to capacity and resource acquisition. For instance, researchers found that if organizations rely on earned income strategies, which suggests a link between public benefit activities and resources sustainability, the organizations were less tied to interorganizational networks and potentially less cooperative (Galaskiewicz, Bielefeld, & Dowell, 2006). While some organizations may share public benefit outcomes, resource issues can thwart cooperation unless organizational sustainability is fostered by cooperative action (Uzzi, 1997). Competitive and cooperative tendencies are complex, and the next section reviews how managers define their operating domains. The definition of public benefit purpose and the organization's role in that domain has implications for competitive behavior.

Analysis of the Task Environment

Three elements guide analysis of the task environment (see **Table 6-1**). First, managers clarify the public benefit purpose of the organization. This may seem obvious, but given the nature and complexity of activities in the nonprofit sector, clarity regarding public benefit objectives and the social value proposition of the nonprofits sets the context to interpret operating domains. The second principle is segmentation of the task environment so as to effectively reflect the resource and public benefits actors. Segmentation is disaggregating domains into subcategories that facilitate understanding. The final step is conducting analysis on the domains. Two techniques are reviewed. Stakeholder analysis provides a method to analyze the nature and character of multiple divergent relationships that influence operations.

TABLE 6-1 Stages in Task Environment Analysis

Criteria	Features
Clarify public benefit purpose	• Define mission and understand need • Set the scope and range of public benefit activities
Segment the operating domains	• Resource and public benefit domains • Disaggregate features of each domain • Identify specific operating context
Analyze characteristics of operating domains	• Assess capacity/depth of market • Stakeholder analysis • Competitive analysis

Competitive analysis explores domain-level forces that influence success. These forces operate at an industry level, and managers gain insight into strategic options and risks by considering the five forces of competitive analysis.

Clarify Public Benefit Purpose

Mission and purpose provide the worldview through which nonprofits define themselves and can capture funder interest and guide public benefit activities. Public benefit classifications improve options in some funding areas while constraining options in another. Environmental organizations, for instance, have different funding opportunities when compared to arts organizations. This requires organizations to refine their organizational identity and use that identity to approach the resource market. Mission translates into services that further refine public benefit features. This mix of values, services, and public benefit purpose is how nonprofits meet the needs and interests of funders (Fischer, Wilsker, & Young, 2011).

Segmenting Operating Domains

Specification of the public benefit purpose facilitates understanding which entities in the task environment might affect performance. The definition of the operating context forms the basis for understanding the dynamics that exist in the task environment. There are various techniques managers can use to help define operating boundaries. One technique is based on customer definitions. Using the customer—beneficiary or target—to define the industry allows managers to understand all other entities that are attending to similar customers or targets. In the public benefit domain, services are a common method to achieve public benefits. Service activities tend to have direct beneficiaries and these beneficiaries can be conceptualized as customers in the public benefit domain. In the resource market, conceptualizing the funding source as a customer has significant intellectual and operational merit. A focus on donors and all manner of funding entities as customers helps define organizational practices as well as the competitive market for resources. Defining industry by attending to customer segments facilitates the formation of strategy to meet customer interests.

Product or service industry classifications are useful to define markets and competitors. This method would use a classification system such as the National Taxonomy of Exempt Entities (NTEE) to identify nonprofits providing similar services. In conjunction with a geographic boundary (i.e., service area), this method is quite useful (Domanski, 2010). These organizations are likely to have similar resource requirements and provide similar services. One of the issues is the need for further clarification of the intensity of services provided by other organizations. This means some entities are focused on services within a particular market niche whereas some providers are more diversified and operate in multiple contexts. Intensity or focus of delivery has significant implications for understanding the behavior of other providers. Review of mission statements can provide clues to how an organization defines its focus. These classification systems facilitate analysis of other providers because there are nationally available compilations of provider characteristics, such as revenue and assets, based on these classifications (e.g., Guidestar).

Defining the features (revenue, assets, or capabilities) of other providers can give managers significant operational guidance. For instance, revenue characteristics are particularly useful for understanding competitive dynamics (Boardman & Vining, 2000). Analyzing the revenue practices of comparable entities allows managers to understand the features of sustainability. Defining the drivers of operational activity allows managers to benchmark their practices to those of other providers. This includes recognizing the prevalence of fee-based income compared to donated income and investment income. Each revenue source is going to imply different organizational capabilities and weaknesses. This analysis suggests the viability and resiliency of other providers and the dynamics of any particular market segment.

There are weaknesses in conducting peer analysis. There is a tendency to consider the practices of large dominant players in the field while ignoring smaller or emergent entities. The small or emergent entities might reflect a new market approach that is not reflected in bigger organizations. It is difficult to fully understand the motivations and purposes of other providers and, consequently, activities can be misinterpreted. Drawing conclusions about operational practices is tricky. For example, there is a tendency to emphasize the financial resource portfolio, which is just one aspect of the comparative advantage. Other providers can build complex operational systems that utilize intangible assets, which are difficult to quantify and interpret (Courtney, 2002). Of particular concern is recognizing the motivations and interests of key actors in the operating environment, and this where stakeholder analysis can be useful.

Analyzing Operating Domains

Analysis of the operating environment seeks to understand the factors that are likely to influence operational success. The capacity and interests of other entities and influential stakeholders is one aspect of the analysis. Stakeholder analysis techniques are useful and informative to rank divergent players and perspectives. Competitive analysis provides insight into the structure of the operating context and the power of significant entities. Both perspectives provide insight into the strategic choices managers confront.

Stakeholder Analysis

Stakeholder analysis techniques help managers understand the interests and preferences of key individuals and groups (see **Table 6-2**). A stakeholder is defined as "any group or individual who can affect or is affected by the achievement of the organization's objectives" (Freeman, 1984, p. 46). Stakeholder perspectives provide guidance about how to make decisions because it is based on understanding, creating, and building *relationships*. By attending to the interests of stakeholders, managers can evaluate their capacity to provide value for different constituencies. Furthermore, this analysis can help managers interpret the viability of different operating domains. Stakeholder perspectives have a great deal of appeal for the nonprofit sector because stakeholder techniques are framed on ethical management principles that extend the interest of the organization beyond profit maximization to consider various priorities that reflect the interests of a range of constituents (stakeholders). Effective stakeholder management practices have economic and social benefits. For example, effective relationship management facilities alliances and partnerships that can control costs, improve reputations, and expand opportunities for service delivery and resource acquisition.

One distinction among stakeholder types is whether the stakeholder is internal (e.g., staff) or external (e.g., funders). Many of the stakeholders listed on Table 6-2 are external to the organization. Commitment and buy-in among influential stakeholder is critical for operational success. This is true for both internal and external stakeholders, but the capacity and potential to support activities is different. Chew and Osborne (2009) investigated factors that managers consider in selecting and implementing services. Governmental actors such as policy makers were dominant factors in the positioning of U.K. social service providers. Beneficiaries and senior leadership were also significant considerations in how nonprofits develop and implement activities. Given these multiple stakeholders, nonprofits need techniques to prioritize stakeholders. The basic process of listing all stakeholders through a brainstorming process is a fairly practical and useful strategy. It is necessary to think about different types of stakeholders and to

TABLE 6-2 Key Stakeholder Categories

Stakeholder Type	Description
Funders	Any entity or individual that pays money to the nonprofit
Users	Individuals that participate in services offered by the organization
Beneficiaries	Individuals or groups that gain advantage through organizational activities (directly or indirectly)
Other providers	Entities in a similar operating domain
Government representatives	Government and political representatives that control resources or legitimacy
Other influential elements	Other constituencies or groups that could provide legitimacy for the nonprofit
Organizational members	Board members, staff, managers, and volunteers

consider how those stakeholders might influence the organization's ability to provide services or raise resources. Disaggregating stakeholder groups to distill unique attributes is critical to analysis. Discussing "stakeholders" as a group provides limited insight whereas detailing particular funder categories and specific actors provides a great deal more perspective and guidance (Ackermann & Eden, 2011a).

An informed and knowledgeable group (e.g., leaders or staff in the organization) can prioritize stakeholders and make judgments about the power and influence of each group within context or project priorities (Bryson, 2004). This helps managers recognize the perspective of different groups and to propose organizational actions in regards to each constituency. Mapping stakeholders across two dimensions of *power* (ability to influence organizational practices) and *interest* in the activities of the organization (see **Figure 6-1**) helps managers assess and prioritize stakeholders. Stakeholders near the top have higher levels of interest or power, while stakeholders near the bottom would reflect lower interest and power. The four categories are depicted that are drawn from work by Ackerman and Eden (2011b). Players would be stakeholders with a high degree of interest and power.

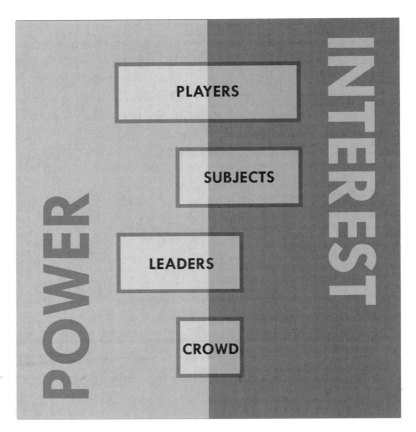

FIGURE 6-1 Stakeholder Power and Interest Map

Data from Ackermann, F., & Eden, C. (2011). Strategic management of stakeholders: Theory and practice. *Long Range Planning, 44,* 179–196.

This might include funders who provide substantial funding to the nonprofit. Managers should manage these relationships closely. Subjects include those individuals that have high interest but limited power to influence organizational actions. This might include beneficiaries who gain advantage though organizational action but do not provide substantial support to the organization. A typical reaction to these stakeholders is making sure they are satisfied with organizational activities. Leaders are those that have significant power and modest interest in the organization. Managers may try to draw these stakeholders into a closer relationship with the organization or at the very least some effort should be made to inform leaders of the activities of the organization. The "crowd" reflects those stakeholders that have low interest and low power. Managers might monitor these types of stakeholders but typically these require little direct action. Through stakeholder analysis managers can provide a guidance for program activities (Deephouse & Carter, 2005).

It is somewhat straightforward to list known stakeholders and consider how they can influence the activities of the organizations. The process starts with known information and is based on perceived interests of key individuals and groups. Engaging these entities provides further guidance to managers as they design and implement organizational activities. The process also helps managers consider who to engage in different types of activities (e.g., information gathering or cooperative planning). Initially, the process doesn't require the management team to overdefine themselves but rather focuses attention on stakeholders and their interests. Interpreting these interests in reference to the priorities of the organization is a more tenuous process that requires judgments and insight into how others perceive the organization and its prospect of future opportunities. Furthermore, the organization must consider how to balance competing interests with inherent resource limitations. Ideally, the process of engaging stakeholders also brings forth strategies to meet interest and create value. Stakeholder analysis is particularly valuable to nonprofits as it helps the organization understand how and to what degree it might suffer legitimacy or trust concerns from different stakeholders.

Competitive Analysis Techniques

Porter (1998) developed a competitive analysis technique to help organizations understand their industry, market focus, and the nature and character of relationships with other providers within particular operating domains. Porter frames his analysis on a competitive market that seeks to exploit market dominance to secure profit, which is not necessarily in alignment with the activities of most nonprofits (Alexander, 2000). Nevertheless, the concept of comparative advantage recognizes that organizations with unique, useful qualities are more likely to sustain success in all the ways that matter. Understanding how other providers operate in particular operating domains is quite useful when prioritizing organizational activities so as to create comparative advantage. Nonprofits confront multiple domains with different objectives. For example, public benefit priorities reflect a desire to have an impact on society. Priorities in resource markets are intended to gain capacity. Industry analysis provides valuable insight into the nature of the task environment and potentially the behavior of other providers, which can guide strategic choices. The competitive analysis model has limitations, such as an emphasis on competitive relationships and limited attention to political influence; nevertheless, the model recognizes several key forces that are valuable to understand and appreciate as nonprofit managers.

Nonprofits operate in complex markets and political contexts that require a mix of cooperative and competitive strategies. Using industry analysis techniques, nonprofit managers can better understand the forces that are likely to encourage or discourage cooperative behavior.

Porter (1998) identifies five forces in the competitive environment, and Oster (1995) adapted the model to the nonprofit context (Tuckman, 1998). Blending these ideas results in the specification of the five forces in nonprofit operating domains (see **Table 6-3**). The model is most useful when specific operating context characteristics are considered. For example, the public funding environment for troubled youth in a particular service area. The following discussion will frame the analysis on issues that are prevalent in the public benefit and funding resource domains. The five forces discussed in this section are threats to new entrants, supplier power, customer/beneficiary power, threat of substitutes, and relation to other providers.

Threats to Entry

Central to understanding the domain boundaries is an ability to ascertain the threats posed by possible new entrants. Organizations tend to exhibit more power in industries that restrict the number of possible new entrants. The introduction of new providers can upset the balance of relationships exhibited in the

TABLE 6-3 Forces in Nonprofit Industry Analysis

Forces	Key Considerations
Threats to entry	How easy it is for other providers or actors to enter an operating context
Supplier power	The influence and power of labor and other required inputs
Customer/ beneficiary power	Considers the power of customers or beneficiaries to influence organizational services and activities
Threats of substitutes	Choices or alternatives that customers and beneficiaries have to seek value from other providers or in other ways
Relation to other providers	The balance of industry factors and interorganizational relationships that inform potential reactions by other providers

Adapted from Porter, M. E. (1998). *Competitive strategy: Techniques for analyzing industries and competitors* (2nd ed.). New York, NY: Free Press.

current operating context. There are seven major barriers to entry that have implications for the nonprofit context. These barriers are differentiation, economies of scale, capital requirements, cost requirements independent of economies of scale, government policy, access to distribution channels, and switching costs.

Differentiation
Differentiation is an attempt to reflect uniqueness that is superior to others in the industry (Barman, 2002). This differentiation gains influence through brand identification, reputation, and customer loyalty. The cost associated with building brand image and reputation is significant, and some of the best-known and trusted brands belong to nonprofit entities. Oster (1995) refers to the importance of reputation as a significant barrier to new entities. Reputation is critical to nonprofit success and, consequently, well-known organizations potentially crowd out the market, making it more difficult for less-recognized entities. Building organizational identity and trust is costly and potentially unrecoverable, so new entrants might be reluctant to enter markets that are dominated by a well-known entity. The importance

of brand and reputation are particularly salient in donor markets such as special events and fundraisers, where prior participation might guide choices. One growth pattern in nonprofits is the tendency to franchise regional entities that benefit from national support and recognition. This is the case for many long-lived nonprofits such as Boy Scouts, Big Brothers Big Sisters, United Way, and Red Cross. Affiliation with national brands can ascribe legitimacy to local entities at relatively modest cost. Regional organizations can, and do at times, override national brands because localized organizations can generate support through informal networks. It is important to recognize that the nature of trust is relationship based, so grassroots efforts can counter the impact of national brands. These same reputational benefits affect the tendency of volunteers to engage and participate with recognized organizations. Nonprofit managers should consider the value of their reputation among important stakeholders and the reputation of other providers.

Economies of Scale

Economies of scale refer to the ability of large, scalable providers to reduce of the cost of per-unit service delivery. For nonprofits, this not as significant of an issue (Coombes, Morris, Allen, & Webb, 2011) because of the labor-intensive nature of the work, but some efficiencies can be achieved through technology, and certain industries might be more affected by technological improvements (e.g., health care). Other activities such as counseling and mentoring are only modestly improved by increased efficiencies achieved through size. A couple of areas where economies of scale might help include the ability of larger entities to create and sustain national brands and thereby transfer that legitimacy to local branches. Furthermore, larger entities allow for specialization among employees, which implies an ability to create better program systems or evaluation methods that might require more specialized talent. Larger entities might also achieve efficiencies in fundraising, again, because of the ability to maintain specialists that are able to employ sophisticated fund development techniques (e.g., prospect research) that smaller firms cannot afford.

Capital Requirements

Capital requirements are related to efficiency of scale in that some industries require large capital expenditures to provide services. For instance, hospitals require large, specialized, costly equipment. Acquisition of capital for nonprofits is particularly difficult because the investment market is not available to nonprofits because they do not provide a financial return. The inability to issue bonds and attract investors that seek a return in profits constrains the growth of most nonprofit entities. Nonprofits typically have to raise significant capital through donor campaigns. So, although all nonprofits confront challenges associated with capital investments, larger firms might gain some advantage by employing individuals capable of carrying out a large fundraising campaign. However, it is fairly common practice for even modest-size organizations to secure consulting assistance in this area. Firms can secure the necessary skills independent of size. They must, however, have a sufficient donor pool to justify the effort. Some other examples of large capital assets include facilities expenditures. Many nonprofits raise capital for land and building purchases. These facilities support the provision of services but also cement (literally) the image of the nonprofit as successful. The benefits of a large campus or facility have implications for service delivery and also reputation and attraction for a labor force. These assets also tend to be fairly illiquid, meaning that they are not readily transferable to cash or other uses. Churches and houses of worship also exhibit the tendency to maintain large physical assets that reflect their success and ability to recruit new members. These capital assets are difficult to develop, but once developed they typically transfer significant benefits (reputational and service delivery efficiencies) to the nonprofit entity. As a result, entering an industry dominated by capital-intensive entities can be very difficult.

Cost Disadvantage Independent of Economies of Scale

Cost disadvantage independent of economies of scale reflects some of the other benefits that large or established firms may gain. Location and facilities could be favorable if acquired before market costs evaluated, thereby making it more expensive for a similar entity to locate nearby. Another example is that some nonprofits own or acquire assets that are rare or noninterchangeable, such as land preserves, historical artifacts, and buildings, which are not accessible at any market cost. Owning or acquiring these assets is central to the distinctive benefits the nonprofit provides. Another example is related to benefits that can be achieved through learning or experience. As organizations operate in industries, they gain experience, develop relationships, and enact practices that help them achieve their objectives. These advantages may not be easily replicated by others trying to operate in a similar context or may take up-front investment of time and resources.

Government Policy
Government policy refers to the tendency of rules or practices to influence industry practices. This can be as simple as licensure requirements that limit quick and easy access to certain service areas, or it can be more complex arrangements whereby nonprofits are created or selected as a primary "partner" to provide services. For example, it is not uncommon that municipalities may share, give, or lease, at a very lost cost, facilities to nonprofits. The city is unable to provide the specialized type of services needed (e.g., youth development, homeless services) and the nonprofit does not have the ability to build or develop the needed facilities. These relationships benefit both entities. Other providers that do not have access to those facilities are at a disadvantage. Sometimes government entities open the arrangement to competitive contracting, but existing relationships and prior learning tend to encourage preference for previously selected nonprofit. These kinds of government subsidies act as barriers to others seeking to operate in similar service areas.

Access to Distribution Channels
Access to distribution channels refers to the tendency of existing networks to exclude those who do not currently operate in the area. For example, nonprofit social services typically operate in complex networks that are cooperative. For instance, one entity

may serve as case manager by negotiating contracts with other entities to provide supportive services (e.g., job training). It is also not uncommon for service providers in similar industries to meet and coordinate services that can achieve efficiencies and educational benefits that may be unavailable to those outside the industry. For example, museums often coordinate and share exhibits so as to benefit from the collections provided by other entities. Another example is the United Way, which, for the longest time, was the only provider of workplace donation campaigns. They had nearly monopolistic operations in workplace donations. Access through the workplace is still constrained, but a number of alternative formats, many of which are available because of the Internet, are now available to employees of large companies. These channels to resources or service delivery methods can be quite difficult to penetrate, and thereby act as barriers to others who wish to operate in similar industries.

Switching Costs

Switching costs refers to the cost users or suppliers might experience if they were to change providers. So in the example of municipal entities providing facilities for nonprofits, there might be fairly significant costs associated with contracting with a new provider. Costs may include updating the facility or providing additional materials already provided by the current entity. Sometimes it is relatively easy for users to switch providers whereas in other instances the number of imbedded relationships makes it very difficult for individuals to change providers. Industries with high switching costs for users or supplies are more difficult for others to enter.

Supplier Power

In reference to suppliers, most nonprofits do not operate in a context that requires abundant natural resources or materials. The critical input for many nonprofits is human capital. Considering the labor pool as a supplier has several implications. It recognizes human capital as the fundamental basis for performance in the sector. Human capital can be compensated or uncompensated (volunteered), but without adequate labor most services are not provided. Consider a youth recreation center that relies on volunteer coaches to provide services. Without reliable volunteers, the agencies cannot afford to provide those services. So, although kids may want a volleyball team, if volunteers are not available to provide that service the organization is constrained. The extent to which volunteers or staff are central to providing services increases their value and power to the agency.

Some overall considerations in relation to suppliers include the extent to which the supplier environment is dominated by a few entities, the size of nonprofit providers, and the degree of fragmentation among supply markets. As suppliers build relationships or institute practices that increase efficiency or effectiveness, suppliers might be reluctant to switch providers due to system costs that are built over time (Oster, 1995). For example, consider a nonprofit that relies on college student volunteers to fulfill particular program objectives (e.g., coaching). The nonprofit might establish a relationship with the community service office or student group that recruits and places volunteers. As the nonprofit demonstrates effectiveness with student volunteers, the community service office is likely to rely on the nonprofit as a reliable placement opportunity and, conversely, the nonprofit relies on student labor while accommodating the constraints of that group. This is a mutually beneficial relationship that is modestly resilient to switching and changes. The central point here is that labor has significant implications for the type and character of services provided.

Customer/Beneficiary Power

Customer/beneficiary power reflects the nature and character of the customer's ability to influence the quality or cost of services. The term *customers* will be used to reflect all entities, individuals, or groups that participate in an exchange relationship with the nonprofit. This will include even those individuals that benefit from services but do not directly exchange monetary value with the nonprofit. So, service beneficiaries, even if they don't pay for services, are conceptualized as a customer of the nonprofit. There are a number of factors that make it difficult to define customers for nonprofit activities because some of what is done exists *indirect*

in a quasi-public space that allows individuals to benefit from nonprofit activities without engaging in any exchange (Steinberg, 2006). Customers in this instance are indirect beneficiaries, hence why *beneficiary* might also be a reasonable nomenclature to capture the exchange relationship. In relation to the financial resource market, donors or any entity that exchanges monetary value is also conceptualized as a customer.

When customer/beneficiary power exists it is typically enacted through the ability to choose among providers. Customer power is exerted by the choice to engage or to withhold that engagement. This has implications for organizational activities and the extent to which the organization wishes to retain that engagement. The ability to switch providers and the significance of that switch (to the nonprofit) reflects higher power. Some issues related to switching include the extent to which services and products from other providers are readily interchangeable (e.g., limited differentiation) or the cost of changing providers is relatively low.

Some other ways that customers can increase their power is by organizing and coordinating among themselves. So, a group of kids with similar interests might petition the agency to provide different or expanded services. The beneficiary group increases power if they can threaten legitimacy of the agency or their absence significantly impacts the agency's ability to secure resources either through fees or support from funders. Other issues include the extent to which the services are highly valued by the beneficiary. Kids may be highly motivated to join recreational and social programs but only modestly interested in the educational programs. Organizations must consider the perceived value of services to effectively provide for the target community. This too can be a bit challenging for nonprofits that have social benefits that might not reflect the highest interests of clients, and they must therefore increase programs that are "fun" so as to provide incentives to participate in educational activities. Providers understand these preferences, and they make choices to consider how and to what degree they must be addressed. Nonprofits might be less responsive to these preferences depending on internal attributes such as wealth, leadership, or philosophical values.

stakeholder analysis

Threat of Substitutes

Substitutes have to do with the number and character of options for customers to attain the same or similar benefits from other sources. That is, can customers receive similar benefits outside the general scope of the industry? For example, when considering a youth recreation center, what other options do kids have in the region for those hours of the day? There could be unstructured opportunities at the local park or even the mall that basically meet the needs of kids to hang out with friends. Furthermore, other entertainment options could include movies, television, video games, and so on. This concept reflects the idea that not only do service providers need to think about the other recreation and educational programs available, they should also recognize that various other activities and arrangements might meet a similar need to keep kids entertained during nonschool hours. In reference to social benefit, however, it might become abundantly clear that some of the substitutes (e.g., illegal behavior) are not optimal for the kids or the community, thereby increasing the preference for retaining children in the program. That, however, is not reflective of user power, but reflects the tendency of funders or government entities to affect services provided and the options and costs for participants.

Relation to Other Providers

Understanding the competitive and cooperative tendencies of entities within a particular nonprofit industry or market is complex. Porter's model depicts some of the most salient forces that managers need to consider. One aspect of defining the public benefit purpose is typically a normative, or values, proposition that prioritizes or promotes a key principle (e.g., healthy lifestyles). At times these principles are widely accepted and somewhat uncontroversial (e.g., help kids succeed). In other instances there can be strong conflict and opposition to different priorities. For instance, pro-life organizations and pro-choice organizations might both function to promote healthy families and healthy babies and work with a similar population of clients, but the techniques and practices are often in strong opposition.

Consequently, an important aspect of the tendency to cooperate is based on the values and public benefit purpose promoted by the organization. Other issues include the number and relative equality (size and scope) of providers. Larger providers tend to exert more influence, although specialized niche providers can exert influence in certain areas. The diversity of providers makes it more difficult to understand and predict how others are going to operate. A group of social service providers that rely on government funding are likely to operate fairly similarly, but faith-based entities or community collaborative organizations might operate in a very different manner, making it more difficult to collaborate and anticipate behaviors. There are also aspects such as cost of providing services and need for high-cost capital resources (e.g., campus, labs, buildings) that can influence provider relations. Investments in high-cost, relatively illiquid assets force providers to continue in the service industry. Similarly, values and historical precedence may also cause some organizations to remain in service areas irrespective of their ability to maintain positive relationships with other providers.

Reaction by Others

Reaction by others is another consideration that managers should understand and anticipate. What will happen with the other providers in response to the presence of new service activities? Much of the competitive environment is predicated on consumer price, so a typical retaliatory response by current providers is to reduce or temporarily undercut price to minimize opportunities. Price is an issue for some nonprofit industries (typically those that have both for-profit and nonprofit providers), but in practice price is a modest influence for most of the industry, given the already-subsidized nature of the many services. Consequently, it is difficult to fully appreciate how certain entities might respond. The two areas where current providers might be concerned include the ability to meet service recipients' needs and the ability to secure necessary resources (funds or labor). Response in each of these areas (services, financial resource, and labor) may be interconnected, and it may unfold in uncertain ways. Government grants and contracts are typically directly tied to particular service delivery methods and markets (direct reimbursable funds). Other funders might not reflect such a direct link to service outputs and resource provision (less direct accountability for specific service activities). Furthermore, some areas are very complex (e.g., homelessness), and demands typically outstrip providers' capabilities. New providers are more likely to be welcomed by current providers and funders if they augment the service infrastructure and don't threaten resource markets. However, there are instances when existing providers perceive competitive forces, and they may look for ways to exclude the new entity from networks or act to minimize the influence of the new entity. Considering how funders might react is also a very important consideration. Some funders may prioritize cooperative and noncompetitive arrangements and thereby discourage others from entering a service industry without clearly demonstrating how they don't "overlap" with other entities. Others may attempt to be more "objective" in the process to evaluate existing and prospective grantees similarly. The tendency of existing entities to ignore, retaliate, or cooperate is an important consideration for programs seeking to enter a new market.

Conclusion

The analysis of competitive and cooperative tendencies within different nonprofit markets and industries is complex. The model developed by Porter has been applied to different kinds of industries and markets, although it is only modestly used by nonprofit scholars. The language and limitations of the model are potentially problematic, but the forces working to explain relations among providers are informative. It is only one model, and the context of a nonprofit's operating environment will influence the applicability of the model. Management techniques can focus on different aspects of the operating environment, and these forces can interact to explain cooperative or competitive behavior. Industry characteristics are one aspect of how organizations can be successful. Some operating contexts are conducive to performance expectations and others are less optimal. The ability of the organization to respond and operate is just as critical as positioning effectively. The qualities and attributes of the organization are reflected in the core competencies that are built and exploited.

Discussion Questions

1. Compare and contrast stakeholder analysis techniques and competitive analysis techniques. Which is more useful to managers when making strategic decisions about programs and activities?
2. Using Guidestar, identify an industry classification (NTEE code) and a geographic region (municipality). This will define the range of providers within a market segment. Identify six comparable (based on revenue) organizations and review the revenue portfolio. Where do they raise funds? How reliant are they on fee-based income versus private foundation grants?
3. What does an analysis such as the one you completed in question 2 tell you about the competitive dynamics in that industry? What about operational standards and principles of effective operation? What other information would you like to know about these providers?

References

Ackermann, F., & Eden, C. (2011a). Strategic management of stakeholders: Theory and practice. *Long Range Planning, 44,* 179–196.

Ackerman, F., & Eden, C. (2011b). *Making strategy: Mapping out strategic success* (2nd ed.). Thousand Oaks, CA: Sage.

Alexander, J. (2000). Adaptive strategies of nonprofit human service organizations in an era of devolution and new public management. *Nonprofit Management and Leadership, 10*(3), 287–303.

Barman, E. A. (2002). Asserting difference: Strategic response of nonprofits to competition. *Social Forces, 80*(4), 1191–1222.

Boardman, A. E., & Vining, A. R. (2000). Using service-customer matrices in strategic analysis of nonprofits. *Nonprofit Management and Leadership, 10*(4), 397–420.

Bryson, J. M. (2004). What to do when stakeholders matter. *Public Management Review, 6*(1), 21–53.

Chen, M. J., & Miller, D. (2012). Competitive dynamics: Themes, trends, and a prospective research platform. *The Academy of Management Annals, 6*(1), 135–210.

Chew, C. (2009). *Strategic positioning in voluntary chariable organizations.* New York, NY: Routledge.

Chew, C., & Osborne, S. P. (2009). Identifying the factors that influence positioning strategy in U.K. charitable organizations that provide public services. *Nonprofit and Voluntary Sector Quarterly, 38*(1), 29–50.

Coombes, S. M. T., Morris, M. H., Allen, J. A., & Webb, J. W. (2011). Behavioural orientations of non-profit boards as a factor in entrepreneurial performance: Does governance matter? *Journal of Management Studies, 48*(4), 829–856.

Courtney, R. (2002). *Strategic management for voluntary nonprofit organizations.* New York, NY: Routledge.

Deephouse, D. L., & Carter, S. M. (2005). An examination of differences between organizational legitimacy and organizational reputation. *Journal of Management Studies, 42*(2), 329–360.

Domanski, J. (2010). Strategic group analysis of Poland's nonprofit organizations. *Nonprofit and Voluntary Sector Quarterly, 39*(6), 1113–1124.

Eggers, J. P., & Kaplan, S. (2013). Cognition and capabilities. *The Academy of Management Annals, 7*(1), 293–338.

Fischer, R. L., Wilsker, A., & Young, D. R. (2011). Exploring the revenue mix of nonprofit organizations: Does it relate to publicness? *Nonprofit and Voluntary Sector Quarterly, 40*(4), 662–681.

Freeman, E. R. (1984). *Strategic management: A stakeholder approach.* Boston, MA: Pitman.

Galaskiewicz, J., Bielefeld, W., & Dowell, M. (2006). Networks and organizational growth: A study of community based nonprofits. *Administrative Science Quarterly, 51*(3), 337–380.

Hasenfeld, Y. (1983). *Human service organizations.* Englewood Cliffs, NJ: Prentice Hall.

Hitt, M. A., Ireland, R. D., & Hoskisson, R. E. (2011). *Strategic management competitiveness and globalization* (9th ed.). Mason, OH: South-Western Cengage.

Lange, D., Lee, P. M., & Dai, Y. (2011). Organizational reputation: A review. *Journal of Management, 37*(1), 153–184.

Loch, C. H., Galunic, D. C., & Schneider, S. (2006). Balancing cooperation and competition in human groups: The role of emotional algorithms and evolution. *Managerial and Decision Economics, 27*(2–3), 217–233.

Oster, S. M. (1995). *Strategic management for nonprofit organizations*. New York, NY: Oxford University Press.

Porter, M. E. (1998). *Competitive strategy: Techniques for analyzing industries and competitors* (2nd ed.). New York, NY: Free Press.

Sosin, M. R. (2012). Social expectations, constraints, and their effect on nonprofit strategies. *Nonprofit and Voluntary Sector Quarterly, 41*(6), 1231–1250.

Steinberg, R. (2006). Economic theories of nonprofit organizaions. In W. W. Powell & R. Steinberg (Eds.), *The nonprofit sector: A research handbook* (2nd ed., pp. 117–139). New Haven, CT: Yale University.

Tuckman, H. P. (1998). Competition, commercialization and the evolution of nonprofit organizational structures. In B. A. Weisbrod (Ed.), *To profit or not to profit* (pp. 25–45). Cambridge, UK: Cambridge University Press.

Uzzi, B. (1997). Social structure and competition in interfirm networks: The paradox of embeddedness. *Administrative Science Quarterly, 42*(1), 35–67.

Corporate Strategy, Structures, and Planning

Learning Objectives

■ Explain and describe corporate strategy decision areas
■ Explain how strategic orientation and structure facilitate implementation of strategic priorities
■ Recognize the role of the board of directors in leading the organization
■ Understand how planning can engage stakeholders in strategic decisions and implementation

The strategic management cycle frames the choices managers confront when forming strategy (see **Figure 7-1**). First, managers address fundamental questions about the operating context. What social problems is the organization going to address and what resource options will sustain the organization? These issues are not considered on a daily basis but are critical to operational success. These choices are defined as *corporate strategy* because they have organization-wide implications. An additional consideration at this level is an accurate interpretation of the socio-political influences that might build or thwart organizational

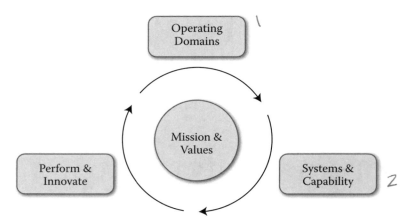

FIGURE 7-1 Strategic Management Cycle

legitimacy. Defining the operational context and interpreting sociopolitical influences facilitate the creation of systems (step two in the strategic management cycle) to enact priorities. These systems include public benefit activities such as a method to deliver human services and fundraising techniques that successfully capture philanthropic interests. Simultaneously, performance expectations are tracked and monitored (step three). All four aspects of performance (social impact, resource sustainability, stakeholder attitudes, and organizational efficiency) operate concurrently. These activities (steps two and three) are defined as *program strategy*. This chapter attends to considerations that managers address in the *formation* of strategic priorities at the corporate level. Corporate strategy reflects the highest levels of decision making in the organization. It is distinguished from program strategies in that corporate decisions tend to have implications throughout the organization, or they involve changes in organizational practices and structures that substantively influence operational practices.

Corporate Strategy

Corporate strategy is concerned with setting in place guiding objectives and priorities that can be enacted by organizational participants as well as understanding how all organizational activities work toward mission objectives. **Table 7-1** summarizes some of the issues corporate decision makers address. These decision areas are reflective of tasks to define and frame the range of operations and activities that the organization carries out. Corporate decisions set boundaries for program strategies. Definitions and boundaries of the operating context are reflected in key guiding statements such as the mission, vision, and values. The analysis of the task environment is instrumental in guiding these decisions. Corporate-level strategy also considers the range of activities that are utilized by the organization. This is conceptualized as diversification and includes diversification within particular operating domains (multiple resource development practices) and diversification across operating areas (identifying synergies between resource development and services). Of particular concern is the use of sociopolitical initiatives that seek to address legitimacy concerns as well as influence social structures and systems. These advocacy-type activities are distinct from direct service activities, and senior leadership should be cognizant of which public benefit functions are implemented by the organization.

advocacy

TABLE 7-1   Issues in Corporate-Level Decision Making

Topic/Area	Critical Questions
Mission definitions	How does the organization define its public benefit purpose and value?
Defining scope and industry	How does the organization define the task/operating environment? Does the organization achieve domain consensus?
Diversification strategy	How do activities in different domain areas relate?
Strategic orientation	How does the organization approach operating domains?
Structure and controls	How is the organization structured and how are operations controlled?
Board of directors	Who is on the board and what tasks are prioritized?
Planning	How are organizational participants engaged in strategic decisions?

Considerations

The mission is how the dominant coalition defines the organization and its role in society. The mission draws on the leaders' philosophical beliefs about society. Typically inspired by interpretation of social deficiencies, a mission is a powerful motivator that distinguishes the organization from others operating in similar markets. Missions are modified and adjusted over time, and how organizations facilitate that adjustment can be critical to success. The tension with organizational missions is that they are fundamentally out of sync with environmental realities. Missions and the associated guiding philosophies (vision and values) reflect idealized perspectives on organizational purposes and consequently must be balanced with environmental forces. Missions reflect a common method to define the operational space of a nonprofit. The translation of the mission to more operational and tactical objectives is difficult, but planning processes can help engage appropriate stakeholders in the development and implementation of those tactics. Periodically revisiting mission objectives in relation to program practices is a critical corporate concern. An organization's articulation of the mission ultimately must be validated by external elements. This is described as domain consensus.

Domain consensus is the degree of agreement among significant stakeholders in the operating environment. This is particularly salient in relation to resource options (Hasenfeld, 1983) and interorganizational relationships (Gulati, 1995). Organizations must demonstrate how they create and add value to a particular operating context. This is a negotiated agreement that reflects interpretations by significant stakeholders, which include funders and major providers. The mechanisms of the market and consumer choice are only modestly salient for nonprofit entities. Rather, sociopolitical elements such as ideological orientation, support by government and regulating entities, access to referral systems to gain clients, and validation by significant funders can be instrumental in an organization's ability to operate (Chew & Osborne, 2009).

Domain consensus illustrates how the competing pressure for legitimacy can mute customer and beneficiary influence because the validation is contingent on significant institutional actions. There are numerous examples of how organizational initiatives are thwarted not by the depth of the social issues but rather by the complex social structures that control resources and legitimacy (Hasenfeld, 1983). Organizations need to demonstrate benefits for dominant stakeholders and seek alignment with cultural values that might influence growth and sustainability. This is clearly a corporate strategic concern and an area that boards are regularly sought to influence (Abzug & Galaskiewicz, 2001). The legitimacy of board members and their social capital can influence key constituencies. Corporate strategy is cognizant of the sociopolitical influences in the task environment and seeks to address those concerns (Bigelow, Stone, & Arndt, 1996).

Diversification

There are two aspects of diversification that merit consideration. The first is the range and complexity of activities within a particular industry. The second is the range of activities and initiatives across industries and domains. The case example of Buckner International provides a good illustration of how a nonprofit social services organization can expand and enrich services both within a particular service domain (at-risk and orphaned children) as well as expand into different service domains (retirement services). Buckner started as a children's home in 1879 and now offers an expansive array of social services to support disadvantaged children and families (see **Exhibit 7-1**). This includes adoptive and foster care services as well as community-based services that help support families in their communities. With a mission that is dedicated to helping children, Buckner services evolved and expanded to provide a range of services. This growth continued throughout the state of Texas into neighboring states as well as internationally.

Diversification within a particular service area can allow an organization to achieve some efficiency due to shared processes and infrastructure, such as information technology and financial management systems that, once established, can be utilized for new services with marginal additional cost. For example,

---

EXHIBIT 7-1 Buckner International

Buckner International is an example of diversification strategies utilized to grow and expand services. Currently, Buckner serves more than 400,000 people a year. They were started in 1879 as Buckner Orphans Home in Dallas, Texas. Intricately linked to the Baptist church, the orphanage was the first organized Baptist charity in Texas (Buckner International, n.d.). The founder, R.C. Buckner, was a Baptist minister who raised resources through alliances with religious congregations. Grounded in Christian values, Buckner is primarily a benevolent charity that ministers to disadvantaged children and families. In 1938 there were about 630 children living at the home across 19 major buildings. The annual report states that the policy has been to "care for more children and do more for children cared for" (Norman, 2013). Over the years Buckner expanded services to include a whole range of family services and community programs. This includes adoption and foster care services, family transition services, and community transformation services. In 1954, Buckner opened its first retirement community in Dallas. Their history suggests that engaging retired ministers and missionaries has been a part of what they have always done at the children's home. By developing a formal retirement services division, Bucker moved into a lucrative and successful service industry. Buckner is one of the largest providers of retirement services in Texas. With program revenue nearing $45 million in 2011, retirement services reflect about one-third of the $120 million in total revenue reported by Buckner and its subsidiaries in 2011 (Buckner International, 2011). Drawing on a long history of international missions, Buckner launched the international programs initiative in 1996. The international programs were launched within the core service area of family and children. Buckner now serves individuals in 13 different countries with a wide array of programs. This growth has resulted in various name changes and an expanded scope of services. They operate two main divisions: retirement services and child and family services, which includes their international work. Each division has goals and strategies to serve particular markets. Division managers develop specific choices about market opportunities and service strategies (business strategies) while the board attends to core values of the organization and major decisions about venturing into new markets (corporate strategies). Part of the growth is fueled by a willingness to merge and incorporate smaller programs and activities. Two examples illustrate how Buckner incorporated localized and emerging programs. The first example involves community centers. In 2012 Buckner acquired Aldine Community Center in Houston. The center was founded in 1990 and joined Buckner as an opportunity to sustain services within the umbrella of a more established organization. The second example involves resource activities. Buckner assumed leadership of a program that gathered shoes for children abroad. The program was started in 1996 by a radio station in Dallas, and by 1999 Buckner assumed leadership to help sustain and grow the initiative. Over the years, with enhanced legitimacy through key stakeholders (Baptist churches), Buckner was able to grow and expand into activities that tapped the interest of supporters and extended the reach of Buckner programs.

providing services for disadvantaged or at-risk children carries numerous regulatory issues that require high levels of sophistication and can be difficult to develop initially. Once in place it is easier to expand the competency into new geographic regions. Diversification and broadening of services in this way reflects corporate strategy because it expands services and thereby risks, which must be understood by senior leadership.

International expansion is different, in that laws and regulations vary considerably as do cultural influences that can substantively change the service delivery strategy. Buckner's expansion of services internationally in 1996 was a risky initiative but it was based on several elements that tied back to the key constituency of supporters. The Baptist church had a long history of international missionary work. There were extensive networks that Buckner was able to utilize as well as a philosophical desire to influence and impact individuals more broadly. Furthermore, as explained by Ken Hall, the long-time CEO and president of Buckner (Collins, 2012), the most significant strategic decision was to move away from Buckner as a place or set of facilities. Hall explained that the growth internationally was fueled by this shift in thinking. Buckner was a movement of people motivated to impact the lives of children. This movement was grounded in a religious perspective about faith and God, and Buckner tends to emphasize service and outreach. The expansion internationally was a natural development that capitalized on key stakeholder interests (Baptist church history of international work) and a desire to impact communities more broadly.

Venturing into new industries, as Buckner did when they moved into retirement services, requires the development of distinctive competencies that are unique to that service domain. Buckner was able to exploit several resource elements that facilitated their success in retirement services. The first was broad-based support and legitimacy through Baptist Churches in Dallas and throughout Texas. They had been working with that constituency for over 70 years before they officially launched the retirement services division. Second, they had extensive housing experience with the children's home as well as experience working with retired ministers. They had been housing elderly individuals for quite some time, as retired ministers and missionaries were associated with the children's home from early in the program's history. Consequently, their customer base was readily accessible through the resource development work and networking in the churches. Compounded with sufficient capital and management expertise, Buckner was able to develop a highly successful but relatively independent division of services that attended to different payment systems and regulations. The demographic shift in society and the retirement of baby boomers promises to further sustain growth in that division. Juggling and interpreting the range of organizational activities can be difficult. Portfolio analysis is proposed as a tool that corporate decision makers can utilize to compare and contrast organizational activities according to selected criteria.

Portfolio Analysis

A portfolio analysis facilitates comparison of disparate organizational activities. The method entails depicting organizational activities on a 2×2 matrix. The selection of criteria to categorize activities is dependent on the needs and priorities of the nonprofit (see **Table 7-2**). One of the first portfolio analysis tools was developed by the Boston Consulting Group (BCG). BCG

TABLE 7-2   Potential Dimensions of Portfolio Matrix

	Description	Issues and Benefits
Market growth	Describe the growth or changes in market features	• How to define market scope • Estimates how demand may change over time
Market share	Consider range of activities in relation to other providers	• Understanding other providers
Profitability or net revenue	Consider revenue gained in relation to the activity	• Aligning revenue with activities • Challenges of linking service activity to charitable donations
Impact or benefit	Describe public benefit and social value of activities	• Long-term impacts are difficult to assess • Indirect beneficiaries are difficult to determine
Mission alignment	Relate activities to organizational objectives and goals	• Distinctions with community needs or impacts

proposes market growth and market share as criteria to guide strategic choices regarding future investments and activities. The matrix map, which is the BCG model adapted to the nonprofit context, proposes social impact and net revenue (Bell, Masaoka, & Zimmerman, 2010) as the ideal criteria to compare and contrast organizational activities. An additional dimension that may be appropriate is mission centrality (Chetkovich & Frumkin, 2003). This may be the same as impact, but not necessarily. It is possible that programs could be impactful but not mission aligned, which would be informative for discussion and would offer the potential for realignment of either the mission or organizational activities.

The benefit of this analysis method is the depiction of all organizational activities on one matrix. It allows senior decision makers and board members an opportunity to compare and contrast activities across operating domains. There are challenges with this method (Day, 1977), such as oversimplification of complex activities operating in complex markets. The process of defining criteria and the placement of activities can be problematic. First is the specification of dimensions to classify activities. There are a number of assumptions inherent in defining and selecting these dimensions. How those dimensions are defined and why they are selected should be vetted and justified. The second challenge is defining and quantifying activities to accurately reflect the dimensions. Whether defining impact or market share, the quantification of program activities may oversimplify some of the subtleties of programs. Placement of program activities inevitably requires judgments about market potential, growth, and so on as some of these elements, including impact, are difficult to assess. Irrespective of potential measurement concerns, some analysis of programs and activities in relation to selected dimensions can be very useful for managers and board members as they seek to conceptualize the range of activities carried out by the organization. Care should be undertaken regarding the decisions based on portfolio analysis, as it is just one method to consider competing and complex issues.

Portfolio analysis allows managers to analyze both public benefit activities (services and advocacy) and resource activities simultaneously. Two models are reviewed that propose different analytical dimensions. A model used in the nonprofit sector uses impact and profitability as the two organizing principles (Bell et al., 2010). *Impact* refers to the extent to which the activities meet community needs. *Profitability* refers to revenue generation and the extent to which activities generate net revenue. This creates four quadrants: "hearts" (high impact, high profitability), "stars" (high impact, low profitability), "money trees" (low impact, high profitability), and "stop signs" (low impact, low profitability). A major fundraising event might have a low impact but generate significant revenue and thereby be classified as a money tree. Alternatively, a special event that provides very little revenue and limited impact might be reflective of an activity that should be "stopped." Similarly, a program activity that has limited impact and limited financial support might be reflective of programs that should be discontinued.

BCG developed one of the original portfolio analysis models. The BCG model analyzed products and services across two key dimensions: market growth and relative share of the market. Market growth reflects an estimate of the growth potential of a market or industry. Markets are defined by organizational participants to explain the operating context that is central to organizational purposes. Managers assess the nature of change occurring within market domains and specifically the potential for expanded activities. Relative market share reflects the extent of activities provided by an organization in relation to other entities operating in the same market domain. This allows managers to classify activities as "dogs," "stars," "cash cows," and "question marks." Dogs have low market share and low growth possibilities and consequently are in line for divestiture. Stars are the opposite, with high market share and high growth potential. These are important activities that should be closely monitored as the market changes. Cash cows operate in a relatively stable market with modest to low growth but the product has a dominant market position. Question marks are products or services that currently hold lower market share but the potential growth is significant. Consequently, some of these products could be potential stars or might represent the future of the organization (Phills, 2005).

Strategic Orientation and Alignment

Strategic orientation is an overall approach to programming (public benefit and resource development) that can be useful for managers as they evaluate programs and activities. Strategic orientation is a philosophical perspective that guides activities in all three phases of the strategic management cycle. To understand an overall strategic approach, Miles and Snow (1978) identified four basic types of organizations: prospectors, defenders, analyzers, and reactors. *Prospectors* are innovators seeking to expand and create new products and services. They are consistently scanning the operating context to identify new customers or are consistently considering new ways to address customer interests. *Defenders* seek efficiency and consistency in a select number of services. They define an operating context and seek to build highly capable and stable systems that allow for efficiency. This works well in industries that are more stable. *Analyzers* are not the first to develop services but are eager to integrate innovations once identified. Analyzers seek to exploit some innovation, while ensuring efficiency. *Reactors* lack a coherent method and are inconsistent and unable to implement tactics reliably. There is empirical research across organizational forms (nonprofit, for-profit, international, small and large firms) to suggest that these organizational "types" are identifiable, and given the operational context, prospectors, defenders, or analyzers can be a reasonable strategic model to frame management decisions (Andrews, Boyne, Law, & Walker, 2009; Ketchen et al., 1997; Miles, Snow, Mathews, Miles, & Coleman, 1997). Reactors, on the other hand, are nonoptimal performers. These "types" are not necessarily pure throughout an organization (Andrews et al., 2009). Different departments and divisions might be more entrepreneurial (i.e., prospector-like) while other departments or divisions are working to improve efficiencies (i.e., defender-like). Even though the typological boundaries are not concrete, they provide a tool to consider how organizational systems work together to improve performance.

While these are not the only types of strategic orientations that managers might choose, they are idealized types that help frame the discussion in this chapter. In addition, managers are unlikely to use these exact words to describe their strategic perspective, but the principles of a prospector or a defender are often prevalent in how strategic options are defined and interpreted. For instance, how the mission is used to inform and guide strategic choices can illustrate the different perspectives. If missions are used to frame operational activities and constrain program choices, this is more reflective of a defender style. Conversely, the perspective that frames the mission as an inspiration for organizational activities is more prospector-like. For those organizations without a philosophical perspective or frame (reactors), directors and managers are likely to approach funding and programming opportunistically. Some may try to build a niche for funding and programming, while others may be more entrepreneurial and seek funding and programming opportunities as they evolve. These perspectives are communicated to managers and line staff through the structures and accountability mechanisms that are developed in the organization.

Organizational Structure and Controls

Strategic orientations are enacted at different levels of the organization (see **Figure 7-2**). For instance, senior executives and board members, at the "corporate" level, contend with defining values perspectives and operating domains. These individuals consider how to frame and interpret the mission so as to guide actions as either a prospector or a defender. An accurate interpretation of external contingencies and how those might influence the organization is particularly critical at this level of decision making. For instance, the board may be reluctant to shift program initiatives away from historical and cultural perspectives that influenced the organization during its founding. If, however, environmental conditions are such that resource and program demands no longer perceive value in organizational activities, then adherence to the mission or program structure is problematic.

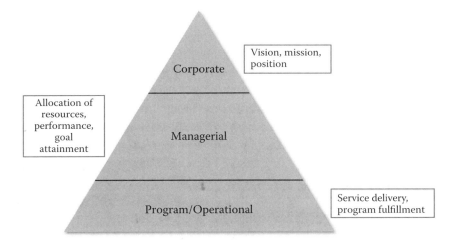

FIGURE 7-2   Levels of Decision Making

Midlevel managers tend to specialize within operating domains. They become experts on providing services or raising funds. They contend with multiple programs within a particular operating domain and allocate resources to optimize activities to achieve organization-wide objectives that are articulated at the corporate level. So, if the corporate strategy suggests that a defender perspective is optimal, midlevel managers would attend to issues of efficiency in program delivery but also ensure that current customers are satisfied with services. Defenders focus efforts on a particular niche or type of customer/beneficiary. Midlevel managers attend to quality and efficiency within that niche.

Program staff, at the operational level, are concerned with the implementation of activities within a particular program area. Consider, for instance, a program provider in a defender organization that has standard procedures to ensure consistency of services. They would be encouraged to get very good at providing a particular kind of service. In prospector-oriented organizations, a program provider might instead be encouraged to be entrepreneurial in developing new program activities or even seeking funds that support innovative ideas.

Figure 7-2 demonstrates how individuals at different levels of the organization are engaged in different aspects of strategy formation (making decisions about what to do) and strategy implementation (creating management systems to achieve objectives). While these distinctions are useful for considering decision making, it is rarely that pure, especially when considering modest-sized nonprofits that tend to require complex decision making at relatively low levels of the organization. Furthermore, with the resource constraints that many nonprofits confront, it is not uncommon that higher-level leadership actively engages in the implementation of resource procurement activities. What is salient for this discussion is that there are different strategic choices, some that have broad, organization-wide implications (e.g., defining mission) and those that are more tactical and impact a particular customer or target group.

Recognizing how different actors are active in strategic decisions is a key factor of creating structures and control systems.

Managers utilize a variety of levers, which are enacted at different levels, such as goals, policies, divisional structures, and position descriptions, to control activities (Hart, 1992). These structural elements clarify reporting relationships and accountability expectations. The level of control is adaptable and managers should consider the extent to which senior leadership sets and prescribes activities or whether program and divisional leadership has the authority to implement and expand programs (Bowditch, Buono, & Stewart, 2008). The distinction between a centralized or decentralized system helps illustrate how prospectors and defenders use structures to enact organizational priorities. A centralized system tends to have tighter and more thorough control systems and authorization structures. In a human service context, highly regulated environments tend to enact tighter control mechanisms to ensure compliance. Centralized systems limit unauthorized behavior by organizational participants but also capitalize on systems and processes that streamline choices to facilitate efficiency. By limiting operational choices, defenders might develop "best practices" to achieve optimal efficiency and replicate these practices throughout the organizational system. A decentralized organizational system is intended to allow a bit more discretionary decision making by organizational participants. Prospectors are more likely to adopt a decentralized structure because it allows for more eyes scanning the external environment to identify opportunities and suggest responses (Brown & Iverson, 2004). A decentralized structure is willing to bear the cost of some inefficiency because independence might foster innovation and gain advantages.

Boards of Directors

A significant consideration for executives is the development and utilization of the board of directors. The literature suggests that high-functioning boards (those that fulfill the duties outlined in the following section) are associated with more effective organizations (Green & Griesinger, 1996; Herman, Renz, & Heimovics, 1996). The exact mechanism of that connection is not clear, but considering the range of research on boards it is apparent that highly capable board members who fulfill their roles are instrumental in strengthening organizations (Herman & Renz, 1999). The vast majority of board members in nonprofits serve as volunteers (Ostrower, 2007). The work of nonprofit boards is increasingly recognized as providing "leadership" (Chait, Ryan, & Taylor, 2005) for the organization. Furthermore, boards need support from executives to achieve their full potential (Herman, 2010). The next section summarizes the basic roles of nonprofit boards and considers how they can function as a strategic asset for the organization.

Roles and Functions

The current literature on nonprofit governance suggests a wide array of potential roles and functions for nonprofit board members. Historically, discussions of ideal board roles have been practice oriented (Carver, 2006; Hopkins, 2009; Houle, 1997) and descriptive with only modest theoretical underpinnings. The developing theoretical literature suggests several perspectives that can guide the priorities of nonprofit board members. Agency theory (Fama & Jensen, 1983), less prominent in non-profit governance literature, is by far the most cited explanation of board governance roles in corporate or legal contexts. Boards have a fiduciary duty to oversee the activities of the organization to ensure shareholder value. Many scholars of nonprofit governance also suggest that resource dependency theory (Pfeffer & Salancik, 1978) is a better way to explain some of the most important activities of nonprofit boards. Additional theories to explain nonprofit governance include group/decision processes theories (Brown, 2005; Zander, 1993), institutional theory (Guo & Acar, 2005; Miller-Millesen, 2003), and democratic theory (Cornforth & Edwards, 1999; Guo & Musso, 2007). These theories provide insight into the different functions of directors, and studies in nonprofit governance have aligned typical roles within the theoretical perspectives (e.g., Brown, 2005; Miller-Millesen, 2003). Findings from these studies are in line with Hillman and Dalziel's (2003) suggestion that monitoring and control (agency functions) and resource and service roles (resource dependence theory) can account for many of the roles carried out by governing boards (see **Table 7-3**).

The Monitoring Role

The monitoring or control function is probably the most widely recognized function in governance. It covers basic fiduciary responsibilities such as overseeing the executive and fiscal assets of the organization. Control and oversight has the potential for conflict, as board members are expected to hold the executive accountable for performance expectations. It appears, however, that many nonprofit boards are limited in their ability to perform effective monitoring activities (Miller, 2002). Boards do not perceive the executive as needing to be monitored, they are not clear to whom they are accountable, and they lack clear performance measures beyond financial performance. These ambiguous expectations that boards have of executives are problematic because it fosters a tendency to go along with current practices and an inability to rigorously attend to performance and accountability expectations. There is some recognition that increased board power in relation to the executive might facilitate oversight, but this is not guaranteed (Olson, 2000). Power is facilitated by increased tenure and expertise, which seems to reflect positively on financial performance. The dynamics of highly functioning boards are complex, and the nonprofit operating environment seems to complicate engagement and participation.

TABLE 7-3   Roles of the Board

Monitoring and Control	Resource and Service
• Oversee financial assets	• Advise and council executive
• Set mission and purpose	• Raise resources
• Set organizational priorities	• Market and promote the organization
• Evaluate the executive	• Link to external constituents
• Monitor program performance	• Recruit new board members
• Monitor strategic direction	• Create strategic direction

The Resource Provision Role

Given the ambiguous nature of accountability in nonprofits and the resource-poor environment, resource acquisition is a high priority for nonprofits. Resource dependency theory suggests that the board is part of both the organization and the resource environment, and that the board functions as a boundary-spanning unit that reduces external dependencies through links to necessary resources (Ostrower & Stone, 2006; Pfeffer & Salancik, 1978). For instance, the board can provide advice and counsel, open channels of communication between the organization and external constituents, and help to acquire resources and lend legitimacy to the organization. Therefore, above and beyond the monitoring function, board members also bring resources and serve as a conduit for the organization.

Other Roles

Abzug and Galaskiewicz (2001) and Guo (2007) suggest that nonprofit boards serve as legitimizing devices that reflect the expectations of important institutional stakeholders in their composition and structure. Board members and their social status can bring increased legitimacy to the organization. So, the idea of high-status board members has salience. The research literature is not effectively developed, however, to fully recognize the value of board member status on perceptions of key stakeholders. A similar strategy is that nonprofits select board members as "representatives" from key constituency groups. Selection of board members can stem from demographic considerations or political alliances. There is substantial literature that recommends that boards should try to "reflect" the community they serve. Again, it is not exactly clear how these areas are ultimately fulfilled in the organization's ability to achieve objectives, but it reflects the board's role in managing the sociopolitical domain.

How to Improve Board Performance

There is support that skilled and capable board members are more effective at performing board roles (Brown, Hillman, & Okun, 2012). It is a relatively modest premise that considering which roles are most pressing for a particular organization and then selecting board members with sufficient experience and capabilities to fill those positions is a good idea. Although this seems simple, most boards engage in relatively constrained recruitment and development practices that do not systematically consider organizational and compositional needs. There are two features that complicate this "simple" recommendation. Specification of goals at the strategic level is tenuous, and translation to individual attributes simplifies complex interpersonal dynamics of recruiting and preparing board members. While there is no silver bullet, boards and executives can systematically improve the performance of the board through efforts that prioritize the engagement of board members (Brown, 2013).

Planning

Planning is the process whereby leaders engage stakeholders in forming strategy. Participation takes place at different times and at different levels in the organization. Planning processes facilitate information gathering, processing concepts, alignment of practices, and commitment to the plan (Bryson, 1995). It is critical that organizational participants are aware of strategic priorities and how their activities are associated with those objectives. Involvement of key stakeholders at the right time can improve planning and strategic decisions. Organizational decision making is inherently political, and building coalitions and alliances can be supported through active planning processes. There is criticism regarding planning as overly time-consuming and unrealistic in the sense that complex organizations can rarely capture all current and *future* activities and functions in a unitary model (Gruber, 2007). Furthermore, there is recognition that strategic choices are a mix between planned objectives and tactical choices to seize opportunities. Recognition that organizational actions are both emergent (bottom up) and planned (top down) places planning as an element in building and implementing organizational strategy.

Planning is a method to grapple with critical choices regarding market domains, organizational systems, and performance expectations. One way to organize planning and strategic decision making is to recognize the different levels of organizational activities. **Figure 7-3** depicts an idealized version of organizational functions in a stair-step pattern, from defining mission to implementing organizational activities. While few organizations are so linear or hierarchical, the components (goals, budgets, programs) are interconnected, and conceptualizing the decision making necessary at different levels suggests appropriate stakeholders for involvement and the mandates or constraints that are placed at different points in the planning process (Hart, 1992). These constraints are framed by corporate decisions at high levels (left side of the diagram). Decisions on the left side are more abstract and broad, while decisions on the right are more tactical and operational. It is important to reiterate that activities on the right side "push back" and inform decisions on the left side as much or more than constraints and controls do from the left. The organizational mission has consistently been recognized as the lens that informs decisions, but missions do not operate independently of organizational actions, and managers must nurture a delicate balance of moving forward long-term goals while promoting actual performance activities in the organization. The

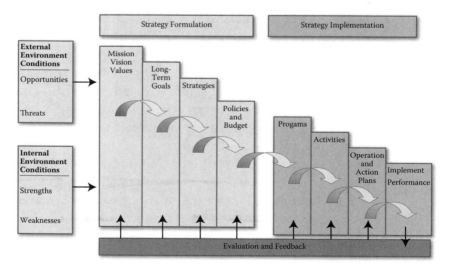

FIGURE 7-3 Levels and Elements of Strategic Planning
Courtesy of David O. Renz, Midwest Center for Nonprofit Leadership at UMKC.

next section describes the features depicted in Figure 7-3 and some methods of engaging internal and external stakeholders.

Information and analysis are the lifeblood of effective strategic planning and decision making. This is depicted by placing external and internal conditions on the far left of the diagram. Other chapters in this text discuss the features of the external and internal environment and how those various factors can be analyzed and utilized. Grappling with these issues and defining them sufficiently to inform decision making is critical to effective planning. Managers and organizations might allocate different levels of effort to information gathering and analysis. Different environmental conditions, as well, might require more or less analysis. Niche markets, for example, that are dominated by a limited number of providers and have strong barriers to new entrants might allow organizations to move forward with information provided by a few knowledgeable individuals. Conversely, more complex environmental conditions that force organizational response, such as shifting expectations from major funders, suggest the need for more complex analysis and information regarding alternative funding options as well as organizational capabilities and how those capabilities compare in relation to other providers. The need for information is different at each level of the organization, but accurate information that blends external and internal factors is used at all levels in strategic decisions. Information and feedback loops are used to guide operations and planning. Mission and vision have already been discussed extensively, so some discussion of strategies and long-term goals is useful. Organizations must consider two issues: who they should include in those discussions and how those discussions might be framed.

Long-term goals and *strategies* are the crux of corporate strategy (Dutton, Fahey, & Narayanan, 1983). This is similar to what Bryson (1995) describes as "strategic issues," or the specification of a few salient priorities. Strategic priorities should address the multiple operating concerns (e.g., public benefit, resource, and sociopolitical) and provide guidance to actors within the organization. Strategic issues are specific enough to guide organizational action and broad enough to allow tactical planning and implementation at lower levels in the organization. Strategic issues are formulated by the dominant coalition of knowledge-able and influential individuals, who hold sufficient knowledge and ability to synthesize complex information and have sufficient influence to facilitate implementation. Specifying members of the dominant coalition is tenuous and is an initial part of the planning process, which clarifies participants and roles.

Conceptualizing strategic issues is not linear, but rather includes inputs, process characteristics, and outputs, which provide a model to disentangle the activities (Dutton et al., 1983) (see **Table 7-4**). As was discussed, information is a key input element, but so is the framing of issues or the "problem." How the problem is conceptualized has implications for how it is reviewed and, ultimately, what is selected as an operational response. Consider, for example, an organization that lost major funding. Is there a problem with the way the organization is confronting its public benefit priorities such that the funder has lost the interest in the organization? If these funders are still operating in prioritized market domains then perhaps the problem is related to organizational practices and services. Alternatively, it could be that the funder is shifting priorities independent of organizational activities. That is, the funder is no longer operating in a market domain that is of interest to the nonprofit. Each of these problems requires different organizational actions, but the stimulus (lost finding) is the same. In the first instance, the organization needs to learn how their service activities are not attending to funder interests. In the second instance, the nonprofit can continue to court the funder, but the nonprofit must recognize that organizational practices may have to shift to follow funder preferences. Another input feature that informs the development of strategic priorities is the recognition that participants have predispositions and interests that guide how they interpret strategic concerns. These can be professional perspectives such that a finance manager is more attentive to costs and resource issues, or they can be power and influence based. Organizational actors are actively concerned about their role and status within the organization. Decision-making inherently brings those conceptions and preferences to the discussion. Accurate interpretation of environmental stimulus is critical and attending to input features facilitates framing and conceptualizing so as to minimize biases and foster discussion and interpretation.

In reference to process characteristics in strategic issues identification, these tend to be complex and multifaceted issues that require sequential review, analysis, and interpretation. Consequently, systematic reinterpretation of primary assumptions is useful. Dutton et al. (1983) refer to the recursive process of revisiting early assumptions based on new analysis and understanding. This can materialize as the reframing of the problem to reflect different interpretations (e.g., funder priorities versus service delivery concerns). This happens with individuals and among coalition participants. It is an individual and collective reinterpretation. Another process feature is the use of both deductive and inductive interpretation. Deduction is commonly referred to as a top-down approach that applies conceptual models to interpretation of problems and issues. These models are used and shared by members of the dominant coalition and might entail perceptions of service beneficiaries. Generally, deductive models are preferred, and they appear rational because they are

TABLE 7-4   Planning Processes

Planning Components	Key Features
Inputs	Information
	Framing
	Predispositions (cognitive, political)
Processes	Analysis
	Interpretation (deductive, inductive, recursive)
	Risk assessment
	Consider alternatives
Outputs	Strategic priorities
	Improved cause-and-effect understanding
	Goals
	Guidelines/Policies

Data from Dutton, J., Fahey, L., & Narayanan, V. K. (1983). Toward understanding strategic issues diagnosis. *Strategic Management Journal, 4*(4), 307–323.

based on shared assumptions of how the market operates. Inductive, or bottom-up, approaches remove conceptual frames and allow for fresh interpretation of data. This is difficult as cognitive frames are useful heuristics to facilitate and expedite decision making. Looking at the data with fresh eyes, so to speak, allows for a potentially different conclusion. Actively recognizing how both frames add value is a critical aspect of how leaders facilitate these processes. One way to facilitate these alternative interpretations is listening to definitions as they are articulated across organizational levels. Frontline workers provide one definition, while board members and community stakeholders provide another. Engaged conversations or forums provide a vehicle to challenge biases and assumptions in key issues confronting the organization.

Strategic issues identification and analysis culminates in guidelines for organizational action. It provides the language and structure for policies and budgeting. A key feature of strategic issues definition is the ability to improve cause-and-effect understanding. What are the antecedents and consequences of organizational actions and environmental influences? These assumptions concerning the causes and consequences of organizational action form the basis for operational strategies. This also provides a coherent language that can be shared and utilized by stakeholders to build programs and provide feedback. The accuracy of these judgments to predict the likelihood of organizational success, or at the very least to suggest guidelines for organizational action, makes the processing so critical. Consider for instance, the example of lost funding and the rationalization of why that happened (e.g., our services versus a shift in funder preferences). If leaders misinterpret the environmental stimulus, the guidelines for organizational action are potentially erroneous. These guidelines are further interpreted by division leaders so as to implement programs and activities, but significant assumptions are more or less taken for granted by division managers in order to ease their planning and implementation. The rest of the diagram reflects how operational decisions are guided by the decisions and interpretations of the dominant coalition. These guidelines are enacted through policies, budgeting, and performance monitoring.

Conclusion

This discussion of planning and corporate strategy has simplified a complex and dynamic process. Planning processes clarify the stages of participation as depicted in the stair-step model of organizational and planning elements (see Figure 7-3). The model allows organizational leadership to see how different stakeholders inside and outside the organization can participate in different aspects of planning and decision making. The model also identifies the different strategic and structural elements that can be utilized: long-term goals, policies, budgets, programs, and so on. An emphasis on strategic issues reflects the need for priorities that facilitate organizational action. Defining and interpreting environmental factors is central to the leaders' role. Placing that understanding within the frame of organizational capabilities is key to effective strategic leadership. The board of directors is active in negotiating and interpreting the task environment, especially the political context of legitimacy. Furthermore, boards act as advocates to gain access to resources. Questions of diversification and the range of services is an ongoing puzzle for senior leadership. The mix of factors, funders, philosophical values, and community needs are constantly in flux. Attending to those interests and interpreting the organization's role is essential for effective strategic decision making.

Discussion Questions

1. Are you familiar with organizations that may have diversified into too many program and resources areas? What about organizations that don't seem to have capitalized on opportunities within their operating areas?
2. A chronic challenge for nonprofit managers is engaging board members in appropriate roles and responsibilities. Why might board member apathy be a problem in small- to modest-sized nonprofits?
3. Sometimes planning seems like a waste of time and energy. What factors might contribute to a wasted effort in strategic planning? What could managers do to utilize planning techniques effectively?

References

Abzug, R., & Galaskiewicz, J. (2001). Nonprofit boards: Crucibles of expertise or symbols of local identities? *Nonprofit and Voluntary Sector Quarterly, 30*(1), 51–73.

Andrews, R., Boyne, G. A., Law, J., & Walker, R. M. (2009). Centralization, organizational strategy, and public service performance. *Journal of Public Administration Research and Theory, 19,* 57–80.

Bell, J., Masaoka, J., & Zimmerman, S. (2010). *Nonprofit sustainability: Making strategic decisions for financial viability.* San Francisco, CA: Jossey-Bass.

Bigelow, B., Stone, M. M., & Arndt, M. (1996). Corporate political strategy: A framework for understanding nonprofit strategy. *Nonprofit Management and Leadership, 7*(1), 29–43.

Bowditch, J. L., Buono, A. F., & Stewart, M. M. (2008). Organizational structure and design. In J. L. Bowditch & A. F. Buono (Eds.), *A primer on organizational behavior* (7th ed., pp. 282–319). Hoboken, NJ: Wiley.

Brown, W. A. (2005). Exploring the association between board and organizational performance in nonprofit organizations. *Nonprofit Management & Leadership, 15*(3), 317–339.

Brown, W. A. (2013). Antecedents to board member engagement and participation in deliberation and decision-making. In C. Cornforth & W. A. Brown (Eds.), *Nonprofit governance: Innovative perspectives and approaches* (p. 288). New York, NY: Routledge.

Brown, W. A., Hillman, A. J., & Okun, M. A. (2012). Factors that influence monitoring and resource provision among nonprofit noard members. *Nonprofit and Voluntary Sector Quarterly, 41*(1), 145–156.

Brown, W. A., & Iverson, J. O. (2004). Exploring strategy and board structure in nonprofit organizations. *Nonprofit and Voluntary Sector Quarterly, 33*(3), 377–400.

Bryson, J. M. (1995). *Strategic planning for public and nonprofit organizations* (Revised ed.). San Francisco, CA: Jossey-Bass.

Buckner International. (n.d.). Our history. Retrieved from http://www.buckner.org/who-we-are/

Buckner International. (2011). *Buckner International: Annual report*. Dallas, TX: Author.

Carver, J. (2006). *Boards that make a difference* (3rd ed.). San Francisco, CA: Jossey-Bass.

Chait, R. P., Ryan, W. P., & Taylor, B. E. (2005). *Governance as leadership: Reframing the work of nonprofit boards*. Hoboken, NJ: Wiley.

Chetkovich, C., & Frumkin, P. (2003). Balancing margin and mission. *Administration & Society, 35*(5), 564–596.

Chew, C., & Osborne, S. P. (2009). Identifying the factors that influence positioning strategy in U.K. charitable organizations that provide public services. *Nonprofit and Voluntary Sector Quarterly, 38*(1), 29–50.

Collins, S. (2012). Nearing home: After 19 years of leading Buckner, Ken Hall still goes back to family. Retrieved from http://www.buckner.org/ken-hall-legacy/

Cornforth, C., & Edwards, C. (1999). Board roles in the strategic managment of non-profit organizations: Theory and practice. *Corporate Governance, 7*(4), 346–363.

Day, G. S. (1977). Diagnosing the product portfolio. *Journal of Marketing, 41*(2), 29–38.

Dutton, J., Fahey, L., & Narayanan, V. K. (1983). Toward understanding strategic issues diagnosis. *Strategic Management Journal, 4*(4), 307–323.

Fama, E. F., & Jensen, M. C. (1983). Agency problems and residual claims. *Journal of Law and Economics, 26*(2), 327–349.

Green, J. C., & Griesinger, D. W. (1996). Board performance and organizational effectiveness in nonprofit social service organizations. *Nonprofit Management & Leadership, 6*, 381–402.

Gruber, M. (2007). Uncovering the value of planning in new venture creation: A process and contingency perspective. *Journal of Business Venturing, 22*(6), 782–807.

Gulati, R. (1995). Social structure and alliance formation patterns: A longitudinal analysis. *Administrative Science Quarterly, 40*(4), 619–652.

Guo, C. (2007). When government becomes the principal philanthropist: The effects of public funding on patterns of nonprofit governance. *Public Administration Review, 67*(3), 458–473.

Guo, C., & Acar, M. (2005). Understanding collaboration among nonprofit organizations: combining resource dependency, institutional, and network perspectives. *Nonprofit and Voluntary Sector Quarterly, 34*(3), 340–361.

Guo, C., & Musso, J. A. (2007). Representation in nonprofit and voluntary organizations: A conceptual framework. *Nonprofit and Voluntary Sector Quarterly, 36*(2), 308–326.

Hart, S. L. (1992). An integrative framework for strategy-making processes. *The Academy of Management Review, 17*(2), 327–351.

Hasenfeld, Y. (1983). *Human service organizations.* Englewood Cliffs, NJ: Prentice Hall.

Herman, R. D. (2010). Executive leadership. In D. O. Renz (Ed.), *The Jossey-Bass handbook of nonprofit leadership and management* (3rd ed., pp. 157–177). San Francisco, CA: Jossey-Bass.

Herman, R. D., & Renz, D. O. (1999). Theses on nonprofit organizational effectiveness. *Nonprofit and Voluntary Sector Quarterly, 28*(2), 107–126.

Herman, R. D., Renz, D. O., & Heimovics, R. D. (1996). Board practices and board effectiveness in local nonprofit organizations. *Nonprofit Management and Leadership, 7*(4), 373–385.

Hillman, A. J., & Dalziel, T. (2003). Boards of directors and firm performance: Integrating agency and resource dependence perspectives. *Academy of Management Review, 28*(3), 383–396.

Hopkins, B. R. (2009). *Legal responsibilties of nonprofit boards* (2nd ed.). Washington, DC: Boardsource.

Houle, C. O. (1997). *Governing boards: Their nature and nurture.* San Francisco, CA: Jossey-Bass.

Ketchen Jr., D. J., Combs, J. G., Russell, C. J., Shook, C., Dean, M. A., Runge, J., et al. (1997). Organiational configurations and performance: A meta-analysis. *Academy of Management Journal, 40*(1), 223–240.

Miles, R. E., & Snow, C. C. (1978). *Organizational strategy structure and process.* New York, NY: McGraw-Hill.

Miles, R. E., Snow, C. S., Mathews, J. A., Miles, G., & Coleman, H. J. (1997). Organizing in the knowledge age: Anticipating the cellular form. *The Academy of Management Executive, 11*(4), 7–20.

Miller, J. L. (2002). The board as a monitor of organizational activity: The applicability of agency theory to nonprofit boards. *Nonprofit Management and Leadership, 12*(4), 429–450.

Miller-Millesen, J. L. (2003). Understanding the behavior of nonprofit boards of directors: A theory-based approach. *Nonprofit and Voluntary Sector Quarterly, 32*(4), 521–547.

Norman, K. (Producer). (2013). Buckner Orphans Home: 1938 annual report [PowerPoint presentation]. Retrieved from http://www.slideshare.net/knorman31/buckner-orphans -home-1938-annual-report

Olson, D. E. (2000). Agency teory in the not-for-profit sector: Its role at independent colleges. *Nonprofit and Voluntary Sector Quarterly, 29*(2), 280–296.

Ostrower, F. (2007). *Nonprofit governance in the United States: Findings on performance and accountability from the first national representative study*. Washinton, DC: Urban Institute.

Ostrower, F., & Stone, M. M. (2006). Boards of nonprofit organizations: Research trends, findings and prospects for future research. In W. W. Powell and R. Steinberg (Eds.), *The nonprofit sector: A research handbook* (2nd ed.). New Haven, CT: Yale University Press.

Our history. Retrieved from http://www.buckner.org/about /history.shtml

Pfeffer, J., & Salancik, G. R. (1978). *The external control of organizations: A resource dependance perspective.* New York, NY: Harper & Row.

Phills, J. A. (2005). *Integrating mission and strategy for nonprofit organizations.* New York, NY: Oxford University Press.

Zander, A. (1993). *Making boards effective: The dynamics of nonprofit governing boards.* San Francisco, CA: Jossey-Bass.

CHAPTER 8

Service Strategies: Designing and Implementing Services for Social Impact

Learning Objectives

- Define the components of a simple logic model
- Explain the rationale for monitoring program activities and outcomes
- Summarize some of the challenges managers confront in measuring program outcomes

This chapter will consider how certain beneficiary populations are the foci of service activities and how those services are implemented to achieve impact. Impact reflects the extent to which services provide positive outcomes for program participants (Sheehan, 2010). The discussion starts with the logic model as a method to understand how activities align to achieve outcomes. The logic model is an integral part of an organization's theory of change. The **theory of change** is the rationale for why and how program services achieve social benefits (Colby, Stone, & Carttar,

2004). The Harlem Children's Zone case example illustrates how managers can focus organizational activities on selected beneficiaries (see **Exhibit 8-1**). While these choices can be difficult and inherently require trade-offs, research suggests that focused attention on particular beneficiaries facilitates an organization's ability to select and create programs that meet the needs and interests of intended beneficiaries. By prioritizing a particular target population program managers can develop a "theory of change" that informs program choices and improves the likelihood of program success (Dobbie & Fryer, 2010). This chapter discusses the practices and principles managers can employ to develop services that fulfill mission objectives.

EXHIBIT 8-1   Case Example: Harlem Children's Zone

Harlem Children's Zone (HCZ), established in 1970, is a comprehensive social service organization located in Harlem, New York. When Geoffrey Canada assumed leadership of the organization, it was providing services to a broad range of individuals in various neighborhoods. Mr. Canada felt the organization lacked sufficient focus to achieve its primary objective: to help children achieve academic success so as to become contributing members in society. Through a series of discussions, the organization reaffirmed its commitment to fostering academic success in children. They defined academic success by enumerating a series of developmental milestones for children at all ages. With objectives and criteria for success, the organization identified the barriers and challenges for the children. By understanding the challenges experienced by children, the organization could develop and modify services to address current gaps. The organization began to create a comprehensive range of services for children at all ages, which extended beyond traditional educational services into the family and the community so as to create a context for success. To design such a comprehensive range of services the organization had to make a number of choices. For instance, they were running a senior center that was well used and a valuable asset, but it became evident that the center fell outside the intended target service beneficiary. Consequently, they transferred responsibility for the senior center to another organization. In addition, as the depth and range of services for the target population increased, it was apparent that the organization needed to impose geographic limitations. They identified a target neighborhood encompassing 90 city blocks and crafted programs to fit their unique needs. These targeted and comprehensive services created impressive results for the children. They were succeeding intellectually as never before and were able to overcome many social and family problems that have derailed so many other children.

Data from Harlem Children's Zone. (2003). Harlem Children's Zone: Growth Plan FY 2001–FY 2009. New York, NY: Harlem Children's Zone.; and Harlem Children's Zone. (n.d.). History. Retrieved from http://www .hcz.org/about-us/history.

Logic of Program Activities

Direct services are program activities targeted at beneficiaries with the intent to improve their condition. The outcome of program activities is the changed status of participants. Through these outcomes the organization creates social value. The core principle is an emphasis on outcomes. This perspective was developed in the evaluation field and relies on objective criteria to assess the benefits created by the nonprofits. Attention to outcomes facilitates program design and delivery because as programs are evaluated managers can adjust and modify services based on indicators of outcome success. These concepts pose several challenges for managers. Fundamentally, it can be very difficult to assess outcome success. A logic model and careful attention to program monitoring can provide significant guidance about the process of service delivery. It informs service options, including the selection and prioritization of program beneficiaries.

Figure 8-1 presents a simple logic model that managers can use to help interpret the reasoning guiding service activities. With just three components (target beneficiary, activities, and outcomes) this model depicts core program features. Logic models were developed by evaluation professionals to facilitate

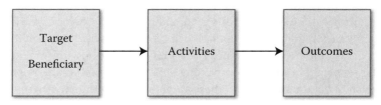

FIGURE 8-1   Logic of Service Activities

program evaluation initiatives (Chen, 2005). Full logic models include additional elements such as resource components on the front end (left side) and long-term community impacts on the far right side, as well as feedback loops and outputs interwoven into the model (W. K. Kellogg Foundation, 2004). A simplified logic model is useful because it reflects the significant decision areas for managers related to developing services. Logic models are based on a causal explanation of how program services result in particular outcomes. Providing service X (e.g., hot meals), participants will change in specific ways Z (e.g., overcome hunger). Logic models facilitate alignment (Schiemann, 2009) among organizational participants because they require clarity on activities to achieve outcomes.

Logic models provide operational guidance to program managers and staff who design and implement program-level strategies. The first step in program planning is defining the "need" for services or the "market" of program activities, which suggest target beneficiaries. The assessment of need forms the basis for activities and is the baseline that will be used to judge program success. Outcomes are an articulation of program benefits that address the defined need. The logic model components are interconnected, and decisions regarding one component affect others. Need should drive program design, and only through the specification of needs can the organization distill its impact and social value (Altschuld & Kumar, 2010). The next section reviews the three components of the simple logic model. First is the selection and identification of program beneficiaries as the target of program activities. Second, outcomes are discussed because clarity regarding outcome priorities informs program activities. Third, program activities are discussed with an emphasis on methods to monitor program elements and assess impact.

Target Beneficiaries

Through the definition of need, beneficiaries are identified. The concern for managers is identifying target populations that are suitable for services. Clarity regarding criteria of participants is critical for operational success. While it is not possible to remove all variability from program participants, it is necessary to have criteria that helps define and describe participants. Participants are the focus of service activities; managers can improve the effectiveness of nonprofits by making organizations more customer friendly (Kara, Spillan, & DeShields, 2004; Vaughan & Shiu, 2001). In this context, the "customer" is the recipient of services provided by the nonprofit. For example, a Boys and Girls Club would focus on the needs and interests of the children who currently participate in organizational activities and simultaneously consider expanding services to other children within a particular geographic region. The club would consider current and prospective participants as the primary customer of public benefit activities. The recommendation contends that nonprofits should focus on who is receiving the services and the benefits that those individuals attain.

There are a number of issues managers confront when providing services to individuals with low "buying" power. If market forces are muted or nonexistent, how does a manager prioritize service recipients? Are managers required to provide services to the most "needy" or to those most likely to succeed? Managers should consider the implications of selecting different program participants and come to terms with how those choices affect program objectives. There are two key dimensions that managers should consider. First is an attention to outcomes; the second relates to the customer experience. In either case nonprofits must make efforts to know their target beneficiary well. They must develop relationships that help the organization listen to customer's interests and preferences.

Focusing on outcomes is a difficult expectation. Most for-profit businesses are not expected to track, document, and demonstrate the benefits of their services. Health care and pharmaceuticals are two highly regulated areas, and there is some expectation of improvement on the part of the customer as a result of services. At the ground level, however, family practice physicians only modestly determine performance success. For instance, how successful is a physician in healing patients? Often, we do not really know. We can make judgments about our own doctor's efficacy when providing service, but often the overall effectiveness of the doctor is not tracked or documented. The doctor can implement a number of practices to make the patient's experience more pleasant, but this may or may not correlate to performance (Brown, 2012). Customers expect businesses to meet preferences and demands. Many nonprofits are not oriented toward their customers in that way. This sets up the dual demands that service beneficiaries place on many nonprofits. Service beneficiaries expect services that are attuned to their interests and demands while achieving long-term benefits and outcomes. The next section reviews outcomes and the subsequent section discusses some issues managers should consider as they develop and implement services.

Defining Outcomes

To understand outcomes, it is good to start with an example. Let's suppose an organization has a mission to improve the lives of older adults. Managers need to determine what it means to "improve" lives. Improve, as an outcome, encompasses a number of different features (see **Table 8-1**). At the simplest level, outcomes alleviate negative aspects of the current condition. If an elderly person is hungry, a nonprofit can provide a meal. These are classified as simple and short-term outcomes. Such activities achieve basic benefits. Managers may often desire to move beyond these basic benefits to consider more substantive benefits such as health status or overall quality of life. As a result, there are short-term benefits (e.g., alleviate hunger) and long-term benefits (e.g., improved health). There are also benefits that move beyond

TABLE 8-1   Types of Outcomes

Type	Description
Short term	Relatively immediate change in participants as a result of services. This may be the elimination of undesirable, physical, social, or emotional status.
Long term	Those benefits that take longer to develop but reflect changes in behavior and improve the condition of participants for a longer period of time.
Simple	Reflecting just one or two proximal benefits.
Complex	Reflecting a combination of proximal and distant elements that build capacity and sustainability of participants.

specific improvements upon the condition of the participant to address root causes of the social problem. Activities that might provide such benefits could include educational services to help the elderly learn about healthy eating or initiatives to facilitate the elderly person's ability to secure healthy food (e.g., lobby for public transportation).

This distinction between alleviating need to facilitating self-sufficiency is important. Intuitively, there is some desire to strive for self-sufficiency outcomes, but social conditions are such that both short- and long-term outcomes are necessary and valuable. This is an important distinction between dependency and independence. Does a nonprofit provide services that make people dependent on them to maintain the social benefits or do they provide services to facilitate independence? Efforts should be made to minimize dependency, but there are situations and populations (e.g., severely disabled) that require long-term ongoing support. **Table 8-2** details a few examples of outcomes nonprofits may hope to attain.

Program Activities

Program activities are the method to create changes in the participants. This section considers how managers are able to monitor and track program delivery. Unpacking the program

TABLE 8-2 Example Outcomes

Category	Description
Knowledge	Changes in understanding through learning
Attitudes	Changes in someone's feeling and emotions, both toward themselves and others
Skills	Ability to apply learning and knowledge, a combination of knowledge and ability
Behaviors	Ability to consistently and reliably engage in appropriate and desired actions
Health and physical	Reflects improvements in individual health or physical condition
Social status	The definition of one's position in society, such as homeless or unemployed; complex mix of individual behaviors and actions as well as opportunities

activities element of the logic model, there are three components to consider: inputs, processes/activities, and outputs (see
Figure 8-2). These three components form the basis of how
managers work to create, monitor, and modify program activities. Inputs are the resources required to deliver services and they

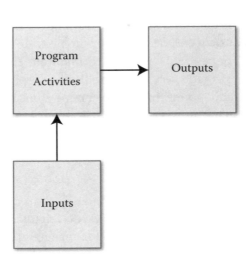

FIGURE 8-2 Elements of Program Activities

include facilities, staff, and equipment. Outputs are indicators of services provided. Outputs specify the type and character of services delivered. Program activities are the actual interaction and delivery of services. It can be difficult to judge service activities because those activities are often intangible and subjective (Parasuraman, Zeithaml, & Berry, 1985). Consider for a moment our ability to judge the quality of a meal versus our ability to judge the quality of the waiter's service. Judgment of the meal is based on a number of tangible indicators, such as color and temperature, as well as some subjective indicators, such as taste. Developing indicators of service quality is difficult. Often we rely on subjective factors (e.g., friendly) that only partially reflect the nature of "service." This is why managers often rely on output and input criteria to assess program quality. This discussion touches on several important areas for managers including service quality, participant satisfaction, performance management, organizational learning, and innovation.

Managers find overseeing services challenging because it is difficult to judge quality. Service quality reflects a number of desirable features. Service quality has to do with implementing the right activities to achieve outcomes as well as attending to perceptions of participants. So a high-quality service is more likely to achieve outcomes and respond to desires and preferences of participants. Consider a counseling session. How would one judge a high-quality counseling session? Focusing on outputs allows managers to consider how many hours were provided in the counseling session. Inputs would consider the professional experience of the counselor. Outcomes might look to see what improvements were reflected in participants after a set period of counseling sessions. Actually judging the quality of counseling is difficult. A manager's technical competence facilitates his or her ability to judge quality of services, but it is often labor intensive to observe and rate services, especially intimate, client-specific services such as counseling. Managers are rarely present for every interaction and therefore must develop methods to ensure quality and consistency of services. **Table 8-3** details some of the strategies managers can use to monitor and track services. No single method is useful in all contexts, and using only one method may

TABLE 8-3   Methods to Monitor Services

Method	Description
Input controls	Manage the type, quality, and quantity of inputs needed to provide services
Monitor and track outputs	Develop indicators of services provided that reflect key drivers of success
Efficiency indicators	Ratios that calculate resource use per some unit of service delivery (e.g., participants)
Track service recipients	Understand who is receiving services and how those individuals respond to services
Customer satisfaction	Participant's perception of the service to meet their expectations (i.e., desires and preferences)
Qualitative assessment of program activities	Talk with providers regularly to remove barriers and refine service activities

result in distortions because it is nearly impossible to develop a single measure that captures the range of nuanced features that reflect high-quality services.

Input controls are used to address the range and quality of resources required to provide services. The idea is that higher-quality inputs are more likely to result in higher-quality services. At the very least, consistency of inputs should result in some degree of consistency in services. Often a high-quality service is customized to the nature of the problem and context. Given the nature of social services, labor is often the most significant resource utilized to provide services. Consequently, managers can work to ensure consistency in the skills and abilities of providers. Training or education in particular skills might be reflective of high-quality inputs. It can be very difficult to ascertain what resource inputs are absolutely necessary for service quality and what is indicative of other norms that guide how services are provided. Furthermore, given the challenges in determining success, managers can find it difficult to prioritize which resource elements are fundamentally required for effective services and which are extraneous to service fulfillment. Given the variety of services provided by nonprofits, it is not possible to articulate a consistent rubric to judge resource requirements. Rather, managers evaluate the range and type of resources required for service delivery and make judgments based on professional experience. A reoccurring theme in providing quality services is that different contexts require different elements and, as a result, managers must engage in an ongoing discussion with providers. Furthermore, it is important to remember that providers often have a vested interest in retaining current resources and skills requirements. Managers are required to negotiate the desires of providers with the practical limitations of the resource environment. Consequently, selection of resource requirements is driven not only by what is needed, but by what is available.

Tracking outputs entails quantifying service delivery activities. This reflects the duration and type of service provided. Managers measure what was done, irrespective of the result or outcome of those activities. While these measures can at times feel bureaucratic or burdensome, these indicators provide the basis for specifying the range and type of services provided. Funders are often concerned with how many individuals the organization served, what type of service they received, and the duration of those services. *Who, what,* and *how long* form basic monitoring outputs. The range of indictors is quite large and, in practice, detailed documentation is often difficult to attain, especially in resource-strapped nonprofits. Consequently, managers must undertake the process of building systems to more easily capture the necessary information. Without accurate and reliable indictors of services, nonprofits cannot document the range and type of services provided, but, perhaps even more importantly, they cannot take the next step to ascertain the results of these activities. Central to the theory of change is that reliable and consistent services are provided and output indicators form the basis of knowing what type of service was provided. Information management systems are a critical element in monitoring service activities.

Efficiency is a production ratio that calculates the cost or amount of services per the appropriate unit of analysis (i.e., per participant). Ideally, these efficiency measures are linked to performance outcomes. So in a smoking cessation program, managers might calculate the cost of "producing" a nonsmoker. Given the difficult nature of determining outcomes, efficiency measures are often based on cost to deliver service (e.g., cost to deliver smoking cessation services per participant). If available, industry standards can also provide guidance on the type of ratios that would be useful. These ratios can be driven by funders, regulatory entities, or industry groups that set guidelines on how many hours, for example, should be allocated to each participant. **Figure 8-3** provides an example of a typical efficiency ratio that calculates the cost to provide services per recipient. This rudimentary efficiency measure can provide insight for managers, especially when compared to industry standards. These ratios are based on reliable outputs and monitoring data. Managers then develop and utilize ratios to interpret and guide activities.

Tracking program participants is regular monitoring of program participants, from initial participation through engagement with services and after separation. Program providers can gather information that facilitates judgments about service effectiveness by monitoring and tracking service recipients. This seems like a relatively obvious objective for nonprofit social services, but the task is very difficult and can be quite expensive. When resources are constrained, the desire is to allocate funds to the direct provision of services and not necessarily to tracking and monitoring program participants. Effective tracking forms the basis of performance assessment. Managers must understand what happened with participants during and subsequent to service activities. Nonprofit organizations need systems to gather information on participants.

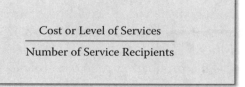

$$\frac{\text{Cost or Level of Services}}{\text{Number of Service Recipients}}$$

FIGURE 8-3   Example of a Service Efficiency Ratio

In the management literature, there is a significant stream of research that considers how organizations can facilitate a relationship with customers (Dwyer, Schurr, & Oh, 1987). This is an attempt to move beyond distinct service interactions to understand the customer more fully. The rationale in a for-profit context is to retain customers and to expand the range and type of services provided. The principle of getting the customer more integrated with the organization is applicable to many nonprofits. Facilitating a partnership of shared responsibility in creating positive outcomes is one method some nonprofits could employ. Participants are committed to the organization as well as the intended outcomes and assume responsibility to negotiate an ongoing relationship because they receive value from the ongoing relationship.

This is some of the wisdom behind the Harlem Children's Zone (HCZ) project, an organization that focuses on a select number of participants to provide intensive and ongoing services within a particular geographic region. They are able to track progress because they provide a range of developmental services that evolve with the program participants. The participants become dedicated to the organization and facilitate tracking and follow-through with program initiatives. The HCZ is a unique model of service delivery that does not apply to all nonprofit contexts, but it illustrates that reconceptualizing services to ensure program benefits is possible. The HCZ has focused on the desired outcome and then worked to build a broad range of services that allow them to track and document participant success.

Customer satisfaction is an aspect of the participant's reaction to service activities. Part of how organizations retain customers is their satisfaction with services. Satisfaction entails many facets related to aesthetics, quality, and perceived value (benefits). Satisfaction is driven by expectations. If organizations are able to meet the expectations of service recipients, they will be satisfied. Satisfaction in and of itself is not an outcome of public benefit services. Rather, satisfaction is a measure of the participant's reaction to services provided. Participant satisfaction can be indicative of services that are more likely to achieve program outcomes, but this is not always the case. For example, patient satisfaction in hospitals is driven by patient and staff interactions as well as responsiveness to demands (Brown, 2012). While patient and staff interactions contribute to a more pleasant experience, they are not sufficient to heal disease. Rather, it is the invasive and often uncomfortable clinical services that ultimately achieve the desired outcome. Hospital stays have multiple objectives that supersede a pleasant experience. Some patients can differentiate quality services, but many are distracted by elements that might not reflect high-quality care (comfortable waiting room). The point is not that participant satisfaction is not important (in fact far too many nonprofits probably ignore this concern); rather, participant satisfaction reflects just one more example of the complex competing demands nonprofits confront when they work to produce public benefits. Prioritizing participant satisfaction is influenced by the choices customers have. If customers have a choice, nonprofits are more likely to attend to customer preferences. If however, customers are in a limited choice context (low buyer power), nonprofits may be less motivated to expend resources on elements that, on the surface, appear to be extraneous to the core service delivery methodology.

Information Management and Measurement

The logic model structures the information needs of managers. The logic model is based on an assumption of a causal link between components. It is difficult to establish causal linkages. Programs must meet three conditions to establish causation. First, there must be an identifiable association between program activities and the intended outcome. That is, as program activities are provided there is a noticeable change in outcome features in participants. Second is a time-order sequence that necessitates that program activities happened *prior* to changes in participants. Finally, and most difficult, is the ability to rule out all other possible explanations for why the changes revealed in the participant were *caused* by program services. These conditions set the stage for the type, range, and quality of information that managers need. Gathering and analyzing information related to each element in the logic model (beneficiary, activities, and outcomes) is the basis for good decision making; furthermore, managers seek to gain knowledge regarding the causal linkages depicted in the logic model diagram.

Managers need to determine what information is desired and available to monitor program services and to track program outcomes. While it is not possible to quantify all program elements, some method to gather and collect information is necessary. **Table 8-4** profiles the steps in developing a measurement strategy to track performance. First is the definition of logic model components. While this may seem rudimentary, the logic model components are not easily defined, and often program managers have multiple, parallel purposes that make depiction of program activities challenging. The next step is the identification of indicators for each feature of the logic model. Indicators are observable manifestations of the logic model concepts. For example, if we are providing services to the elderly (target) to improve their health (outcome), we might measure and track some basic health statistics such as blood pressure and cholesterol level. Finally, managers need to establish methods to collect accurate and timely information. This entails record-keeping systems as

TABLE 8-4   Steps in Measurement

Steps	Definition
1. Define the logic model components	Clear definition of target beneficiary, service activities, and outcomes facilitates tracking and measurement.
2. Identify measurable indicators	Indicators are features of a more complex idea or concept (i.e., logic model component) that you are able to measure and track.
3. Data collection methods	Determine the strategies to gather and compile information about indicators. This includes timing of data collection and methods to collect the data (surveys, intake forms, etc.).

well as different tactics to capture information needs. There are a broad range of potential practices that are discussed in relation to the logic model components. How the information is collected facilitates judgments regarding performance outcomes.

Types of Indicators

Once the logic model components are defined, managers devise a system to collect information that provides insights into the nature and character of those components. This suggests the need to have proximal indicators that reflect aspects of the larger and more complex logic model component. Consider, for example, a desire to provide services to "disadvantaged youth" (target beneficiary). Managers would develop indicators or criteria to define "disadvantaged" and "youth." Defining youth is usually fairly straightforward and typically entails chronological age, although other indicators should be proposed, such as developmental stage. Age is a reasonable objective indicator of "youth." Indictors of disadvantage could entail any number of features such as family income, single-parent family, poor academic performance, and so on. Selecting these indicators provides confidence to providers and funders that the logic model components are present and operating according to the planned intervention. Five types of indicators are reviewed (see **Table 8-5**).

Indicators can be either subjective or objective. Objective indicators are those features that are less influenced by perception or judgment. Considering the example of selecting disadvantaged youth for a program, an objective indictor might be family income. Objective indictors are not based on opinion or attitudes. Subjective indictors are based on judgments or perceptions. So program providers might ask school counselors to nominate a few disadvantaged youth for the program without necessarily detailing all criteria for those judgments, but rather allow the counselor to make nominations based on impressions. Such a perception may be the only available indicator. For instance, consider a program that wants disadvantaged

TABLE 8-5 Types of Indicators

Types of Indicators	Issues and Considerations
Subjective	These are perceptions of individuals and reflect attitudes about participants or the services (e.g., satisfaction).
Objective	Are independent of individual perceptions, such as a score on a test or independent observations.
Quantitative	These are indicators that can be depicted as numbers, which facilitates analysis and comparison.
Qualitative	Are typically more descriptive and reflect words, pictures, or videos that can provide significant detail but can be difficult to analyze and compare.
Reliable	This reflects the ability to get good information consistently over time.

youth that reflect more subtle features, such as ambition or leadership potential. While the program may develop an assessment tool, it is not uncommon to rely on more subjective indictors, such as the impressions given by knowledgeable individuals. Satisfaction with program services is another example of subjective impressions by program participants. Those impressions are valid indictors of the participant's opinion of program features. So while objective indictors are often desirable, there is a role for subjective indicators as well.

Another distinction among indicators is the extent to which they are quantitative or qualitative. Quantitative indictors are based on numbers and can be easily compared and ranked (e.g., family income). Qualitative indictors are based on words and tend to be more descriptive. While words carry more complexity, it is typically difficult to easily compare written descriptions. Sometimes it is useful to have quantitative indicators with qualitative description to provide more detail. Consider, for example, medical records that rely on numerical, visual, and descriptive narratives to detail patient health. It is the compilation of various indicators that provides the best assessment. The final criterion to consider is reliability. Reliability has to do with accuracy and consistency over time. Reliable indicators provide accurate and consistent measurements. Indicators form the basis of performance management practices that managers utilize to monitor and track program activities and outcomes. This is a brief review of some measure concerns that managers confront when trying to monitor program activities as reflected in the logic model.

Learning and Innovation

Up to this point, this chapter has highlighted the importance of developing logic models and indicators of service quality, which include resource inputs, specification of program outputs, and tracking participants. The compilation of indicators provides a basis for understanding performance in nonprofits. It is difficult to quantifiably assess the success of nonprofit social service programs. Consequently, the methods outlined should be used to engage program providers, participants, and other knowledgeable stakeholders in reflection and discussion to interpret the implications. Program evaluation and monitoring do not necessarily represent the "truth." Rather, these practices provide a basis to understand difficult and complex services with multiple objectives. It is critical to engage individuals in conversations to facilitate interpretation and to guide future activities. The focus is taking the information and learning what works, what needs more information, and what does not seem to provide the intended benefits. Without good information individual biases and the contending forces in strategic decision making can influence program choices. Far too often, the tracking of services is provided for others and not used to improve services and understanding in the organization. It is this orientation toward learning and adaptation that is potentially the most important lesson in the chapter (Crutchfield & Grant, 2008). The collection of information must be translated into knowledge and learning for the organization or its value is lost.

Managers need to address several elements of organizational learning and knowledge management (Argote, McEvily, & Reagans, 2003). The methods of creation, retention, and transfer of knowledge are complex and involve an iterative process of formal and informal mechanisms to support learning by organizational participants. At the most fundamental level there has to be the creation of knowledge and understanding regarding service quality. Frontline providers often have a great deal of wisdom and understanding of what works. If managers support this knowledge it can be used to guide and inform others. Managers need to ensure that providers at all levels increase their expertise and sophistication of service delivery strategies. This requires systems that facilitate learning, sharing, and retention of high-quality service delivery practices. How does an organization capture and define "best practice" strategies used to provide services? If frontline managers have an understanding of quality services, they need to distill and describe the practice to facilitate sharing. Often, but not always, sharing among providers in one unit is fairly easy and spontaneous. Managers can facilitate and encourage organizational providers to engage in information sharing. Organizational members must be motivated to share information and learning. Consider, for example, a classroom teacher. What are the elements that facilitate retention and sharing of information and knowledge about teaching practices? How can supervisors move beyond informal lunchroom conversations? Part of it has to do with the culture of the organization and the formal systems to reward and support providers to create, articulate, and share knowledge about best practices. The data and information gained through monitoring program activities are critical, as is the "logic" or theory of change employed by organizational participants. Learning and innovation entail adapting and adjusting services to facilitate higher-quality services to achieve program objectives and to create substantive benefits in program participants.

Conclusion

A simplified logic model with three components (target beneficiary, service activities, and intended outcomes) informs the development of service strategies. While these features interact and operate in the broader organizational and environmental context, attending to program outcomes guides choices to support public benefit purposes. Nonprofits need to build service strategies that address community needs that emphasize outcomes because typical customer-based market forces are not sufficient to guide service delivery strategies. Outcomes become the "other bottom line." Nonprofit managers have a philosophical and moral responsibility to strive toward producing public benefits, and developing outcomes for service recipients is a significant component of that responsibility. The simple logic model is an abstraction of complex service strategies so as to facilitate a focus on outcomes. A model that attends to outcomes can be applied to a number of service contexts. Providers must describe the "logic" behind their service activities. This rationale for services facilitates the allocation of resources and prioritization of service beneficiaries. Multiple contending forces (most notably resource constraints) can wreak havoc on clear linear models. An attention to outcomes and the logic that guides service activities facilitate the alignment of resources. This alignment is critical for organizational participants because the focus on outcomes serves to motivate organizational members. Goal-based objectives that address the fundamental social purpose of the organization are incredibly motivating for organizational participants. Furthermore, in resource-poor contexts where there are endless demands, a focus on objectives can help frontline providers prioritize their activities. Without some definition of program objectives, service providers can feel overwhelmed and undersupported.

There are a number of challenges associated with creating and implementing high-quality services to obtain social benefits. This includes attending to resource inputs and tracking indictors of service delivery (outputs). There is no single method to guarantee that service activities will achieve long-term benefits (social value). Conscientious efforts to manage the service delivery process increase the likelihood of success. Managers should monitor service beneficiaries to understand what benefits they receive from program activities. **Figure 8-4** presents an expanded logic model diagram to include inputs, outputs, and feedback loops. Program providers must share and

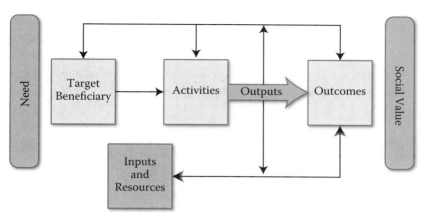

FIGURE 8-4 Expanded Logic Model

interpret information gained through monitoring activities. It is the process of feedback and refinement that improves programs, creating systems and a culture that supports learning and improvement. The feedback loops are recursive, because program activities evolve and develop as informed by operations and contextual factors. This includes the resource environment that is conceptualized as program inputs. Furthermore, the diagram places the logic model in the context of community needs to produce social value. Program activities are designed to address community needs with the intent of providing social value. Placing service activities as operating in the broader environmental context provides guidance to managers and organizational leaders. Strategic leaders help interpret social needs as the market for services and social value as the culmination of organizational objectives. The ability to produce social value is the justification for acquiring resources.

Discussion Questions

1. Consider a nonprofit social service program that you are familiar with and identify the three elements of a basic logic model (target, activities, and outcomes).
2. If it is difficult to track program participants, how much effort should nonprofit managers employ to assess program outcomes?

Can you think of examples where it might be OK to operate without an ability to track outcomes? What could managers monitor instead?

3. What practices could managers employ to support learning and information sharing in an organization?

References

Altschuld, J. W., & Kumar, D. D. (2010). *Needs assessment: An overview.* Los Angeles, CA: Sage.

Argote, L., McEvily, B., & Reagans, R. (2003). Managing knowledge in organizations: An integrative framework and review of emerging themes. *Management Science, 49*(4), 571–582.

Brown, T. (2012, March 14). Hospitals aren't hotels. *New York Times.* Retrieved from http://www.nytimes.com/2012/03/15 /opinion/hospitals-must-first-hurt-to-heal.html?_r=0

Chen, H. T. (2005). *Practical program evaluation.* Thousand Oaks, CA: Sage.

Colby, S., Stone, N., & Carttar, P. (2004, Fall). Zeroing in on impact. *Stanford Social Innovation review,* 24–33.

Crutchfield, L. R., & Grant, H. M. (2008). *Forces for good: The six practices of high-impact nonprofits.* San Francisco, CA: Jossey-Bass.

Dobbie, W., & Fryer, R. G. (2010). *Are high-quality schools enough to increase achievement among the poor? Evidence from the Harlem Children's Zone.* Cambridge, MA: Harvard University. Retrieved from http://scholar.harvard.edu/files/fryer /files/hcz_nov_2010.pdf

Dwyer, F. R., Schurr, P. H., & Oh, S. (1987). Developing buyer-seller relationships. *Journal of Marketing, 51*(2), 11–27.

Harlem Children's Zone. (n.d.). History. Retrieved from http:// www.hcz.org/about-us/history

Harlem Children's Zone. (2003). Harlem Children's Zone: Growth plan FY 2001–FY 2009. New York, NY: Harlem Children's Zone.

Kara, A., Spillan, J. E., & DeShields, J. O. W. (2004). An empirical investigation of the link between market orientation and business performance in nonprofit service providers. *Journal of Marketing Theory & Practice, 12*(2), 59–72.

Parasuraman, A., Zeithaml, V. A., & Berry, L. L. (1985). A conceptual model of service quality and its implications for future research. *The Journal of Marketing, 49*(4), 41–50.

Schiemann, W. A. (2009). Aligning performance with organizational strategy, values and goals. In J. W. Smither & M. London (Eds.), *Performance management* (pp. 45–87). San Francisco, CA: Jossey Bass.

Sheehan, R. M. (2010). *Mission impact: Breakthrough strategies for nonprofits.* Hoboken, NJ: John Wiley & Sons.

Vaughan, L., & Shiu, E. (2001). ARCHSECRET: A multi-item scale to measure service quality within the voluntary sector. *International Journal of Nonprofit and Voluntary Sector Marketing, 6*(2), 131–144.

W. K. Kellogg Foundation. (2004). *W. K. Kellogg Foundation evaluation handbook.* Battle Creek, MI: Author.

CHAPTER 9

Social and Political Strategies: Community Building and Advocacy

Learning Objectives

- Describe the range of advocacy activities available to nonprofits
- Consider the key decisions in social and political strategy development
- Recognize the different targets of advocacy activities
- Employ methods toward different social, political, and economic entities

This chapter introduces techniques and strategies that nonprofits can utilize to influence their social, political, and economic environments. These strategies move beyond services to beneficiaries to consider how nonprofits influence social and political processes to achieve public benefits. These activities are often conceptualized as advocacy and lobbying and include such things as community grassroots organizing, direct lobbying to influence government entities, and petitioning corporations to shift their production and distribution practices. Advocacy activities confront social, political, and economic systems that control or influence rules and resources (see **Exhibit 9-1**). Some nonprofit entities specialize in these practices, but much of what is discussed can be used by any nonprofit. Whether it is a social service, arts, or environmental organization almost all nonprofits have priorities that can be advanced through activities in the sociopolitical domain. If chosen effectively and utilized appropriately, social and political activities can influence all aspects of nonprofit performance (financial, mission, and legitimacy) (Bigelow, Stone, & Arndt, 1996; Libby, 2012; Lux, Crook, & Woehr, 2011).

Within the public policy context, "small nonprofits . . . are the backbone of political voice in communities around the country" (Reid, 1999, p. 292). Nonprofits generate excitement for elections and help with voter registration. They inform communities of important communal issues. They raise awareness of the needs of the communities they serve. The U.S. political process is inherently driven by the engagement of nonprofits and their constituencies. Nonprofits have been instrumental in supporting significant achievement in civil rights, nondiscrimination, environmental issues, trade issues, labor, and countless other issues. Long-term social priorities are often most effectively achieved through systematic and strategic use of advocacy strategies. There is an increasing plurality of social priorities, and often nonprofits are an important resource to ensure that different voices and concerns are elevated and engaged in political processes. While corporate influences dominate in many political situations (Golden, 1998), nonprofits are a primary method that individuals and community groups can use to influence political decision making. In many ways nonprofits have philosophical and moral requirements to advance social issues that are a priority for their constituencies.

EXHIBIT 9-1   Mothers Against Drunk Driving

Mothers Against Drunk Driving (MADD) is an example of a nonprofit that prioritizes advocacy activities to change the rules about drunk driving. By organizing and campaigning they helped changed the way Americans thought about drinking and driving. They were instrumental in crafting and instituting extensive legislation at state and federal levels that strengthened standards and toughened enforcement. MADD wasn't just about victim services and supporting mothers who had lost children; they were about changing the system so that there were fewer deaths and fewer grieving mothers (Davis, 2005; "Secrets to Success," 2005). Mothers Against Drunk Driving was started by Candy Lightner, who lost her daughter to a repeat drunk-driving offender in May of 1980. Ms. Lightner and several friends began the tedious work of untangling a massive social problem (it was estimated that alcohol was involved in 60% of fatal crashes in 1980). By researching the issue, MADD was able to understand the complexity of the system that allowed, and in many instances encouraged, individuals to drive when impaired. They were also able to get a sense of just how big the problem was. Using this research and heartfelt messages of lost loved ones, they gathered attention and built a coalition of concerned individuals. They garnered media attention and the attention of lawmakers. Local chapters were started in communities around the country. These chapters were the backbone of volunteers that provided support to grieving families and fueled the desire to change the system. They took the message to the White House and ultimately gained the support of President Reagan, who signed the Uniform Drinking Age Act in July 1984. They also confronted major corporations that resisted regulations on alcohol use and availability. The growth and success was not without struggles and challenges that strained management capabilities and the volunteer spirit. MADD reflects the continued professionalization of interest groups. The organization that started as a grassroots social movement is now a multimillion dollar organization with complex organizational structures and formalized strategic priorities. The policy accomplishments are impressive, and the outcomes of those policies also seem to have substantially benefited society (Eisenberg, 2003). Alcohol-related fatalities have been significantly curtailed, and the work to address underage drinking and driving also seems to have shown positive impacts for driver safety. MADD reflects both the challenges and benefits of active involvement in policy activities.

Advocacy and Political Strategy

This chapter covers activities that are intended to produce public benefits by influencing and modifying institutional practices and social norms. These activities can be conceptualized as advocacy or corporate political strategy. Advocacy refers to a range of activities that organizations participate in to shape public policy (Reid, 2000). There are three distinct "targets" of advocacy work. First, nonprofits can work to organize and mobilize community members. Second, nonprofits can engage public institutions to influence policy creation and implementation. Finally, nonprofits can confront private entities so as to influence how they function and operate. For instance, environmental organizations target companies and businesses that are operating in a way that the nonprofit perceives as threatening or damaging to the environment.

Advocacy can be defined as "support for an idea or issue" (Avner, 2010, p. 349) or "the act of pleading for or against a cause, as well as supporting or recommending a position" (Hopkins, 1992, p. 32). Advocacy is "any attempt to influence the decisions of any institutional elite on behalf of a collective interest" (Jenkins, 2006, p. 297). Nonprofits use advocacy-type activities to influence public opinion, engage constituents, guide the creation and implementation of rules and laws, and influence corporations to behave in ways that align with the interests of the nonprofit. These types of activities are important because it is often not possible to achieve mission objectives solely by providing services. At times it is necessary to change social, political, and economic systems to reallocate resources, change norms and beliefs, change behaviors of individuals and institutions, or create rules that support the priorities of the nonprofit. Negotiating the social and political context to influence stakeholder perceptions about the organization and the "cause" is vital for organizational and social performance. The next section further defines lobbying as a type of advocacy activity and then discusses a couple of different organizational forms that nonprofits can utilize to achieve social and policy objectives.

Background

Lobbying is a type of advocacy. Lobbying is "asking elected officials or others who can make policy decisions to act in a particular way on a specific policy proposal" (Avner, 2010, p. 351). The Center for Lobbying in the Public Interest defines lobbying as "a specific, legally defined activity that involves stating your position on specific legislation to legislators and/or asking them to support your position"(*Make a Difference for Your Cause*, 2006). There are two types: (1) direct lobbying, stating positions on specific legislation to legislators; and (2) grassroots lobbying, communicating with the public on specific legislation to invite them to contact their elected representative. This chapter discusses direct lobbying activities in relation to public entities. Grassroots lobbying is discussed in relation to community organizing and public education initiatives that are targeted at community members and significant stakeholders.

501(c)(3) organizations can indeed engage in advocacy activities, but there are some restrictions on the range and type of activities that are allowed. Many of the educational strategies discussed later are not considered lobbying. Only the direct involvement in the political process, especially campaigns, and direct lobbying of law makers is restricted. It is not necessary to get into the nitty-gritty of legal guidelines; a list of resources is provided at the end of the chapter. Fundamentally, the U.S. government does not want charitable donations diverted to political purposes (Reid, 2006). The laws can be confusing and complex. One alternative is to join a collaborative or use a different organizational form, which allows more active and unlimited participation in political elections and lobbying activities. A common alternative form is 501(c)(4), for social welfare organizations, which do not benefit from tax-deductible contributions. Many major nonprofit organizations in the United States operate as both a 501(c)(3) and a 501(c)(4). These "social welfare" organizations have more leeway in how they engage in the political process while still gaining some benefits of the nonprofit status (see **Table 9-1**).

The other common organizational form is member and trade associations (often 501[c][6], but not always), and these are discussed below as an option available to nonprofits in implementing political activities. There are other organizational classifications (527s, labor unions 501[c][5]s), but it is not absolutely necessary to discuss all these variations of legal formation. The intent is to explore strategic options to influence institutional

TABLE 9-1   Comparison of 501(c)(3) Versus 501(c)(4) Organizations

Description	501(c)(3) Charitable Organizations	501(c)(4) Social Welfare Organizations
Key tax rules	May receive deductible contributions. No federal gift tax on contributions.	Tax-exempt but contributors do not receive deduction. Donor may owe federal gift tax on contributions over $10,000. Organizations taxed on investment income to the extent of electioneering expenditures.
Permitted activities	Charitable and educational activities, including public education, and lobbying (for public charities).	May engage in any activity permitted for a 501(c)(3) organization, plus any activity that serves public purposes, such as lobbying and advocacy in the public interest.
Is lobbying allowed?	Public charities: Yes, to a limited extent—subject either to the substantial or expenditure test. Private foundations: No lobbying allowed.	Yes, lobbying may even be the organization's exclusive activity.
What campaign-related activities are allowed?	Nonpartisan voter registration, voter education, and get-out-the-vote efforts. Campaign intervention is strictly prohibited.	May engage in nonpartisan activities. May engage in electioneering as long as it is not the organization's primary activity.

Modified from Reid, E. J. (2006). Nonprofit advocacy and political participation. In E. Boris & C. E. Steuerie (Eds.), *Nonprofits and government: Collaboration and conflict* (pp. 357–360). Washington, DC: Urban Institute.

actors and to engage the general public in political and social action. It is true that at times the engagement in advocacy can appear legally confusing, but there is tremendous opportunity, and in many ways a responsibility, for nonprofits to attend to the political and social context. Furthermore, the enactment of political and social priorities can be fulfilled through alliances with other organizations—whether a 501(c)(4) or 501(c)(6)— trade, professional organization, or a labor union. The chapter introduces the strategic decisions managers should consider in this area and introduces some of the operational techniques managers can use to fulfill their strategic priorities.

Key Decisions in Developing a Social and Political Strategy

Nonprofits need to consider four key decision areas (see **Table 9-2**). The areas range from high-level strategic decisions regarding overall approach to tactical decisions about targets and methods to achieve social and organizational objectives. While there is a logical progression from high-level decisions on approach to tactical decisions about methods, there are various instances when the questions answered at an operational level are going to have implications for overall approach. Though each of these areas is discussed separately, they interact and inform each other. Furthermore, responses will shift based on the issues under consideration.

TABLE 9-2 Strategic Decisions in Advocacy Activities

Decision Areas	Options and Considerations
Approach to political activities	Reactive versus proactive
	Autonomously versus collectively
Select and prioritize issues	Describe the problem
	Understand the different sides of the issue
	Consider costs and benefits
	Learn leverage points
	Ascertain the stage of policy action
Prioritize targets	Community members
	Public entities
	Private entities
Determine strategy	Educating and mobilizing community members
	Influencing the policy agenda and monitoring implementation
	Shifting activities and practices of corporations

Approach to Political Action

This section explores decisions that organizations have to make regarding their overall approach to advocacy and political action. Two broad areas are discussed as overarching strategic questions. The first area addresses that organizations tend to be either reactive or more proactive. The second area relates to how organizations implement those strategies and whether they operate more or less autonomously (single-entity initiatives) or more collectively (multiple organizational initiatives).

Reactive Versus Proactive

There are different schools of thought regarding the most appropriate way for organizations to approach advocacy and political activities (Hillman & Hitt, 1999). The reactive approach addresses social or political issues as they evolve. As issues arise, organizations respond to address those concerns. So, as budget cuts are discussed at the state capital, for example, nonprofit managers recognize that policy decisions will impact their ability to provide services, and they mobilize to mute the impact of those potential budget cuts. This reaction is appropriate and at times unavoidable. An alternative approach, taking a proactive stance, requires long-term perspective to systematically prioritize and deal with policy issues. This approach requires monitoring policy issues and actively crafting a political and social agenda. It is typically based on relationships with individuals and institutions. These relationships form the basis of advocacy initiatives and alert nonprofits to potential concerns or priorities. From a strategic decision standpoint, nonprofits are more likely to be effective if they are able to build the infrastructure of proactive advocacy (Independent Sector, 2012), but these capabilities are complex and costly.

There are a number of factors that will influence how nonprofits approach political action. Dependence on different institutional actors is a factor that will affect political action. For instance, nonprofits that rely on government funding are more likely to take an engaged and relational stance in trying to modify and influence allocation practices (O'Regan &

Oster, 2002). Nonprofits that are less dependent on government funding might be more likely to take a transactional (reactive) approach to engage government entities as issues arise that are related to their mission or purpose. Organizational purpose is also likely to influence participation in advocacy. For instance, environmental organizations are typically more likely to engage in advocacy-type activities and consequently may employ both transactional and relational approaches.

In 2000, the Center for Lobbying in the Public Interest surveyed nonprofit organizations to investigate factors that influence nonprofits' engagement in advocacy. The Strengthening Nonprofit Advocacy Project (SNAP) (Bass, Arons, Guinane, & Carter, 2007) found several factors that influence whether nonprofits will participate in advocacy (see **Table 9-3**). Larger organizations are more likely to engage in advocacy activities and may have a designated staff member who is primarily responsible for

TABLE 9-3 Factors Influencing Participation in Advocacy

	Likely Participators	Not Likely Participators
Mission/industry	Health, environment, social actions	Arts, recreations, religious, philanthropic
Budget	Bigger budget	Smaller budget
Staffing	Someone responsible for government relations	No staff person or volunteer assigned to government relations
Source of funds	Multiple funding sources	Single funding source
Type of funding	Foundation and government funding	Other types of funding
Membership	Has members	No membership
Trade or professional association membership	Joins associations and coalitions that engage in public policy	Does not join associations and coalition that engage in public policy
Connection between advocacy and mission	Sees advocacy as important to protecting programs and serving constituents	Views advocacy as a diversion from organizational mission and impairs service delivery

government relations. The existence of members is also indicative of a propensity to engage in political activities. So is the tendency to join groups or associations that engage in public policy. The process of bringing together common interests and advocating for those interests is central to what member benefit organizations often try to accomplish. Member benefit organizations can help define issue concerns as well as engage in active lobbying. This allows member entities to focus on services while supporting political action.

The final indicator relates to how nonprofits define and perceive their role and mission. If nonprofit managers can perceive how engagement in policy and advocacy activities is instrumental to achieving mission objectives then, of course, they are more likely to allocate resources (time and money) to implement these practices. Many 501(c)(3) nonprofits primarily define themselves as service organizations without an active political agenda. They frame their work as meeting direct needs and interests of service beneficiaries. Using advocacy methods requires nonprofit managers to see the connection between direct service activities and advocacy in political contexts. For a service-oriented nonprofit, elevating the conversation to recognize system and institutional forces can be difficult. Consider, for instance, an art museum that specializes in period art pieces. The focus and expertise of museum staff is related to curating, preserving the art, and educating community members. Recognizing how social attitudes about art affect their work is difficult. Asking staff to attend to decision making in city hall or the state house can be a significant shift in thinking. Again, this might be the role of a membership group that brings together all arts organizations in the region and then engages in some of the advocacy and public education activities. It is potentially beneficial for all nonprofits to see their work as not only operating in direct services but also elevating those concerns to the political and social context.

Autonomously Versus Collectively

Another question about organizational approach relates to how the nonprofit plans to implement political activities. Is the organization going to operate more or less independently or are they going to participate in a coordinated multiorganizational initiative? Coordinated initiatives can take a variety of forms, but they all reflect organized efforts among two or more entities to operate cooperatively in the sociopolitical domain. Trade and professional associations are examples of collective entities that might facilitate coordinated political action (Balassiano & Chandler, 2010). Each method has its advantages and disadvantages. Operating independently allows the organization to focus exclusively on their interests and concerns. They can prioritize and focus the message to reflect concerns that are central to their priorities. On the other hand, it can be costly and time-consuming to build and sustain an advocacy initiative independently. Organizations can also potentially access a broad base of support through multiorganizational initiatives, which are often more powerful than individual institutional efforts. These options (autonomous versus collective action) are not exclusive, and nonprofits can join coalitions geared toward particular issues and then move independently as other issues become pressing (Independent Sector, 2012). The next section discusses three overarching strategies that organizations can use to influence the political process. If an entity has the financial wherewithal to mount a full-scale approach it can be quite effective operating autonomously. Large organizations are more capable of implementing individual initiatives. They can afford both human and financial capital requirements. This allows the organization to control messages and prioritize their issues. Collective action allows organizations to off-load some of the specialized skills to an independent entity that can help carry out these activities. The task of defining and prioritizing policy and social issues is complex. Shared or cooperative initiatives may facilitate an organization's engagement by overcoming resource barriers.

Select and Prioritize Issues

Issue definition is the primary method to focus and direct advocacy activities. Issue identification is the process of defining and understanding the issue or "problem" that the nonprofit wishes to address. Using information from an intensive needs assessment that explores causes of social problems can be instrumental in framing social issues. Advocacy activities are targeted at resolving the issue and how it is defined. Preliminary background research often reveals a number of subtleties that might not always be obvious. Organizations must determine which issues they will prioritize and which aspects of the social issue they will address. The nonprofit's mission is central to identifying issues. Inherent in defining issues is the fact that they are informed by concerns of organizational priorities.

Thorough research of an issue entails describing the size, scope, and features of the issue. The process of gathering secondary and primary data, conducting analysis, and developing and reviewing countless reports to get a handle on issues is critical to the success of an initiative. The definitions of social issues also arise from the concerns of constituents. Professionals actively try to define issues, and they also listen to and understand the concerns of constituents (Pilisuk, McAllister, & Rothman, 1996). The case summary of MADD provides a good illustration of how defining and unpacking issues helps identify methods to engage constituents. MADD identified the prevalence of drunk drivers as the focus of their activities. As they further defined and understood the issue, they realized there were several layers to the issue, including inconsistent enforcement, lax laws, and social norms that accepted and tolerated drunk driving. MADD gathered data to help educate others on the size and depth of the problem. This research identified a number of potential leverage points where MADD constituents could apply pressure to shift practices, laws, and enforcement.

A prominent news story or a particularly tragic case can move issues to the forefront of public attention. The case of Chelsea's Law in California is an example of how a particularly tragic rape and murder of a teenage girl can galvanize public support for highly punitive laws that, in many ways, do not address the *real* problem (Libby, 2012). The desire for action can run counter to appropriate interventions that balance costs and benefits. Through research, it is possible to understand the aspects of the issue that are amenable to action. Some issues may seem simple or straightforward, but rarely do others outside the industry understand those concerns in the same way industry experts do. Furthermore, obvious solutions might exist, but implementation will require cooperation from others outside the organization. If implementation did not require such cooperation, why would we need advocacy? There are few "simple" solutions with complex social issues, but easier interventions may exist. As a result, the process of research and prioritization is intended to identify those actions, how to put them into place, who needs to be involved, and how much it will cost. Policy activities inherently have costs, and organizations must understand who is likely to bear that cost. One feature of a successful policy tactic is to have clear and easily identifiable winners while having fewer or more-ambiguous losers (Independent Sector, 2012).

A fundamental feature of most advocacy activities is the existence of conflict. There are different ideas about how issues should be defined and what kinds of solutions will be the most effective. That is why it is a *political* process. There are competing agendas, ideas about how to move those agendas forward, and limited resources. It is inherently messy and at times controversial and risky. It requires the nonprofit to take a position, articulate a justification, and move issues toward the desired solution. In the case of identifying winners and losers, sometimes a nonprofit can be instrumental in putting a face and story to the "losers." Defining the individuals and communities that will pay the cost of policy objectives can be quite powerful as political decision makers rarely want to alienate significant constituencies.

Research activities also help understand the "stage" of the issue in relation to political elites and the general public. Lobbying and advocacy activities follow three basic stages. First, those participating in advocacy activities must have an awareness and knowledge regarding the issue. Of concern is the level of awareness among policy decision makers, the general public, and the media. Is the issue even on the agenda of policy makers? Once an issue gains attention, efforts shift to influencing decision making and policy options. How are the targets (community members, policy makers, or corporations) going to respond, and what strategies will they deploy to identify and prioritize solutions? This phase is crucial as it requires careful monitoring and attention to the actions of multiple constituencies. The final phase (although it's not quite that simple) relates to ramifications of decisions and actions (or inaction). During this phase, nonprofits monitor progress or they seek to redefine the issue and raise concerns anew. This "life-cycle" of issues repeats as priorities are identified and championed (Bigelow et al., 1996). Organizations modify and use tactics based on the stage of the issue. They prioritize different activities and targets depending on how the issue is defined and conceptualized.

Prioritize Targets

There are three primary targets of nonprofit advocacy activities: community members, public entities, and private entities (see **Table 9-4**). Advocacy activities targeted at community members have several objectives including raising awareness about a social problem or issue, shifting perceptions about appropriate behavior, and trying to unite and mobilize constituents into action to influence other targets (government or corporations). Public entities can be the focus of political action. This is a common focus of many advocacy and lobbying activities and includes all levels of public entities: local governments, oversight

TABLE 9-4   Targets and Objectives of Advocacy

Target	Objectives: What Is Intended to Change?
Community members, general public, and key stakeholders	Knowledge, awareness, attitudes, social capital, social norms, behavior, and engagement
Public entities	Election results, resource allocation, law creation, policy implementation, regulatory action, and enforcement behavior
Private entities	Organizational practices related to product development, labor, distribution, and so on; support for social policies; industry standards

boards, county government, state and federal government. The objectives in this area relate to influencing all phases of the legislative and governing processes, including attempts to influence election results, shift allocation practices, and guide the creation and implementation of laws and policies. There are also advocacy-type activities targeted at private institutions. Private institutions are the target of advocacy activities when their activities may negatively impact priorities of the nonprofit. This includes environmental practices, consumer rights, and labor issues. The next section explores these targets and the tactics nonprofits can utilize to achieve objectives.

Advocacy Strategies

To influence targets and achieve objectives, nonprofits need to elevate their power. Political and social processes are complex and multifaceted, but entities with more social power have more influence in these contexts. How those in power exert their influence depends on the issue. Power is the ability to exert influence in the actions and decisions of others. Organizations can gain influence through financial resources that can more or less buy the attention of key stakeholders. Alternatively, organizations can gain influence by increasing their social power (see **Table 9-5**). The first principle of social power relates to elevating bargaining

TABLE 9-5 Sources of Social Power

Source of Power	Key Issues
Coordinated action	Joining constituents together can increase bargaining power.
Set the policy agenda	Ability to guide and structure policy discussion.
Creation of shared norms	Create a sense of shared understanding and assumptions regarding social issues.

Data from Speer, P. W., & Hughey, J. (1995). Community organizing: An ecological route to empowerment and power. *American Journal of Community Psychology*, 23(5), 729.

clout (Speer & Hughey, 1995). The power to influence political decisions increases when nonprofits can organize constituents and other entities around particular social issues. Coordinated and organized activities, compared to those of individual actors, fundamentally increase influence. This is why community and grassroots organizing is critical to the advocacy puzzle.

The second source of influence relates to the ability to set the agenda or frame issues for discussion. If an entity can influence what gets discussed and how that topic is discussed, they can exhibit significant influence in policy areas. Agenda-setting power comes from external pressure exerted through public opinion and an organization's internal access to decision makers. Nonprofits gain access by providing valuable information to decision makers (Hillman & Hitt, 1999). That information includes policy options and guidance about the preferences of key constituents. A nonprofit's ability to place concerns on the policy agenda is partially influenced by the type of information they can provide.

The third source of power originates from shared norms and consensus regarding the ever-changing state of social rules and principles of accepted behaviors. Global warming is an example of how attitudes and beliefs regarding the existence and potential causes of global warming have shifted over time. The ability to influence and shift the assumptions about social issues is powerful but difficult. Shared norms are often based on philosophies about human behavior and society, which can be difficult to shift and alter. Shared norms are powerful because they exclude certain questions based on a sense of shared/popular consensus. If certain beliefs about society are assumed to be "true" then they are less likely to be questioned and evaluated in political debates and policy making. Social power (Speer & Hughey, 1995) provides the basis for understanding the tactics that nonprofits can use to elevate social issues onto the policy agenda and influence the process of enacting policy. Using the target and objectives presented earlier (see Table 9-4) facilitates the discussion of these tactics. The next section is organized according to the different objectives and tactics, which focus on particular targets.

Educating and Mobilizing Community Members

In relation to the community members and the general public as a target of initiatives, two activities are discussed (see **Table 9-6**). The first is public education and awareness initiatives; the second is community organizing tactics. Public education and awareness intend to increase understanding of social issues and potentially the work of the nonprofit (Randolph & Viswanath, 2004). Drawing on experiences in public health provides some key principles that are likely to improve success. Public education campaigns are expensive, and when compared to the corporate marketing tactics, public interest educational initiatives are just fractions of the mass media messaging present in society (Pallotta, 2008). It is important to gain sufficient exposure with the target audience. Defining the recipient of the message facilitates determinations regarding messages and methods so as to gain sufficient access. The use of social media also is instrumental in lower-cost promotional activities.

The KONY 2012 initiative spearheaded by Invisible Children is an example of a successful viral video that garnered more than 3 million supporters ("KONY 2012," n.d.). The KONY 2012 initiative also demonstrated another important feature of successful public education initiatives, and that is a comprehensive system

TABLE 9-6   Educating and Mobilizing Community Members

Activities	Methods and Strategies
Public education	Increasing awareness of social issues
	Promoting behaviors
	Targeting subpopulations
Community organizing	Individual and organizational entities
	Understand issues from constituents' perspective
	Increase awareness
	Build social capital among constituents
	Create systems to engage
	Careful use of mobilization initiatives

of supportive structures. Invisible Children has a comprehensive campus network of both high school and college-age students that are active in fundraising and grassroots engagement. There were a number of easy and often local options to support the desired response. Another key aspect of public education tactics is the content of the message, which should be based on the best available empirical and behavior knowledge. The nonprofit should position itself as a content expert and credible source of information, consequently, accuracy in the public benefit message is important. This was a point of contention with the KONY 2012 message, as some constituencies felt the message misrepresented their interests (Roopanarine, 2012). The final aspect of public education initiatives is ongoing monitoring and tracking of message components and receptivity among target audiences. Broad-based public education initiatives are probably beyond the scope of most nonprofits and they are not without risk, but targeted and focused educational initiatives are absolutely in the purview of many nonprofits, and they can serve as a critical tactic in sociopolitical domain (Andreasen & Kotler, 2008).

The next area to consider is how to form coalitions. Organizing and coordinating constituency groups elevates social power. This includes community organizing activities that attempt to form coalitions of individuals, and it also includes activities to bring together organizational entities to create broad-based institutional support. These activities can influence both the ability to set the agenda for policy discussions as well as the creation of shared norms among members. Grassroots advocacy efforts attempt to "shape public opinion and mobilize individuals and collective action" (Reid, 1999, p. 298). It is "the most essential of the strategies central to effective nonprofit advocacy to achieve short-term and long-term policy reforms" (Avner, 2010, p. 367). Through grassroots organizing, people can improve their leadership, emphasize specific communal issues, and increase the base supported by the nonprofit. President Obama worked as a community organizer in Chicago. He described the effect that grassroots organizing can have: "It holds the power to make politicians, agencies and corporations more responsive to community needs. Equally important, it enables people to break their crippling isolation from each other, to reshape their mutual values and expectations and rediscover the possibilities of acting collaboratively—the prerequisites for any successful self-help initiative" (Obama, 1988).

There are multiple facets to community building, but it is possible to distill a few key features that facilitate success (Guierrez & Lewis, 2012; Speer & Hughey, 1995). It is important to gather input from constituents to understand their concerns, priorities, and issues that they seek to address. Community members will not engage in issues that are not central to their concerns. The next feature is public education regarding the issue. Educational initiatives carry various messages including information about the problem as well as strategies to mitigate the concerns. The third area is related to building social capital among community members. Community organizing is about building the capacity of individuals and communities. Individuals' commitment to the issue or cause is important and their social connections are significant factors that support engagement. The fourth area relates to building systems and mechanisms to engage participants. This entails building the infrastructure to support community members as well as the communication methods to connect members. Communication practices are enabled by information and technology systems that have transformed methods of engaging community members (Hanna, 2010). There are a number of basic systems of volunteer coordination that are required for organized engagement. The final area for consideration is engagement and participation. When should community members be mobilized and in what way should they participate? These practices to engage and coordinate community members are critical for support and enactment in many of the other aspects of advocacy.

Grassroots organizing is not the root of all political action but it forms a vital source of power and legitimacy that is instrumental for success in many areas. Nonprofits need to understand which group/community is interested and willing to rally support. The support doesn't just materialize because it is important; it takes care and feeding to build support and social connections that are resilient. To effectively advocate through grassroots, organizations need to have a strong base of participants. The local health services center is unlikely to drum up support for their issues unless they have strong support from the community. If they decide one day to attempt to advocate, they would likely fail unless they have sustained an active base of support.

Influencing the Policy Agenda and Monitoring Implementation

There are numerous methods to influence the policy discussion. These activities are typically conceptualized as lobbying, but they entail a broad range of tactics that involve direct engagement in policy making as well as information and research activities that form the backbone of knowledge that guides advocacy activities. One way to organize these activities is to think about the political, legislative, and regulatory process from the beginning to the end (see **Table 9-7**). The "beginning" is the process of electing or appointing policy makers. The middle steps are associated with creating laws, policies, and rules that will be enacted either through administrative or legislative action. The "end" of the process entails implementation of these policies and the tedious work of creating and interpreting how the rules will be carried out. It is not quite that simple, but the three areas provide a framework to consider nonprofit advocacy activities.

TABLE 9-7   Influencing the Policy Process

Stages	Example Activities
Election-related activities	Registering voters
	Endorsing candidates
Policy and rule making	Lobbying
	Agenda setting
	Policy making
Monitoring implementation	Watchdog groups
	Legal action
	Evaluation

Election-Related Activities

Efforts to influence elections and participation of constituents have a long history in nonprofit advocacy work. Nonprofits have been active in promoting voter rights as well as ensuring that voters have access to polls. This includes monitoring election practices and employing a whole range of activities intended to educate voters about the issues. There are different threads of activity in this area and many nonprofits are anxious about too much activity in this area given the restrictions on charity lobbying. There is also risk associated with involvement in election results. If nonprofits are perceived as too partisan, it can come back to threaten nonprofit survival. Often nonprofits seek to provide information about the candidates and the issues without necessarily promoting a particular candidate ("Preaching Politics," 2010). These activities take place throughout the levels of government, from local through federal systems, and many nonprofits play critical roles in educating community members in localized elections. These election-related activities link directly to the coalition activities just described because the ability to mobilize voters demonstrates the influence and potential power of the nonprofit.

Direct Lobbying

Engagement in policy making through lobbying entails efforts to frame the discussion so as to ensure that topics and issues salient to the nonprofit are indeed discussed (Jenkins, 2006). In some cases, lobbying activities work to keep items off the agenda (Jenkins, 2006). For instance, on the federal level, nonprofit groups are quite vocal in keeping discussions about removing deductions on charitable contributions off the table. The process is called agenda setting, and it happens in two ways. It can be exerted through external pressure (e.g., protests and high-profile media attention) and it can come from gaining access to decision makers—internal influence. Access to decision makers is facilitated by three factors: interpersonal relationships, financial incentives, or the ability to provide information that helps guide decision makers. Interpersonal and social ties provide access to decision makers. This was discussed as a fundamental decision in how an organization is going to approach advocacy. Is the organization going to be reactive and exert influence from the outside, or proactive to develop the relationships that provide access to key decision makers? Financial influence comes in the form of political campaign contributions and other perks, such as offering employment following political service, that are often highly regulated. Information that educates decision makers on how their constituents feel about certain issues is very valuable to decision makers and can be used to gain access to policy discussions (Hillman & Hitt, 1999).

External efforts seek to elevate issues so as to force action by institutional actors. Grassroots mobilization efforts such as asking constituents to call their congressman or legislator can be quite influential. Protests can have mixed results because the media portrayal of those actions is critical to influencing action. Media attention also can be very influential in policy discussions (Wallack & Dorfman, 1996). Media outlets are inherently difficult to control and nonprofits need to actively work to frame messages so as to capture the attention of news outlets. Media outlets do not want to be manipulated and are unwilling to be the mouthpiece of advocacy groups. Attention-grabbing news articles are absolutely necessary and nonprofit groups must consider how to use the media to reflect the systemic issues as well as the personal trauma resulting from decisions that might capture popular media outlets. While the number of media outlets continues to grow, social media outlets can also be quite powerful to motivate action. However, managing and guiding those messages can require a great amount of time and resources.

Internal activities, as well, are instrumental in guiding policy discussions. Access to decision makers is fundamental to successful lobbying initiatives. This access is costly and difficult to acquire. Federal efforts are awash with financial incentives and backroom deals that seem well beyond the operations of most nonprofits. National-level organizations do actively engage in various efforts to garner the attention of government officials. Lobbying and access take place at state and local levels as well. Attention to school board and city council discussions and decisions can be just as important for many nonprofits. In addition to money, information is the other currency that can guide these conversations. Nonprofits can be active in providing key information and knowledge that informs and guides decision makers. The existence of "facts" is not the only kind of information policy makers need; they also need information that helps them understand their constituencies. This is a critical role that nonprofits can often uniquely fulfill. Taking on pharmaceutical companies dollar for dollar is probably well beyond the ability of most nonprofit entities, but gathering the sentiments of members and voicing those sentiments to decision makers can have significant implications.

Personal relationships are critical if nonprofits want to influence the policy-making process. It might be possible to elevate significant policy concerns through media and active constituents, but participation in the rule-making process also benefits from careful attention to the nuts and bolts of committee work. Working to create rules that fulfill advocacy objectives requires attention and specialized knowledge of how budgeting and allocation practices are carried out. There are countless steps and processes that lobbying groups must monitor. Without reliable internal relationships, most groups cannot be aware of the decisions and potential actions that might occur. Lobbyists must actively nurture relationships to be knowledgeable of current and potential action. Furthermore, these relationships facilitate sharing information and research that is necessary for crafting legislation. The information is used to craft language for legislation and to bring solutions to the table. Neither of these can be accomplished without the existence of working relationships.

Implementation and Monitoring of Policy

Advocacy groups can also actively monitor the implementation of policy rules. Environmental groups, for instance, allocate significant resources to monitor the actions of the Environmental Protection Agency and the associated actors throughout the system all the way to the local level (Jenkins, 2006). Nonprofit watchdog groups are critical to ensure that policies and rules are enacted and enforced. They gather important information and data on the implications of these practices. Nonprofit groups are often active in tracking the impact of policy decisions and they use this information to further engage constituents. Legal action is an option and some nonprofit groups will rely on courts to force action on certain legislation or challenge the legality of current practices. Litigation is most effective at stopping undesired behaviors and when used in conjunction with other lobbying efforts can be effective at moving legislative issues forward. Gaining the attention of legislators is increasingly competitive. Numerous nonprofit groups and industry groups are active in the process and gaining attention requires coordinated and sustained effort that blends outside agitation and internal access to achieve political success.

Shifting the Activities and Practices of Corporations

Private corporations and industry trade groups can also be the focus of nonprofit advocacy activities. Consumer markets and global corporations are instrumental actors in many issues that are of salience to nonprofit groups. Environmental concerns are often a focus of attention, but nonprofit groups can raise attention for labor practices and product safety. These activities range from attempts to shift consumer behaviors (e.g., boycotts) to reward or punish corporations that are potentially engaged in practices counter to the nonprofit's mission, to alliances that allow nonprofits to influence organizational practices and industry standards. One of the fundamental tools in the nonprofit advocacy toolbox is engaging constituencies in organized and targeted efforts to influence institutional action. Most corporations are sensitive to bad publicity and most strive to reflect some aspect of corporate citizenship, at least in the public realm. As a result, nonprofit groups often highlight corporate behaviors they find unacceptable. Mobilizing consumers and media to draw attention to corporate malfeasance can be effective. Translating consumer frustrations into tangible, corporate actions is the critical element in facilitating the desired transitions. Corporations operate in complex multistakeholder environments, and they balance pressure from media, regulatory bodies, advocacy groups, and market forces (Waldron, Navis, & Fisher, 2012). Nonprofits also use legal action to control the actions of corporations (see **Table 9-8**). There are countless examples of how courts can intervene. While courts can intervene to curtail inappropriate corporate actions, multinational corporations are massive and powerful entities that can often overpower the judicial system.

Nonprofit organizations must see corporations holistically to achieve the desired outcomes. Doing so allows nonprofits to engage in confrontational as well as cooperative activities that can be mutually beneficial. Nonprofits desire social outcomes as well as increased organizational legitimacy and resource stability. Alliance with corporations can be tricky, but if managed appropriately, nonprofits can facilitate socially desirable outcomes while gaining presence in consumer markets. Nonprofits can challenge corporations from the "outside" and they can operate cooperatively to foster changes in institutional practices from the "inside."

TABLE 9-8 Shifting the Activities and Practices of Corporations

Tactics	Issues
Increase public awareness	Help constituents understand corporate practices.
Mobilize consumers (punish/reward)	Careful consideration of when and how to engage constituents. Sustaining interest is difficult.
Legal action	Costly and long, involved process. Need for substantial technical expertise.
Alliances with corporations	Potential to "sell-out" in favor of legitimacy or financial incentives. Potential to influence through increased association with powerful corporations.
Influence industry standards	Difficult to gain access from the "outside." Significant potential to influence industry norms.

Another channel of activity focuses on the quasi-institutional entities that create and monitor industry standards. In addition to government regulatory bodies, corporations create and comply with industry-created standards and accreditation practices. These trade and industry groups balance competitive interests and attend to the complex interrelationship among producers, suppliers, regulators, and buying groups to create, modify, and often enforce industry practices. Nonprofit advocacy groups can target these institutional entities to expand their influence beyond an individual corporation to influence industry-wide practices. As with all these tactics, there are multiple and conflicting priorities and actors and nonprofit groups should be knowledgeable of the process and prioritize potential leverage points. It is not always clear how these practices are enacted and enforced, and prioritizing particular targets facilitates success in messaging and social outcomes.

Conclusion

There are a number benefits nonprofits can obtain through strategic use of sociopolitical activities. Working with the city or school board to encourage funding for particular beneficiary groups is just one level of engagement in political and social advocacy. Exclusive focus on service-based programs and activities is unlikely to achieve all of the mission objectives of the nonprofit. Recognizing the institutional and systemic forces that create, support, or allow social issues and concerns to persist is absolutely in the realm of tasks nonprofits should address. Engagement of community members through coalition building is likely to foster social power and organizational legitimacy. Social media can, at times, dramatically mobilize constituents, but that does not circumvent the need for old-school grassroots organizing. The strength of interpersonal relationships to motivate participation is critical for sustained action among members. The commitment of community members provides a unique competitive advantage that is the basis for action in successful campaigns. Connecting with community members regarding social issues and engaging those members is, in some ways, one of the most important elements of nonprofit success. Those members are willing to support the nonprofit in multiple ways. This includes financial contributions and voluntary labor, both of which strengthen organizational action and contribute to organizational survival. One of the conclusions is that nonmarket actors are going to be instrumental to organizational success. Managers should build systems that engage those actors. This will facilitate the production of social outcomes and impact.

Achieving these benefits is not all roses and sunshine. There a number of challenges that can thwart work in this area. Building coalitions is long-term, hard work, especially if social bonds among constituents are limited, as is often the case. Social issues and rational arguments bring together concerned citizens, but long-standing engagement is supported by social relationships, which are not easily created, sustained, or controlled. Consequently, nonprofits can find that these activities take a tremendous amount of effort that strains organizational resources. With pressure for performance and impact, long-term constituency building can be relegated to the back burner of organizational activities. These initiatives take time, and it can be difficult to document tangible outcomes. These activities, if focused around mission priorities, can galvanize constituents, but to do so organizations must clearly prioritize mission objectives, and such clarity can be difficult. Nonprofits operate in multiple contexts and across multiple levels, and distilling priorities and values requires consensus among organizational members that may not always be present. Furthermore, advocacy engagement requires taking a stand on issues that may be controversial. The political arena is messy and taking a position is likely to alienate some individuals. This can appear risky for organizations that don't want to alienate donors and funders. As values-based organizations that strive to achieve social benefits, nonprofit organizations should systematically assess the range of advocacy activities available to them. This often means partnering with other organizations so as to share the costs and risks.

Discussion Questions

1. In what way does community and grassroots organizing form the basis of political action for nonprofits?
2. Why should a nonprofit define and build a community of support that is ready and willing to mobilize? How would they go about doing that?
3. What specialized attributes and assets should nonprofits develop to be effective in lobbying activities?
4. What factors would you weigh as you advise a nonprofit to engage in advocacy activities?
5. Think about the choice to operate independently versus collectively. How might you advise a nonprofit about the benefits and challenges of each approach?

Additional Resources

Center for Lobbying in the Public Interest: http://www.clpi.org/
Independent Sector: http://www.independentsector.org/advocacy
Internal Revenue Service: http://www.irs.gov/Charities-&-Non-Profits /Lobbying
Minnesota Council of Nonprofits: http://www.minnesotanonprofits .org/nonprofit-resources/public-policy-advocacy/federal-law-and -nonprofit-lobbying

References

Andreasen, A. R., & Kotler, P. (2008). *Strategic marketing for non-profit organizations* (7th ed.). Upper Saddle Rover, NJ: Pearson, Prentice Hall.

Avner, M. (2010). Advocacy, lobbying, and social change. In D. Renz & R. D. Herman (Eds.), *The Jossey-Bass handbook of nonprofit leadership and management* (Vol. 18). San Francisco, CA: Jossey-Bass.

Balassiano, K., & Chandler, S. M. (2010). The emerging role of nonprofit associations in advocacy and public policy: Trends, issues, and prospects. *Nonprofit and Voluntary Sector Quarterly, 39*(5), 946–955.

Bass, G. D., Arons, D. F., Guinane, K., & Carter, M. F. (2007). *Seen but not heard: Strengthening nonprofit advocacy.* Washington, DC: Aspen Institute.

Bigelow, B., Stone, M. M., & Arndt, M. (1996). Corporate political strategy: A framework for understanding nonprofit strategy. *Nonprofit Management and Leadership, 7*(1), 29–43.

Davis, L. (2005, Fall). 25 years of saving lives. *Driven,* 8–17. Retrieved from http://www.madd.org/about-us/history/madd25thhistory.pdf

Eisenberg, D. (2003). Evaluating the effectiveness of policies related to drunk driving. *Journal of Policy Analysis and Management, 22*(2), 249–274.

Golden, M. M. (1998). Interest groups in the rule-making process: Who participates? Whose voices get heard? *Journal of Public Administration Research and Theory, 8*(2), 245–270.

Guierrez, L. M., & Lewis, E. A. (2012). Education, participation, and capacity building in community organizing. In M. Minkler (Ed.), *Community organizing and community building for health and welfare* (p. 215). New Brunswick, NJ: Rutgers University Press.

Hanna, N. (2010). *Transforming government and building the information society.* New York, NY: Springer.

Hillman, A. J., & Hitt, M. A. (1999). Corporate political strategy formulation: A model of approach, participation, and strategy decisions. *Academy of Management Review, 24*(4), 825–842.

Hopkins, B. R. (1992). *Charity, advocacy, and the law.* Hoboken, NJ: Wiley Law Publications.

Independent Sector. (2012). *Beyond the cause: The art and science of advocacy.* Washington, DC: Author.

Jenkins, J. C. (2006). Nonprofit organizations and political advocacy. In W. W. Powell & R. Steinberg (Eds.), *The nonprofit sector research handbook* (2nd ed., pp. 307–332). New Haven, CT: Yale University.

KONY 2012. (n.d.). Invisible Children. Retrieved from http://invisiblechildren.com/kony/

Libby, P. (Ed.). (2012). *The lobbying strategy handbook*. Los Angeles, CA: Sage.

Lux, S., Crook, T. R., & Woehr, D. J. (2011). Mixing business with politics: A meta-analysis of the antecedents and outcomes of corporate political activity. *Journal of Management, 37*(1), 223–247.

Make a difference for your cause. (2006). Washington, DC: Center for Lobbying in the Public Interest.

Obama, B. (1988, August/September). Why organize? Problems and promise in the inner city. *Illinois Issues*, 40–42.

O'Regan, K., & Oster, S. M. (2002). Does government funding alter nonprofit governance? Evidence from New York City nonprofit contractors. *Journal of Policy Analysis and Management, 21*(3), 359–379.

Pallotta, D. (2008). *Uncharitable: How restraints on nonprofits undermine their potential*. Medford, MA: Tufts University.

Pilisuk, M., McAllister, J., & Rothman, J. (1996). Coming together for action: The challenge of contemporary grassroots community organizing. *Journal of Social Issues, 52*(1), 15–37.

Preaching politics from the pulpit. (2010). Pew Forum. Retrieved from http://www.pewforum.org/2012/10/02/preaching-politics-from-the-pulpit-2012/

Randolph, W., & Viswanath, K. (2004). Lessons learned from public health mass media campaigns: Marketing health in a crowded media world. *Annual Review of Public Health, 25*(1), 419–437.

Reid, E. J. (1999). Nonprofit advocacy and political participation. In E. Boris & C. E. Steuerie (Eds.), *Nonprofits and government: Collaboration and conflict* (pp. 291–325). Washington, DC: Urban Institute.

Reid, E. J. (Ed.). (2000). *Structuring the inquiry into advocacy*. Washington, DC: Urban Institute.

Reid, E. J. (2006). Advocacy and the challenges it presents for nonprofits. In E. Boris & C. E. Steuerle (Eds.), *Nonprofits and government: Collaboration and conflict* (2nd ed., pp. 343–372). Washington, DC: Urban Institute.

Roopanarine, L. (2012). Kony 2012—The anti-LRA video that went viral. *The Gaurdian: Poverty Matters Blog*. Retrieved from

http://www.guardian.co.uk/global-development/poverty
-matters/2012/dec/31/kony-2012-lra-video-viral

Secrets to success. (2005, Fall). *Driven,* 23–24. Retrieved from
http://www.madd.org/about-us/history/how-madd-has
-been-successful.pdf

Speer, P. W., & Hughey, J. (1995). Community organizing: An ecological route to empowerment and power. *American Journal
of Community Psychology, 23*(5), 729.

Waldron, T., Navis, C., & Fisher, G. (2012). Explaining differences
in firms' response to activism. *Academy of Management
Review, 38*(3), 397–417.

Wallack, L., & Dorfman, L. (1996). Media advocacy: A strategy
for advancing policy and promoting health. *Health Education
& Behavior, 23*(3), 293–317.

CHAPTER **10**

Financial Resource Strategies

Learning Objectives

- ▪ Understand the issues and challenges managers confront in resource markets
- ▪ Consider how competitive forces influence resource options
- ▪ Use the features of business relationships to analyze resource options
- ▪ Employ these analysis techniques to prioritize stable and reliable resources

It almost does not matter how effective a nonprofit organization is at providing high-quality, impactful programs; if it does not have sufficient resources it will not survive. There is a link among mission performance, impact, and financial success, but that relationship is rarely direct. This chapter primarily discusses financial resource markets, but other resources are considered including in-kind gifts of services and materials. This includes both earned and donated income. Managers must address a number of issues and concerns regarding the resource market. Principles from Porter's (1998) competitive analysis model are instrumental in understanding the different forces at play in these relationships, as are a number of other issues related to stakeholder management. The chapter starts with a discussion of the key concerns nonprofit managers confront in relation to securing reliable and stable resources. There is a brief review regarding the sources and types of resources available to nonprofit managers. The features of those resources influence the nature of the relationships that are developed. It is the ability to develop and maintain relationships with funding entities that is the key to financial stability. The nature of business relationships are discussed in detail, and the methods managers can utilize to overcome the challenges and minimize risks are presented.

Issues and Challenges for Managers

Fundamentally, the resource market for nonprofit management is about gaining capacity and reducing risk. Managers seek reliable, predictable resource streams that allow for optimal internal control and utilization. The nature of nonprofit services necessitates that nonprofits operate in not only basic customer exchange relationships but more complex and ambiguous arrangements that involve third-party payers and donated resources. Each type of revenue stream provides different levels of autonomy and predictability for nonprofit managers (Grønbjerg, 1991). **Figure 10-1** illustrates the forces that confront managers in a resource market—the degree of autonomy the resource allows and the degree of predictability related to the resource. Managers want high levels of autonomy and high levels of reliability (upper-right quadrant). Reliability relates to confidence in receiving the revenue on a consistent basis (predictability). Managers need reliable, stable funds so as to effectively plan. Control or autonomy reflects the extent to which managers can use the funds more or less as they see fit to meet strategic priorities. Some funds come with significant restrictions, some of which are imposed by funders whereas others may have been negotiated by the nonprofit. Control considers how much autonomy the manager has to use the funds as they see fit and to adjust those uses over time. Managers can use

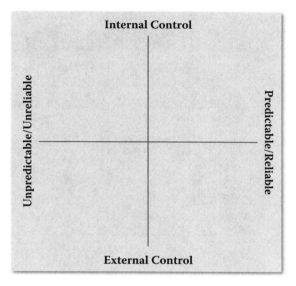

FIGURE 10-1 Matrix of Financial Resources

Figure 10-1 to map funding sources. This allows managers to evaluate funding sources and consider options to shift or modify the funding portfolio to meet organizational interests.

In addition to the preference for internal control and reliability, managers are guided by a desire to secure funds that require limited management oversight, provide sufficient cash flow, and align with the purposes of the organization (see **Table 10-1**). These issues are discussed next.

Complexity of Management

The administrative requirements of funding sources can vary substantially, and managers must be astute to the costs associated with different funders. Management complexity tends to reflect costs of using the funds or the cost of securing the funds. Management complexity issues include accountability reporting and monitoring compliance of funding expenditures. These accountability expectations can be the most stringent in regard to public funds. Effectively accounting for how dollars were utilized as well as the outcomes or benefits of those expenditures is costly. Another management cost is associated with the need for

TABLE 10-1   Resource Issues and Challenges for Managers

Issue/Challenge	Description
Autonomy	Resources can be used as the manager determines without constraints or demands from the funder.
Predictability	Resources are consistently accessible to managers and they can plan accordingly.
Complexity of management	The funds can be secured or managed without high cost.
Cash flow	There are sufficient funds available to handle day-to-day expenses.
Mission drift	The funds supplement the purposes of the organization without requiring extraneous services or activities.

extensive negotiation and preplanning. This can be the case with major gifts, which require managers to nurture relationships over the long term. This requires significant professionalized services without a clear sense of the return on those activities. Consequently, managers must consider how different revenue sources require the agency to handle reporting requirements and how difficult it is to develop relationships.

Cash Flow

Cash flow is a significant concern for many nonprofit managers and relates to having sufficient cash on hand to cover expenses on a daily basis. A couple of things contribute to poor cash flow. Some donation patterns are cyclical, where more money comes in during particular parts of the year. Without careful planning managers may be constrained when funding is less generous. Another concern is that some funds may be restricted. Restricted funds are those that can only be expended for particular purposes. If a manager has funds but is not allowed to expend those funds on pressing issues they may be inclined to forgo those arrangements because of demands to meet daily operating costs. Cash flow issues are particularly challenging for contracts that are based on reimbursement arrangements. Nonprofits are required to provide services, document expenses, and then seek payment. It is not uncommon that payments can be delayed 60 to 90 days beyond the date those services are provided or, in extreme instances, the date they are invoiced. These delays can cause significant challenges for managers as they try to meet daily operation needs. Managers may trade autonomy for predictability because reliable and consistent sources of funds help with cash flow issues, allowing managers to plan according to anticipated revenue flows.

Mission Drift

Another concern for managers relates to autonomy and how funding sources may impose priorities on the nonprofit. Do managers lose control of organizational goals based on the preferences of funders? If funders mandate activities and outcomes, nonprofit managers are required to adopt those requirements as a stipulation for accepting the funds. This will be discussed in more detail as it relates to adaptations that are required in business relationships on the part of both funders and recipients. The point here is that nonprofits have philosophical priorities that might or might not fully align to funder desires. As a result, defining how mission priorities are reinforced or obfuscated by funder goals is important. The more funding sources a nonprofit accepts, the more likely externally imposed goals may distract from mission objectives (Jonker & Meehan, 2008). In the day-to-day functioning of organizations it might be difficult to ascertain how and to what degree particular funding sources might shift organizational practices over time. Concerns regarding mission drift can be addressed by periodically using a portfolio analysis to consider issues such as mission alignment versus stability or some other criteria that is significant for nonprofit managers. This review of funding sources helps leaders consider how funding options are related to strategic priorities.

Managing Funding Resources

Given the range of resources available to nonprofits, managers and senior leadership need to evaluate and respond to the various resource options. The dominant management advice is that nonprofits should diversify their revenue sources (Carroll & Stater,

2009). They should develop a portfolio of revenue streams that complement each other. This includes earned income through fees, contributions, and investment income. A diverse portfolio of revenue options reduces the risk imposed by any one source and is more likely to create a composite revenue stream that is consistent and reliable over time. Larger organizations seem more capable to manage the dynamics of multiple revenue streams. This makes sense in that larger organizations are able to secure the specialized talent that is necessary to manage the intricacies of different revenue sources. They can more effectively manage those complexities and, consequently, benefit from the diversity of funds, which minimizes the impact of shifts or reductions in one funding source.

An interesting study revealed a potential contradiction in this advice. Researchers found that nonprofits that had grown very large (over the last 30 years) did not diversify the type of resources they secured (Foster, 2007). Rather, those nonprofits utilized a particular type of resource and became very good at meeting the needs and interests of those funders. Partly this reflects that relatively few funding options exist for nonprofits to grow into large entities. The two dominant funding sources are government funding and fees, and these sources tended to dominate the activities of really big nonprofits. The study was interesting because it excluded institutions of higher education and hospitals, which tend to rely very heavily on fees and tuition. Within a particular type of revenue source (e.g., government), however, the really big nonprofits did diversify. Those that secured the majority of their funding from governments, for example, would work with a large number of government entities and divisions. Some of the large nonprofits that they analyzed were involved in international development; consequently they would seek funds from not only the U.S. government but also from international government entities. The nonprofits tailored their activities to the needs of particular funders and developed specializations and technical competencies that minimized the costs of managing the resource.

Strategically utilizing funds allows managers to create a sustainable revenue model (Foster, Kim, & Christiansen, 2009). The next section reviews six common revenue streams in relation to the five criteria that are important to nonprofit managers (see **Table 10-2**). The classification of particular funding sources across any of these criteria is difficult because of the heterogeneity in funding markets, but the table reflects overarching tendencies. The sources are also classified as earned, donated, or mixed. Earned funds are based on an exchange arrangement. Services are provided and the customer pays for those services. Donated funds are provided with no direct service provided. This distinction between earned and donated reflects an important consideration in funding choices—the motivation of the funder. What is the desired intent or objective of different funders? In an earned-income model the interest is related to funder interests and level of services. Funders pay a fee or buy services because they have particular needs that the nonprofit can provide. Donated funds, however, address a different motivation. Donors still have needs that the nonprofit can fulfill, but they are less direct than providing a particular service. Some donors want to "give back"; some have needs related to personal identity and who they are as a person, and donating helps fulfill that need (Boenigk & Helmig, 2013). Recognizing these different interests allows managers to

TABLE 10-2   Source of Funds Compared Across Management Priorities

Source of Funds	Type	Reliable	Autonomy	Cost	Cash	Mission
Private source fee	Earned	Yes	Yes	Lower	Yes	Maybe
Third-party fee	Earned	Yes	No	High	No	Maybe
Public funds	Earned	Yes	No	High	No	Maybe
Individual donated	Donated	Maybe	Yes	Moderate	Maybe	Yes
Individual major gift	Donated	No	Maybe	High	No	Maybe
Private grants	Mix	No	Maybe	Moderate	No	Maybe

develop systems that address funder needs and thereby build more stability into the funding model. The next section briefly summarizes common funding streams and considers the dominant tendency across the six dimensions.

Private Source Fees

Private source fees are revenue generated directly from the provision of services. Individuals pay a fee to receive a particular service. This is the most common type of earned income. Reliability is dependent on the nature of competition in the service market. To be successful a nonprofit must develop a reasonable set of services that capture a particular customer market. This is a significant qualification and should not be minimized. *If* a nonprofit can do that, then they are likely to have reliable income that can be used according to the demands of the organization. Effective organizations do need to attend to customer preferences to ensure that fee-paying customers are not going to shift to an alternative provider. Private source fees can reflect positively for cash flow because services are directly linked to revenue. Private fee income requires relatively modest management over and above typical accounting. There are few external forces that will demand accountability for these funds (think fees at art museums). However, certain industries, such as health care, might have high regulatory requirements that do exert costly demands on an agency. There is some contention that a nonprofit that relies exclusively on fee-based revenue from consumers are not all that different from a for-profit business selling a service. While the nature of specific industries will influence the enactment of charitable purposes, it is reasonable to consider how revenue income might reflect the extent to which nonprofits are functioning for charitable purposes.

Third-Party Fees

The same caveat regarding the ability to operate effectively in a competitive market applies to third-party fees. If a nonprofit can secure market dominance, these funds can be quite reliable. The challenge with these funds is that third-party entities tend to exert significant power and influence in the market because they have strong buying power. They can push prices down, which exerts a demand for efficiency. Third-party entities can require significant documentation regarding payments because they are not the direct recipient of services. These entities need accountability measures to demonstrate the level and quality of services. Third-party entities tend to "reimburse" for services, and this can cause cash flow issues. Organizations often provide services prior to payment, which at times can be delayed for months. This arrangement may directly align with mission purposes, but selection of beneficiaries is partially controlled by the third-party entity that determines eligibility. This too reflects the potential loss of control that can occur in this funding context.

Public Funds

Public funds contracted to nonprofits have historically been a reliable source of funds, especially if there is some alignment between the nonprofit mission and public purposes. Typically, public entities have an agenda of priorities and perceive the nonprofit as instrumental in fulfilling their objectives. The nonprofit loses some control of their service options as public funds also tend to come with various restrictions and beneficiary requirements. Nonprofits also may have difficulty managing accountability demands as they can be tedious. Cash flow can also be a concern as these contracts are typically paid through cost reimbursement and can result in massive financial outlays that governments pay months after services are provided. As long as managers are careful in what kinds of grants they receive, the funds can be aligned with mission purposes. However, nonprofits often extend operations to access more funds and, consequently, can see shifts in mission priorities as they seek more and more funds that stretch the bounds of their mission priorities.

Individual Donations

Individual donations in and of themselves are inherently unreliable, but managers overcome the unreliability of particular donors by broadening the base of individuals who give on a regular basis.

By creating a large pool of individuals giving modest sums on a regular basis, nonprofit managers can create a fairly stable source of income that typically has few external controls. There are fairly significant costs associated with operating and managing such a fundraising system. This is partly reflected in complexity of donor interests and the need to develop systems that fulfill those interests. Nonprofits cannot address all donor motivations, so choices regarding message and target are critical. If donated funds can be secured on a regular basis, it might address cash flow concerns because donations tend to come without strings attached. Donated funds also allow managers to focus on mission purposes as the draw for funds.

Major Gifts

Major gifts are inherently unreliable. They are contingent on the preferences and interests of donors, and even on their health because some of the most significant gifts come after the death of the donor. Organizations can negotiate the amount of donor influence, but many major gifts require the nonprofit to make modifications and adjustments. The cost of securing major gifts is significant as they require substantial staff support. Major gifts should reinforce the mission, but there are numerous instances when donors have private intentions that seek to shift organizational priorities, so nonprofit managers must control for those contingencies.

Private Grants

Privately funded grants and contracts are typically perceived as less reliable. The funds are often short term and project specific. There is, however, a great deal of heterogeneity in private funding sources. Some major foundations function as highly professionalized organizations that require extensive accountability. The funds are restricted to purposes outlined in the proposal, and application procedures are competitive and rigorous. Private granting entities do not receive direct benefits in exchange for the funds provided; there are often very clear deliverable expectations that must be performed by the nonprofit. So while these funds are not technically "earned" they are provided with the expectation of clearly outlined performance expectations. Conversely, some private family foundations function and operate as an organizing system of individual or family philanthropic priorities. There are numerous instances where foundations can provide regular and consistent support to selected nonprofits. Shifting from the competitive, formalized process of grant seeking to the insider system is critical to increase reliability and autonomy. There are fairly high management requirements as these contracts can require substantive evaluations and reporting, as well as enduring the process of soliciting grant funds. Foundations do not typically require reimbursement for services, but the funds can be restricted to specific purposes, which can limit cash flow. Mission alignment depends upon careful selection of funding sources. Similar to public funds, private funds can shift mission priorities, so nonprofits should carefully select funding partners.

Methods to Analyze Funding Options

Two types of analysis are considered. First is a market analysis, which considers Porter's competitive analysis model to understand market forces and the availability of alternatives. Such analysis considers the number, range, density, and competitive demand on various resource options. Second are relationship-based analysis techniques, which consider aspects of funding relationships and how nonprofits can manage those relationships. Through market analysis managers identify potentially viable funding sources, and through relationship management managers determine the costs associated with securing funding.

Market Determinants

Managers should use the market and industry analysis techniques discussed earlier to understand industry-level factors that can influence success in the funding market. A discussion of the private foundation market might be illustrative. The number and variety of private foundations can be readily accessed through foundation directories. Using the boundary-defining attributes of mission and geographic service area allows managers to define the size of the potential resource market. The foundation directory is a sophisticated tool that helps summarize critical information about assets, prior history of grant funding, and much more. A similar analysis is possible with public funding sources. Depending on the capabilities of the nonprofit, different filters can be applied to screen funders to create a manageable list of options. This analysis defines the size of the potential funding market in a particular niche area. Not all markets are so readily defined or interpreted.

Individual donor markets are much more difficult to conceptualize and define (Sargeant, 1999). There is no readily available database of donors and their interests. Consequently, nonprofits approach the donor market from the perspective of known entities (e.g., Who has given to the nonprofit before? Who has some prior relationship with the nonprofit?). The donor market is typically defined by the operating context, but broad-based general attempts to gain additional donors can be utilized by nonprofits. In the past, these efforts were initiated through mail and phone campaigns but, increasingly, social media allows for access to a large number of potential donors. Generic descriptions of potential donors are only modestly useful as donors are motivated by specialized attributes, which are not necessarily readily apparent. Some of the generic attributes that tend to be associated with donor behavior include age, gender, and religious background. Similarly, social class and income provide a sense of how viable the donor market might be. The intrinsic determinants of why individuals give are more difficult to ascertain, but are much stronger predictors of actual behavior (Sargeant, West, & Ford, 2001). Attitudes toward the organization, the sector, and "helping others" provide significant insight into donor behavior; unpacking and understanding these attitudes, however, are quite challenging. This highlights the need for specialized and skilled staff to catalogue information, maintain relationships, and craft solicitation strategies.

Fee markets are complex and require a different set of skills and analysis when compared to donor markets, government grants, or private foundations. Fee markets require nonprofits to engage in a direct exchange of services for revenue. The introduction of third-party payment systems complicates the arrangement because nonprofits must negotiate a primary relationship with the payment agency (public or private) and then engage in practices to attract customers. Furthermore, the complexities of the competitive forces are often amplified in the fee market because many of the services suitable to this market are also offered by for-profit providers. So no longer are nonprofit entities competing for resources among other nonprofits—they are operating in an open market. Fee-resource markets are not applicable for every type of nonprofit, but considering which beneficiaries (or potential beneficiaries) have the capacity to pay for services might add a level of rigor to the services that is at times absent. Analysis of third-party entities is easier because there are typically fewer of them, which implies that those third-party entities have more power to negotiate price and service issues. Private party–fee revenue suffers from some of the challenges articulated in the donor market. Demand might be diffuse and not easily defined.

Relationship Management

Defining and analyzing the funding market opportunities is just part of understanding resource options for nonprofits. The ability to establish and nurture an ongoing relationship with funding entities is central to success. The next section considers the features of healthy business relationships. Maintaining relationships with individuals requires different competencies and capabilities than maintaining relationships with organizations, but there are a number features that operate in both individual and institutional relationships (see **Table 10-3**). One thing to remember is that even individual relationships operate on multiple levels. There are dynamics between individuals and there are dynamics with the organization as an entity. For instance, individual donors have attachments to their alma mater (the organization). They harbor fond memories of their collegiate life, which often reflects strong attachments to the institution, and these attitudes

TABLE 10-3 Issues Related to Managing Resource Relationships

Features	Key Attributes
Existing working relationship	• Length of relationship • Significance
Nature of entities	• Mission focus • Public vs. private • Size and power
Legal and formal arrangements	• Contracts • Donor rights • Monitoring options
Nature of trust	• Attitudes of partners

Performance and satisfaction	• Ability to meet demands of beneficiaries
	  • Service quality (outcomes)
	• Ability to provide benefits to donors
	  • Donor motivations
	  • Control costs

Communication and information sharing	• General and targeted messages • Reputation and image management • Efficacy of information
Adaptations allowed or required	• Norms of cooperation • Systems and practices

have significant implications on philanthropic behavior. In addition, donors establish relationships with the development officer or some other point of contact at the institution. The behavior of the point of contact also has implications on the actions of the donor. Institutional attachment leads to interest in supporting the organization, but the actions of the organizational representatives facilitate the ability of individuals to actually contribute in substantive ways. The complexities of relationship management practices are magnified when nonprofits build funding relationships with public or private organizations. There are interpersonal aspects, and there are also interorganizational features. These interorganizational features tend to formalize the relationships, which can lead to increased stability, but institutional relationships often require extensive monitoring and adjustments. The nature of business relationships is dependent on the power differential between partners. The market analysis just discussed helps managers understand the power differential between the nonprofit and the funding entity. Defining the features of business relationships further suggests how managers can secure funds that are reliable and come with fewer operational requirements.

Existing Working Relationships

It is generally good advice to nurture and support existing relationships. This section explores methods to maintain the funding relationship because this tends to be more cost effective than developing a new relationship (Lewis & Williams, 2011). Recognizing the importance of maintaining existing relationships does not negate the need to engage in prospecting of potential donors and funders. Nonprofit managers need to do both: prospect for new funding options (some of which is accomplished through the market analysis strategies just discussed) and nurture existing relationships. Lewis and Williams (2011) explored how much was "lost" by nonprofits year to year versus what was reported as "gains" in donations. Lost donations were those donors that had given in the past, but had either downgraded or stopped giving. Gains included new, recaptured, and upgraded donors. In many instances the losses superseded the gains. Attention to existing relationships should be a priority.

This section emphasizes features and practices to maintain and strengthen effective funding relationships. These features apply to both individual and organizational funders, but understanding how to manage an organizational versus individual funder typically takes slightly different techniques. There are a number of attributes to consider. First is the basic attributes of the funding entity and the nonprofit. This recognizes how dispositional characteristics influence relationship strength. Next, the extent to which relationships are bound by legal and formal contracts is explored. Then the nature of trust in business relationships is addressed as well as how trust is fundamentally the backbone of relationship management practices. While there are a number of features that support and build trust, three concepts are presented: (1) performance and satisfaction, (2) information sharing, and (3) the extent to which adaptations by either partner are required or allowed. These three elements are vital to building trust and reflect the methods through which managers can create stronger business relationships.

Nature of the Entities

Features of both the nonprofit and the funding entity will suggest the feasibility and potential strength of the funding relationship. One of the most pressing is similarity of goals and purposes. The role of mission is central to defining potential funding markets. Additionally, managers need to identify funding entities that reflect more subtle values and priorities that are similar to the interests and priorities of the nonprofit. Funding entities that share a common purpose are much more likely to engage in a long-term relationship. It is easier for nonprofit managers to maintain this relationship because the purposes of the organizations are aligned and both entities are motivated toward the same end. The clarity and focus of the priorities influences the potential strength of the relationship. If a funding entity has multiple priorities then the strength of ties within any one priority area might not be quite as strong, especially if the entity reevaluates and adjusts funding priorities. This relates to the challenges of maintaining a relationship with public entities, which have multiple purposes. Any particular nonprofit is likely to reflect just one of the objectives for public managers. Depending on the political and economic context, funding may be fairly stable or managers may find that public funds shift priorities depending on political mood.

Funders are often conceptualized as maintaining power or influence in the relationship, but there are attributes of the nonprofit that can shift power from the funder to the recipient. The size or capacity of the nonprofit can influence relationship characteristics, because larger, more capable nonprofits maintain stronger legitimacy. This legitimacy reflects the dominant nature of a nonprofit in certain issues, industries, or causes. In comparison to some funding entities, highly desirable or attractive nonprofits can exert more influence. This influence means the nonprofit can direct the nature of the funding relationship. The power dynamics are complex and reflect characteristics of the market, such as alternative funders and nonprofit providers, as well as organizational attributes such as wealth and legitimacy. For example, the Catholic Church is a massive entity with a long history and significant wealth. This stability and history place the Church in a unique position with potential donors such that the church is not inclined to accept restrictions or allow modifications to operations in exchange for funds. While the Church is an extreme example, there are instances when small and modest nonprofits maintain unique capabilities that are attractive to certain funders, and this allows the nonprofit to exert more influence in the relationship.

The organizational attributes just discussed are the basis for conceptualizing the quality and nature of relationships that nonprofits develop and nurture with funding entities. Knowing features of the nonprofit and the funder and how those features influence funding arrangements is important, but in some ways these attributes reflect the current "state" and are only modestly mutable for either funders or nonprofit recipients. The next section discusses aspects of the relationship. How either partner is able to influence the arrangements depends on their position in the relationship. If they are smaller, less significant, and more "needy," then they are less able to make demands, but if they are institutionally strong, clear on mission priorities, and operating from a basis of independence, then there is significant room to negotiate and operate effectively in a funding relationship. These features are reflective of both institutional and individual funding partners. Obviously, small individual donors are less able to negotiate. Nevertheless small donors rely on market forces and relationship attributes as part of their decision making. Individual donors form impressions about funding options, performance, and trustworthiness, and if they are unsatisfied they will be inclined to discontinue or shift giving.

Legal and Formal Arrangement

Legal controls have several implications for how to manage relationships (Shabbir, Palihawadana, & Thwaites, 2007). Legal controls provide a degree of predictably and reliability in a relationship, especially if the parties have limited prior operating experience. Typically articulated in contract arrangements, the clarity of partner expectations and the formalized agreement of these arrangements provide a sense of security to the partners. These contracts specify performance expectations, deliverables, anticipated outcomes, timelines, and the like. The arrangement moves beyond individual agreements and utilizes formalized and institutional agreements recognized by entities outside the partner entities. The ability to seek outside help for grievances or noncompliance with relationship arrangements tends to ensure compliance by both parties. Public entities tend to depend on legal controls and formalized accountability mechanisms throughout the funding arrangement. Due to the demands of accounting for funds, public managers need objective and systematic controls. Public entities are much more likely to use legal and contractual arrangement even with long-standing partners, while private foundations often have two levels of relationships (Grønbjerg, Martell, & Paarlberg, 2000). They rely on formal controls initially, but over time, as the relationship develops, they can shift to a more cooperative, trust-based arrangement.

Individual donors have the right to specify the purposes of the donation, and nonprofits must respect those purposes. Nonprofit managers undertake a long process with major donors in determining how to attend to donor interests while operating within the constraints of the organization. This ability and willingness to negotiate is discussed as a separate feature and reflects the adaptability of both partners. As an example of major gift negotiations, a donor gave $15 million to the University of Virginia for a yoga center. The university was initially reluctant and then worked to reconceptualize the donor's interests into a Contemplative Sciences Center (Rice, 2012). These negotiations take time, and when the nonprofit begins implementing the gift, implied, stated, or intended expectations can sometimes be difficult to operationalize. Often there are written expectations, but there have been a number of high-profile cases that demonstrate how complex donor intent can be (even with written guidelines). The difficulties of interpreting donor purposes, especially after the donor has passed away, can be quite challenging (Gary, 2010). Conflict tends to occur in circumstances that have changed substantially since the gift was provided and the originally stated preferences are no longer feasible or reasonable. The interpretation of purposes and viability of those purposes form the crux of the conflict. Who determines what was ultimately intended in word or spirit, and what is feasible? Nonprofits have a vested interest to use the funds according to their priorities while meeting the intent of the donor. Donor families can have priorities and interpretations that are not organization specific, which can cause problems for nonprofits. While legal and formal controls are useful for both funding entities and donors, they are not sufficient to guide all funding relationships.

Nature of Trust

The nature of trust in each partner at both the individual and institutional levels has significant implications for the success, cost, and reliability of the relationship arrangement. Trust is the basis for a healthy relationship. Trust is defined as a genuine concern for the interest of others (Mayer, Davis, & Schoorman, 1995), and to be viable, trust must exist at the interpersonal and the institutional levels. Promises of the development officer must align with institutional actions. Developing and nurturing trust in funding relationships is complex and multifaceted. Trust reduces complexity because there is less demand to verify and document all actions and activities. Rather, institutional partners can rely on good intentions as the mechanisms by which to judge actions. Consequently, managers at the individual and institutional levels should actively work to create and support trusting relationships. Developing quality relationships is costly and, consequently, partner entities estimate the potential benefits of any relationship (Doney & Cannon, 1997). Partners also make judgments about the potential value of and the implications for what is lost without a strong partnership. Confidence in behaviors and an ability to accurately predict the actions of others is the basis of a sound, trusting relationship. This is typically formed through longer and broader relationships. As funders witness the actions of an organization over time, they gain a greater sense of confidence in their ability to understand the motivations and actions of the other entities. While individual and institutional actions are not the same, partner entities do tend to shift between confidence in the institution and attitudes about the individual. Trust in individuals can transfer to positive attitudes about the institution.

There are a number of things that are inferred from this brief discussion of the roles and drivers of trust. Consistency and quality of both individual and institutional actions are key and will be discussed more in the next section. Increasing the likelihood that partners can accurately predict your actions is critical. There are also institutional attributes that tend to predict trust. This includes institutional size and the reputation of the entity. Reputation of the nonprofit and funding entity serves as a strong proxy for the trustworthiness of the organization. The level and nature of information sharing as well are strong predictors of trust. The more information that partners share has significant implications for how entities perceive and trust each other. The extent to which partners are provided "inside" information reinforces the sense of trust in a relationship. The concept of integrity is a guiding principle for individual and institutional action. The more frequently individuals and institutions uphold their word, the more likely others are to develop trust in the relationship. Individuals hold relatively ambiguous impressions of nonprofit organizations, and yet these impressions have significant implications for engagement (Venable, Rose, Bush, & Gilbert, 2005). Donors and partners base their willingness to engage in the relationship partly on the perceived reputation of the organization. The next section discusses three critical features of a trusting relationship. The first is related to meeting and satisfying *performance expectations* of partners and service beneficiaries. The second is sharing accurate *information* that informs performance expectations and helps donors better understand the processes and practices of the nonprofit. The third feature is *level adaptations* that are required or allowed by both parties. The extent to which donors believe the nonprofit is listening to their preferences and working to accommodate those interests builds trust. Similarly, nonprofits will gain trust in the funder through efforts to accommodate organizational preferences and interests.

Performance and Satisfaction

There are two aspects of performance and satisfaction that are of interest to resource providers. One is related to the ability of the nonprofit to provide high-quality services to beneficiaries. Funding entities expect to learn how the organization is successful in achieving public benefit outcomes. This information takes a full range of forms from the number and quality of programs, to a discussion of the impact and outcomes produced through organizational activities. This aspect of performance is important and significant to funders in different ways. For example, those that pay fees for services want to hear that the activities and services of the organization are beneficial and effective. Understanding potential performance outcomes creates expectations of program quality. Third-party entities might even make payments contingent on performance outcomes. Donors, on the other hand, can prioritize service effectiveness to differing degrees. Individual donors who provide modest gifts might have only limited capacity or interest to understand the performance effectiveness of organizational activities. These donors are often distant from beneficiaries, their investment is modest, and detailed understanding of performance can be complex. Major donors might have more interest in performance outcomes but they often are just as concerned about their own personal priorities, such as the establishment of new initiatives or supporting programs of personal interest. This suggests that other features about performance influence donor decisions.

The second area of performance and satisfaction that drives funder decisions is related to the nonprofit's ability to meet the interests and preferences of funders. These interests are varied and at times complex. One that is discussed quite often is the ability to provide services that are cost effective. The most common method to demonstrate efficiency is a calculation of "program" expense compared to "management" or administration expense. The general rule of thumb used by national charity watchdog entities and now adopted by many public funding entities is that all administrative expenses, which include fundraising expense and management expense, should be no more than 25% of the total expenses of the organization. The pros and cons of this ratio can be debated, but the fact is that many funders are interested in the cost ratio and believe that most of the money donated to the organization should go to provide program services. Third-party entities as well are fundamentally concerned with efficiencies and can exert significant pressure on nonprofits to operate with thin margins (Frumkin & Andre-Clark, 2000). The exact allocation of expenses across the categories (program, management, fundraising) is based on cost allocation policies and judgments of accountants in discussions with managers. Making these judgments can be difficult, and managers are motivated to report increased efficiency, but auditing firms provide professional guidance and monitor the rules for allocating funds across expense categories. The standard is, at times, crude, but it is also quite powerful for funding entities and serves to rule out nonprofits that are deemed inefficient (Ashley & Faulk, 2010).

The ability of the nonprofit to meet donor motivations and interests is the other area that drives decision making (Lindahl, 2010). This can prove difficult for nonprofit managers that must balance service activities and donor services that require nonprofits to consider the preferences and interests of donors. The ability of nonprofits to meet the preferences of funders is critical. The motivations of donors are varied but have been defined in four categories (Shabbir et al., 2007). In the functional category, donors want to feel like they are helping a cause or a program that is bigger than them. They want to make a difference and expect the nonprofit to help them recognize how they are benefiting and helping the community and society. In the familial category, donors desire to help a family member. This can either be direct, such as support for a school club of which your child is a member, or indirect, such as the desire to fund breast cancer research because your mom is a survivor. Memorial gifts as well are driven by familial ties that relate giving to support the memory of a family member or someone who is close to you. The third motivation is related to demonstrable benefits such as recognition and tax benefits that can influence decision making. Finally, there are emotional reasons that relate to self-image and emotional attitudes toward guilt and salvation. There are a range of emotional drivers that motivate individuals to give so they can elevate negative feelings or highlight positive attributes of their personality. Interpreting how and what motivations are prominent for donors is difficult. Development professionals work to communicate messages that reinforce the performance expectations of donors and funding entities.

Communication and Information Sharing

Nonprofit managers must address different levels of information sharing and communication (Sargeant, Hudson, & West, 2008). Managers must attend to public relations and communications to manage and develop positive impressions about the organization. This higher-level messaging is embedded in the context of attitudes about the sector and attitudes about the industry or cause to which the organization belongs. Managers must also target communication toward particular partner entities and customized information sharing that addresses practical and operational issues related to the fulfillment of partnership agreements. Both levels of communication are instrumental in building relationships and trust of the nonprofit. Through trust and positive impressions of the organization, funding entities (individuals and organizations) are more inclined to support and engage with the nonprofit.

Broad-based communication is directed at the general public, donors, and program participants. The messaging is similar to marketing initiatives of for-profit corporations although the message is moderated to reflect the nature and character of the nonprofit. For instance, in a study of direct mail materials to donors, it was found that simplified materials as opposed to excessive graphics and high-gloss materials were more effective in the number of respondents and the value of donations (Bekkers & Crutzen, 2007). The author's interpretation was that many donors prefer nonprofit materials that reflect a frugality or simplicity. This implies that the nonprofit is not wasting resources on marketing and fundraising, but allocates funds to meet public purposes. Nonprofit marketing is complex and multifaceted. In a marketing study to explore the dimensions of brand identity among charitable nonprofits, this complexity is revealed in the four dimensions of brand personality that nonprofits must try to control (Venable et al., 2005). For instance, nonprofits must reflect a frugal orientation, but also sophistication. Donors want to believe the nonprofit is capable operationally and instrumentally. Integrity is also a critical aspect of nonprofit identity. Given the complex and indeterminate aspects of nonprofit performance, many donors and fee-paying clients seek indicators that suggest the organization is a faithful and honest steward. The very *nature* of a nonprofit is that it is trustworthy and yet the general public has substantive reservations about exactly how trustworthy nonprofits are (Herzlinger, 1996), especially in relation to the good use of resources. Another important feature relates to compassion and nurturance. Communicating and explaining how the nonprofit cares for the beneficiaries is critical. There are other aspects of the nonprofit's brand or personality that reflect the unique qualities of the organization that seek to further reinforce these key principles, which fundamentally seek to build trust in the organization.

Targeted messaging is intended to respond to the interests and demands of particular partner entities. This includes communications with major donors and organizational partners who have moved beyond the general messaging just described and seek more detailed and intimate information about performance. A study of supplier markets (Anderson & Narus, 1990) finds that the efficacy of communication and information is key to supporting relationships that build trust. Adequate information has no universal level of frequency or timing, rather it requires providing accurate and valuable information that is sought by the partner entity when and how they prefer to receive that information. In doing so, the nonprofit demonstrates their ability to meet the interests and preferences of the funding entity, and these messages fundamentally convey performance metrics that are important to the partner. The ability to monitor and track which stakeholders merit individualized communication and messaging is challenging. Organizations that are highly successful at gaining major gifts allocate significant staff resources to manage and track key relationships and actively work to develop volunteer infrastructures to support necessary communication. Increasingly, organizational partners are seeking consistent and reliable information that is linked to their information management requirements. Nonprofits need to consider their ability to respond and provide accurate and complete information in the format required by the funding organization. These communication requirements form the crux of the management demands that managers need to balance when entering complex funding arrangements.

Adaptations Allowed or Required
As nonprofit managers negotiate funding arrangements with major entities, either individual donors or organizational partners, they must determine performance requirements and expectations. As these investments and relationships develop, one partner may expect organizational or institutional adaptations of the other. This gets to the nitty-gritty of attending to the capabilities of the partner entities and how those capabilities can be exploited, strengthened, and utilized to achieve objectives of the other entity. This relates to the example of refining and shifting a concept of a Yoga Center into a Contemplative Sciences Center at the University of Virginia. The University of Virginia modified and created a number of institutional features to respond to this gift, but the school also had expectations that the donor would adjust priorities and requirements to accommodate the capabilities of the university (Cannon, 2012). Partner entities have very real expectations of quality, reliability, and benefits. The extent to which one partner imposes those accommodations and requires a partner entity to shift depends upon many of the features already discussed, primarily as they relate to power. The norms of cooperation (or lack thereof) in these arrangements have significant implications for the nature of the relationship and the autonomy of either partner (Cannon & Perreault, 1999). These norms take time to develop and are indeed contingent on

a number of factors. A common complaint or concern with some nonprofits is that they are too compliant to funder preferences. The idea that the nonprofit is not a truly independent entity, but rather a broker or agent for a major funder, has implications for strategic decisions and the establishment of priorities. The control and compliance expectations and the systems operating on either side of the partner relationship might indicate the nature of the partnership. Partnerships that allow for accommodations with both partners can provide reliability and predictability for both entities.

Conclusion

Managing resource options for nonprofits is complex because of the multiple funding options available. Analysis of both earned and donated income options is critical. There are fundamental differences between fee-based markets and donor markets. This is further complicated by the individual and organizational attributes operating in those funding arrangements. The practices managers utilize in fee-based markets are distinct from the skills required to manage major gifts or to comply with complex public contracts. This chapter refined the definition of resource markets, reviewed market analysis techniques, and introduced methods by which managers can evaluate relationship requirements. Considering the resource options from a strategic perspective allows managers to compare and contrast various funding options as part of the portfolio of revenue streams in the organization.

Do nonprofit managers have simplified guidelines in reference to seeking and prioritizing funds? Yes and no. Nonprofit managers want reliable, consistent funds that come with few strings attached, that are relatively easy to manage, and that can be expended as needed to support the mission. What methods can managers employ to achieve that? They must first start with a clear and simple definition of their purpose and actively manage that image and reputation. This requires messaging and strong networks that are willing and able to articulate organizational priorities. Furthermore, the organization needs a clear values proposition. How do they operate efficiently and impact the community? What benefits do nonprofits create and how can funders be a part of the solutions advocated by the organization? People need an emotional reason to attach to the organization and to invest in those activities (Stater, 2009). Fee-based markets might be more transactional and instrumental, but the unique opportunity for most nonprofits is to garner public trust in the organization's ethical proposition. Failing to create and generate trust is a fundamental issue confronting nonprofits.

Discussion Questions

1. What considerations might prioritize certain funding requirements (e.g., cash flow, autonomy) for nonprofit managers?
2. Should a nonprofit manager prioritize market factors or relationship factors to secure funds? Why? What are the implications of these different practices?
3. Building trust in funding relationships requires significant management expertise. How can managers facilitate effectiveness in this area?
4. What are the trade-offs of a diverse revenue portfolio compared to a focused revenue strategy that relies on limited number of sources?

References

Anderson, J. C., & Narus, J. A. (1990). A model of distributor firm and manufacturer firm working partnerships. *Journal of Marketing, 54*(1), 42–58.

Ashley, S., & Faulk, L. (2010). Nonprofit competition in the grants marketplace. *Nonprofit Management and Leadership, 21*(1), 43–57.

Bekkers, R., & Crutzen, O. (2007). Just keep it simple: A field experiment on fundraising letters. *International Journal of Nonprofit & Voluntary Sector Marketing, 12*(4), 371–378.

Boenigk, S., & Helmig, B. (2013). Why do donors donate? Examining the effects of organizational identification and identity salience on the relationships among satisfaction, loyalty, and donation behavior. *Journal of Service Research.* doi: 10.1177/1094670513486169

Cannon, H. B. (2012). U.Va. to launch contemplative sciences center. Retrieved from http://news.virginia.edu/print/content /uva-launch-contemplative-sciences-center

Cannon, J. P., & Perreault, W. D. J. (1999). Buyer-seller relationships in business markets. *Journal of Marketing Research, 36*(4), 439–460.

Carroll, D. A., & Stater, K. J. (2009). Revenue diversification in nonprofit organizations: Does it lead to financial stability? *Journal of Public Administration Research and Theory, 19*(4), 947–966.

Doney, P. M., & Cannon, J. P. (1997). An examination of the nature of trust in buyer-seller relationships. *Journal of Marketing, 61*(2), 35–51.

Foster, W. L. (2007, Spring). How nonprofits get really big. *Stanford Social Innovation Review,* 46–55.

Foster, W. L., Kim, P., & Christiansen, B. (2009, Spring). Ten nonprofit funding models. *Stanford Social Innovation Review, 7,* 32–39.

Frumkin, P., & Andre-Clark, A. (2000). When missions, markets, and politics collide: Values and strategy in the nonprofit human services. *Nonprofit and Voluntary Sector Quarterly, 29*(suppl 1), 141–163.

Gary, S. H. (2010). The problems with donor intent: Interpretation, enforcement, and doing the right thing. *Chicago-Kent Law Review, 85*(3), 977–1043.

Grønbjerg, K. A. (1991). How nonprofit human service organizations manage their funding sources: Key findings and policy implications. *Nonprofit Management & Leadership, 2*(2), 159–175.

Grønbjerg, K. A., Martell, L., & Paarlberg, L. (2000). Philanthropic funding of human services: Solving ambiguity through the two-stage competitive process. *Nonprofit and Voluntary Sector Quarterly, 29*(suppl 1), 9–40.

Herzlinger, R. E. (1996). Can public trust in nonprofits and governments be restored? *Harvard Business Review, 74*(2), 97–107.

Jonker, K., & Meehan, W. F. (2008). Curbing mission creep. *Stanford Social Innovation Review, 6*(1), 60–65.

Lewis, W., & Williams, C. (2011). *A better measure of success.* Washington, DC: Urban Institute.

Lindahl, W. E. (2010). *Principles of fundraising; Theory and practice.* Sudbury, MA: Jones and Bartlett.

Mayer, R. C., Davis, J. H., & Schoorman, F. D. (1995). An integrative model of organizational trust. *The Academy of Management Review, 20*(3), 709–734.

Porter, M. E. (1998). *Competitive strategy: Techniques for analyzing industries and competitors* (2nd ed.). New York, NY: Free Press.

Rice, A. (2012). Anatomy of campus coup. *The New York Times Magzine,* September 10, 56–62, 65–67.

Sargeant, A. (1999). Charitable giving: Towards a model of donor behaviour. *Journal of Marketing Management, 15*(4), 215–238.

Sargeant, A., Hudson, J., & West, D. C. (2008). Conceptualizing brand values in the charity sector: The relationship between sector, cause and organization. *Service Industries Journal, 28*(5), 615–632.

Sargeant, A., West, D. C., & Ford, J. (2001). The role of perceptions in predicting donor value. *Journal of Marketing Management, 17*(3-4), 407–428.

Shabbir, H., Palihawadana, D., & Thwaites, D. (2007). Determining the antecedents and consequences of donor perceived relationship quality—A dimensional qualitative research approach. *Psychology & Marketing, 24*(3), 271–293.

Stater, K. J. (2009). The impact of revenue sources on marketing behavior: Examining web-promotion and place-marketing in nonprofit organizations. *Journal of Nonprofit & Public Sector Marketing, 21*(2), 202–224.

Venable, B. T., Rose, G. M., Bush, V. D., & Gilbert, F. W. (2005). The role of brand personality in charitable giving: An assessment and validation. *Journal of the Academy of Marketing Science, 33*(3), 295–312.

Interorganizational Relationships

Learning Objectives

- Explore the range of interorganizational relationships
- Understand the purposes of interorganizational relationships
- Review management strategies to achieve benefits and minimize costs

Joining forces with other organizations is a powerful strategy for nonprofits to achieve objectives; whether social impact priorities, political objectives, or resource needs, interorganizational efforts are often instrumental for success. Interorganizational relationships take a range of forms (networks, partnerships), operate under countless terms (collaboration, coordination, alliance), and are defined as a relationship between two or more independent entities that are designed to achieve mutual and individual objectives by sharing and/or creating resources (Tjemkes, Vos, & Burgers, 2012). There are numerous benefits and challenges that make managing these relationships difficult. Interorganizational alliances are prized in the social sector as they can facilitate efficient use of resources, limit redundant efforts, and reduce funding uncertainties. This chapter reviews the range of interorganizational relationships that are possible and considers the conditions and methods that facilitate success in what is often a complex and indeterminate operational method.

There is limited consistency on nomenclature, so something called collaboration in one context is called a network in another context and a partnership in another. The term *interorganizational relationship* is used to refer to all types and phases of collaborative and cooperative arrangements between organizations. These relationships operate across sectors and can focus on all the various aspects of operating an organization. So there are institutional arrangements related to providing back-office support (e.g., finance, human resources), and there are arrangements focused on funding, advocacy, and services. Given these variations, the chapter tends to focus on interorganizational relationships that are related to service delivery objectives, although there are instances when examples related to advocacy and resource objectives are more appropriate. Managers approach interorganizational relationships from different perspectives. Many managers see collaborations and alliances as the optimal method to achieve organizational and social objectives. From this perspective it is only through coordinated and interconnected initiatives that major social problems are going to be addressed. Given the lack of dominant market forces, sharing and cooperating is perceived to be the *right thing* to do. Other managers come to collaborations reluctantly. Experiencing limited success with individual initiatives, many managers realize that achieving organizational priorities are often unattainable without cooperation and coordination. Furthermore, some funding options are only available to organizations that operate in cooperative arrangements. In order to achieve mission objectives and reduce funding risks, most nonprofit managers are going to have to collaborate and coordinate with some partner entities. That is, managers approach collaboration by choice (it is the way to do "business") or by force (it is required because independent effort is incapable of achieving many of the objectives they value, and powerful institutional actors believe it is the right thing to do) (Bryson, Crosby, & Stone, 2006). Either way, interorganizational alliances and partnerships are a fundamental feature in nonprofit services and advocacy. As was discussed in the chapter on advocacy, political power and influence is increased through alliances and collaborations. Similarly, nonprofits are rarely in a position to achieve broad-based social impact through their own activities.

Levels of Engagement

Classifying all possible interorganizational relationships is difficult because of the multiple purposes, structures, and partners. Thinking about relationship intensity is one method to organize alliances (see **Table 11-1**). At one end (level one) are relatively modest arrangements that require limited institutional resources and pose modest risk. These types of arrangements might be conceptualized as *information networks*. The use of common terms is problematic because there is significant variation in structural

TABLE 11-1 Levels of Interorganizational Relationships

	LEVEL 1 Modest	**LEVEL 2** Intermediate	**LEVEL 3** Extensive
Common terms	Networks	Collaboration, alliance	Partnerships and mergers
Structural adjustments	Limited	Modest	Substantial
Resource requirements	Limited	Variable	Extensive
Negotiated goals	Limited	Yes	Extensive
Institutional controls	Limited	Modest	Intense
Management complexity	Limited	Modest to extensive	Extensive
Interdependence	Loosely coupled	Increased interdependence	Tightly coupled

Based on Murray, V. (1998). Interorganizational collaborations in the nonprofit sector. *International Encyclopaedia of Public Policy and Administration, 2,* 1192–1196.

features among commonly used terms. The terms used here are intended to be illustrative of different levels of engagement. In the middle, level two arrangements require more coordinated effort and share joint objectives. This might be conceptualized as *collaborations*. At the far end of the continuum are arrangements that entail the creation of new or joint organizational forms. This includes *partnerships* and mergers. Recognizing the continuum of arrangements is helpful as it facilitates the analysis of alliance options. Different alliance structures provide different benefits and costs. The next section explores the features of these different types (Bailey & Koney, 2000; Guo & Acar, 2005; Murray, 1998).

Level one relationships allow organizations to operate almost entirely independently but facilitate information sharing and coordination (Provan & Milward, 2002). Information networks are common, flexible, and facilitate learning and coordination because organizations increase awareness of other entities that are operating in a similar area. There are a variety of organizing principles that might instigate a network. It can be similarity of beneficiaries, geographic area, or service delivery strategies. Human service networks exist to facilitate referral of clients with specialized needs. For example, organizations that are providing services for homeless individuals and families in a particular region may form a network to coordinate services and facilitate access for beneficiaries. Demand often outstrips capabilities of service providers, so efforts to fill unique service niches and limit redundancy might drive managers to remain aware of organizational partners through service networks. The development of information patterns and communication channels is a key feature of networks. The use of social media can facilitate the establishment and ongoing viability of networks (Scearce, Kasper, & Grant, 2010). Network arrangements facilitate learning because participants can share practices that relate to the activities of others. Furthermore, these networks can be instrumental in gaining access to service beneficiaries. A key feature is network location and the extent to which participants are central to communication patterns or are peripheral (see **Figure 11-1**). Central locations suggest multiple contacts with participants and importance of information provided. Central location in a network

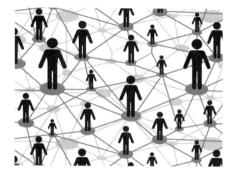

© iStockphoto/Thinkstock   © Sweet Lana/Shutterstock, Inc.

FIGURE 11-1   Network Structures

requires more organizational resources. Peripheral participants demand fewer organizational resources, but the points of contact are limited to a select number of participants, often one of the central partners. Extracting value from networks can be challenging, especially after initial learning of key players is established, because participants are typically only modestly committed to the network structure.

Another benefit of networks is the ability to gain legitimacy. Nonprofits can gain legitimacy though participation in networks, especially if the network contains dominant entities in the area of coordination. So if a major hospital is part of a healthcare network, other providers may join the network to associate with the major provider. There are also risks as networks can allow organizations to gain benefits (knowledge, understanding, and access), while not necessarily contributing much. So, new and younger organizations may gain substantial benefits from a network, while larger established entities may experience costs and risks associated with information sharing. To maintain dominance, organizations have to attend to other institutional participants and networks can be a method to sustain influence among other partners. Networks can also function as a forum to identify partners for more advanced interorganizational relationships.

Networks can also include the beneficiaries and/or targets of organizational objectives. As nonprofits try to organize communities, networks are instrumental to support communication and activation. Networks facilitate mobilization and activation of participates. As issues are identified, networks are the method to engage and educate participants. Furthermore, beneficiaries can share information with each other. For instance, the Environmental Defense Fund created a network of environmentally conscious corporations to share practices and ideas for sustainability.

Level two interorganizational relationships, commonly referred to as collaborations, entail purposeful, negotiated, and shared expectations of performance from participants. These arrangements may be formal or ad hoc and can last for extended periods of time or can be focused on particular program activities that are more short term. The example of homeless service providers illustrates how an information-sharing network can lead to negotiated arrangements among some partners to coordinate efforts. The determination to provide particular services and not provide others is influenced by discussion and negotiation with other organizational entities. A homeless shelter might negotiate an arrangement with a job-training program. The shelter agrees to send residents to the training program, and the training program prioritizes access for those participants. The arrangement can entail even more sophisticated activities and use of resources and practices, such as arranging for the training program to offer services in the shelter facility. Objectives in these arrangements are typically focused on cost saving and efficiency. The shelter does not have the capabilities to offer training programs, and the training program needs a consistent and reliable source of participants. Both organizations benefit and can emphasize their capabilities. These arrangements are also focused on achieving mission objectives. Providers recognize the need for additional services that they are not able to provide. Coordinating with another entity improves outcome success for program beneficiaries and minimizes the need to add program features. These arrangements require ongoing communication and continued negotiation to ensure benefits and avoid costs. Control and accountability can be difficult to manage because the partners remain independent and there are limited joint structural arrangements.

The third level of interorganizational relationships relates to increased formality and institutional commitment (i.e., partnerships). These arrangements are longer term and may reflect substantive structural changes negotiated between entities. What distinguishes these arrangements is the intensity of dependence and structural adjustments in accountability and control. This might entail forming a separate organizational entity or some sort of oversight and coordinating entity that has responsibility for managing partner relationships and monitoring program success. Partner organizations in these arrangements forgo institutional autonomy in certain areas in favor of increased controls. These arrangements might even culminate in situations where one partner integrates the services and programs into the organization. The arrangement with the homeless services shelter and the training organization could culminate in the partners merging so as to provide a more unified service portfolio and minimize some of the disadvantages inherent in interorganizational relationships. The distinction is increased interdependence and loss of autonomy in favor of reliability and control.

Types of Interorganizational Relationships

Distinct from level of engagement is the range of partner entities in interorganizational relationships. Thinking about the exchange between partners facilitates understanding the dynamics inherent in different structural options (see **Table 11-2**). A fundamental feature is the power differential of organizational actors (Hallen, Johanson, & Seyed-Mohamed, 1991). There are interorganizational relationships among roughly equivalent entities (peer to peer). These arrangements can consist of just a limited number of entities (e.g., one organization partnering with another) or broader arrangements and networks. These arrangements require negotiation and some form of governance and accountability that recognizes the independence of organizational partners (Provan & Kenis, 2008). An alternative structure is an asymmetrical arrangement between significantly different-sized institutions. This signifies a lead organization, and such arrangements imply significant power differentials based on dependence of the smaller entity. As a result, governance and accountability

TABLE 11-2 Common Types of Interorganizational Relationships

Type	Description
Peer to peer	Arrangements among roughly equivalent entities
Asymmetrical	Significant power/size differential among members
Multistakeholder	Includes a broad range of participants offering different levels of engagements
Cross sector	Arrangements between different organizational types such as public–private partnerships and corporate–nonprofit partnerships

can be imposed by larger, more powerful partners. Multistakeholder arrangements suggest diffuse power arrangements that might include a variety of organizational participants. Some of these might be large and others are small, but with complex multistakeholder arrangements, accountability and governance are difficult to manage or control. Consequently, these arrangements often result in creating governing boards or independent structures that facilitate negotiation and oversight (Provan & Kenis, 2008). Cross-sector relationships include arrangements such as public–private partnerships and corporate–nonprofit agreements. These arrangements imply a different set of power and cultural dynamics that are likely to influence autonomy. Cross-sector arrangements add complexity because of different organizational cultures and purposes (Bryson et al., 2006).

Interorganizational relationships may develop over time, passing through different stages, but not all arrangements evolve. Furthermore, arrangements are not linear. Managers may identify a potential partner and move quickly to merge or integrate services at a more advanced level without necessarily operating in a level two arrangement. Considering these levels and types provides a framework to discuss several other issues regarding interorganizational relationships, such as the rationale for interorganizational relationships and the challenges associated with managing these arrangements. Different levels and types of engagement are going to result in different benefits and present different challenges.

Paradoxes of Interorganizational Arrangements

When considering different collaborative arrangements, there are a number of paradoxes that make interorganizational relationships particularly challenging. Managers balance three fundamental paradoxes (see **Table 11-3**) in regard to interorganizational relationships (Tjemkes et al., 2012). The first relates to competition versus cooperation. Managers consider whether particular actions are in the interest of their organization (to improve their capabilities) or in the interest of the collective. It is not one or the other, but there are instances when cooperative action costs some organizations and benefits others. While many nonprofit managers might minimize competitive tendencies, there are a number of areas in which nonprofits compete. The most pressing is related to financial resources either through fees, contracts, or donated income. Engaging other nonprofits is inherently risky because partners may learn your practices and can potentially increase their viability in relation to funders. There are certain opportunities only available to collaborative and cooperative initiatives, so it is possible that collective action may indeed provide access to resources not currently accessible to an independent organization. Furthermore, the nature of nonprofit markets suggests that cooperative tendencies are appropriate and necessary. It is the balance of gaining organizational benefits while contributing to the collective good.

TABLE 11-3   Management Paradoxes in Cooperative Arrangements

Paradox	Description
Competitive vs. cooperative	Balancing the interests of collaborative priorities against the recognition that shared engagement facilities another organization's potential for success
Economic vs. social	Balancing economic costs against softer social benefits such as reputation
Deliberate vs. emergent	Seizing opportunities as they develop while also ensuring that planned long-term priorities are nurtured

The second paradox relates to economic costs versus social benefits. As discussed, interorganizational relationships are difficult to manage, and they are predicated on healthy social relationships. Social benefits are qualitatively different from clear cost-benefit calculations based on financial returns. The importance of social capital, especially bridging relationships, is difficult to quantify, and cooperative interorganizational relationships can be a key feature of organizational assets and capabilities. Nonprofits build social capital for a number of reasons related to legitimacy and reputation. The alliances built with other organizations are an important feature of an organization's success in the sociopolitical domain. Strong collaborative relationships are not based on pure calculations of financial costs and rewards. All relationships require investments, and interorganizational arrangements are no different. It can be difficult for managers to ascertain when a collaborative arrangement is no longer worth investment, especially because determination is based on social and economic calculations. This issue is apparent in efforts to be inclusive and participatory in decision making. Is it better to slow the process to include all constituents (often less central and less powerful members) or is it better to move forward quickly and efficiently, potentially at the cost of excluding some from the decision-making process (Human & Provan, 2000)? This paradox also might reflect more immediate costs related to staff time and long-term potential benefits of increased institutional legitimacy. Balancing real direct cost against potential long-term gain is difficult.

The third paradox is related to choices that managers make regarding planned engagements versus emergent opportunities: deciding between a unique opportunity that develops more or less unexpectedly versus carrying out a sequential process to build and nurture relationships that will eventually develop into a valuable arrangement. This paradox also relates to structures that tend to be hierarchical and formalized versus arrangements that are flexible and responsive. Management of interorganizational relationships requires ongoing adjustments that balance planned objectives with practical limitations, barriers, and opportunities. Judgments in these areas are based on analysis, intuition, and prior experience. It is difficult to know how different opportunities might develop versus the enactment of a plan. It doesn't always have to be a trade-off but there are limited organizational resources, and following new opportunities might come at the expense of planned activities. These paradoxes illustrate the strategic contingencies leaders, managers, and volunteers grapple with as they seek to attain and advance organizational and societal benefits. Thinking about objectives and opportunities influences how managers approach these arrangements. Collaborating for the sake of collaborating is not a good idea. The next section reviews some of the common rationales for interorganizational arrangements.

Reasons for Interorganizational Arrangements

Participation in interorganizational relationships is based on an assessment of current and future benefits and costs. Evaluating costs and benefits is difficult because these elements resist clear quantification and because they are not easily compared as they reflect a range of issues. Consequently, managers should identify a few elements that are most pressing in relation to a specific collaboration opportunity and then monitor indicators that can signal developments in those areas. So if a prospective collaborative opportunity is likely to facilitate learning new service methods, then a periodic report on what new methods are discussed and the degree to which those features can be or have been incorporated into organizational practices is necessary. Without objectives and priorities it is nearly impossible to assess the success of collaboration activities. With a few prioritized elements managers are more likely to track these features and evaluate the relationship. The next section describes typical rationales for joining interorganizational relationships. A hypothetical jobs training program is used to illustrate the benefits, detailed in **Table 11-4**.

Achieve Social Impact

Organizations participate in collaboration initiatives to improve outcome success of target beneficiaries (Bailey & Koney, 2000).

TABLE 11-4 Reasons for Interorganizational Alliances

Purpose	Description
Achieve social impact	Many mission objectives are beyond the scope of one organization.
Cost efficiency	Achieves efficiencies in providing complex services and reduce risks inherent in new initiatives.
Strategic adaptation	Allows for exploration and adaptation to complex or changing environmental conditions.
	Provides access to industries, service areas, or opportunities that are outside current capabilities.
Learning	Assess partners' capabilities, strengths, and weaknesses.
	Opportunity to learn practices and techniques from partners.
	Creates new knowledge about service activities.
Access to resources	Secures capital and skills needed to achieve objectives.
Stakeholder management	Increases reputation and legitimation by partnering with influential and powerful entities.
	Maintain domain authority by influencing competitors or key actors in areas of expertise.

Data from Barringer, B. R., & Harrison, J. S. (2000). Walking a tightrope: Creating value through interorganizational relationships. *Journal of Management, 26*(3), 367–403.; and Tjemkes, B., Vos, P., & Burgers, K. (2012). *Strategic alliance management*. Florance, KY: Routledge.

Collaborative efforts may extend the range of services available to particular target groups so as to provide a more comprehensive system that addresses underlying causes and barriers to success. Organizations reach beyond their activities to facilitate broader social benefits. This idea is fundamentally socially and community oriented rather than organizational. It is socially responsible to join collaboration efforts because the issues that are importance to the organization (e.g., poverty, health) can be more fully achieved by partnering with others. So a job training organization may help participants gain skills and eventually employment, but they might join a collaborative so as to provide access to a spectrum of services that address poverty more broadly. There are a number of "related" issues that the training organization might not address but that are going to influence the success of participants. This can include childcare concerns and transportation, for instance, as well as broader economic development concerns about the number and type of employers. So while the training organization might not gain organizational benefits, program participants gain because they have access to comprehensive services.

If improving social impact is a priority there must be attention to monitoring and tracking the benefits obtained by participants. Managers should identify what services and outcomes are provided through collective elements, which may not have been available through organizational services. Managers should ascertain how those services improve outcomes for participants. Social impact and outcome performance is a complex phenomenon that entails a range of assessment methods. These initiatives can facilitate data collection and analysis. This is critical because interorganizational initiatives are nearly impossible for individual organizations to monitor. Furthermore, disentangling unique features of the service delivery mix is challenging. While this rationale for joining collaboratives is primarily about social benefits, the next couple of rationales are related to organizational benefits.

Cost Efficiency

The ability to provide services more efficiently is a common objective in collaborative initiatives. Efficiencies are achieved through increased capacity and specialization. Collaborative efforts may facilitate purchasing and other operational efficiencies that can be amalgamated through joint effort. Tracking costs and budget expectations for program-related expenses is often the best method to understand the financial efficiencies achieved. Thinking about the job training, program managers might seek alliances with computer and information technology providers so students can have access to the newest technologies. This improves the quality of training services provided and mitigates some of technology costs associated with providing access to the newest machines and programs. Consequently, relationships in this area are intended to facilitate service delivery, which may also expand options. The focus is shifting to managing costs related to offering program services while attending to quality concerns. There are also alliances that can share operational costs, such as personnel services or health-benefit collaboratives that let organizations share risk and limit costs.

Strategic Adaptations

Interorganizational relationships facilitate access to service areas and industries not currently accessible to providers (Tjemkes et al., 2012). So while cost efficiencies are primarily concerned with providing existing services, and social impact is focused on beneficiary outcomes, this objective considers how organizations can gain industry advantages and grow the range of services they provide. First, because of limited capabilities and prohibitive cost structures managers can use interorganizational relationships to open service opportunities. By utilizing the skills and relationships of partner entities, managers can gain access to potential markets that they cannot currently serve. This facilitates learning, which is discussed next, because organizations can learn about challenges and costs related to different service areas without necessarily assuming all the risk. So this is about strategic growth and expansion of services, which includes geographic expansion (markets) and methods. The job training program may collaborate with local businesses to explore training needs and demands within different industries. So while they may work extensively in training students to work with technology they may explore other industries and the training needs of new businesses to offer a broader, more expansive set of services. Interorganizational benefits in this context provide flexibility to explore new markets by sharing risk and cost with organizational partners.

Learning

Learning opportunities are often prevalent in interorganizational relationships because seeing and understanding the operations of others can result in a number of learning opportunities. This is referenced in the discussion about using alliances to facilitate strategic adaptations. Through collaborative arrangements, managers are provided the opportunity to learn about a number of different topics. Learning can take place in reference to new markets or new service delivery strategies. The challenge is to ensure that knowledge and learning are incorporated by the organization. While learning is often an implied benefit of interorganizational relationships, without clear methods to incorporate or adapt, organizations are often constrained to capitalize on new opportunities. Take, for instance, a desire to learn about other providers so as to evaluate potential collaborative and merger opportunities. If there is not a system in-house to evaluate, plan, and implement new joint ventures, the learning cannot be utilized. Another way that learning takes place in collaborative initiatives is through joint efforts that are exploratory so that neither entity is necessarily more knowledgeable, but by joining together they can share costs to develop new and innovative practices (Hardy, Phillips, & Lawrence, 2003; Phelps, 2010).

Access to Resources

Interorganizational arrangements can facilitate access to and reliability of resources because of the shared agreements and purposes. Whether those arrangements are contractual or negotiated ad hoc, there are a variety of potential resource options that can be gained through interorganizational relationships. As was discussed, fundraising and fund development is fundamentally based on relationships that garner support for organizational priorities. It is the ability to identify shared priorities that facilitates resource provision from donors and partners. In addition to financial contributions, managers can garner in-kind resources such as pro-bono professional services and access to desirable facilities. In addition to establishing relationships with resource providers, organizations that work with other providers are able to access resources that are only available to collaboratives or multi-institutional cooperatives. Many funders, both private and public, require nonprofits to demonstrate that they are working with other organizations and engaged in active collaborative arrangements.

Managing Stakeholder Relations

The last area to consider is that organizations may participate in interorganizational partnerships to manage or maintain relationships with significant stakeholders. There are two areas where this can be instrumental. One is that by joining with others an organization may be able to increase legitimacy through these affiliations. Even if there are not necessarily accreditation standards or entrance criteria, organizations benefit by being affiliated with other influential participants in the field. Accreditation and certification standards further enforce legitimacy because they demonstrate recognition by an independent entity, often consisting of peers that have verified your practices. So, the first potential benefit is that by affiliating with peer institutions, an organization can establish itself as legitimate to others outside of that network (e.g., funders, community members). The second area is related to managing relationships within the network. As a participant in these collaboratives, organizations can influence institutional practices and demonstrate their influence in the field. It really comes down to power and interorganizational relationships as a method to demonstrate dominance or controls on other providers. Whether that is through the establishment of accreditation standards or other peer-to-peer controls, dominant institutional players can influence the range and type of other entities that operate in similar industries. So, the second way that interorganizational relationships help organizations manage stakeholder relationships is that dominant organizations might have more influence in how other providers deliver services. If nonprofits are perceived as an industry leader they gain respect from those outside the network and deference from those in the network (Tjemkes et al., 2012).

Challenges of Interorganizational Relationships

There are a number of reasons for joining interorganizational relationships, and the nature of the nonprofit sector makes it inevitable that managers are going to utilize a range of interorganizational structures to achieve mission and organizational objectives. Clarity regarding purposes facilitates management, but there are a number significant challenges associated with collaborative arrangements (see **Table 11-5**). Depending on the level of engagement, many of these arrangements require a loss of autonomy because organizational interests are balanced against collective priorities. Organizations also put themselves in a potentially dependent relationship as they may not develop independent capabilities if they rely on partners to fulfill certain functions. There are a variety of risks in these arrangements, such as the potential for partners to learn organizational practices that could make them more competitive, or they could put demands on resources that take away from organizational interests.

These relationships are inherently difficult to manage. They are difficult to control and guide as participants have multiple interests. The oversight and governance challenges are substantial, and managers should work through the phases in collaboration, as described in the next section. These phases allow managers to prioritize their interests and consider the practices

TABLE 11-5 Challenges of Interorganizational Alliances

Disadvantage	Description
Loss of autonomy	Requires shared decision making and balancing institutional and partner objectives.
Risk of dependency	Potential for organizations to rely on capabilities of partners without the ability to develop those capabilities internally.
Organizational risk	Potential opportunistic behavior of partners to tap organizational resources.
Management complexities	Requires coordination and communication among various entities outside the organization. Different philosophies about organizational practices can lead to conflict.

Data from Barringer, B. R., & Harrison, J. S. (2000). Walking a tightrope: Creating value through interorganizational relationships. *Journal of Management, 26*(3), 367–403.; and Tjemkes, B., Vos, P., & Burgers, K. (2012). *Strategic alliance management.* Florance, KY: Routledge.

required to achieve objectives. Before discussing specific management practices, it is necessary to evaluate the influence of operating contexts likely to foster or inhibit collective action. If the operating context is nonsupportive of collective action then collective work is more difficult. Conversely, if these forces support collective action then it is much more likely to succeed (Chen, 2010).

External Contingencies and Preconditions

There are a number of external factors that are going to influence the range and scope of interorganizational relationships (see **Table 11-6**) (Bryson et al., 2006). The operating context provides the opportunity and motivation for collaborative action (Hanleybrown, Kania, & Kramer, 2012). Managers should ascertain the factors that are likely to foster or inhibit success. Issues to consider include industry factors such as the number and type of other providers. Is the industry heavily or thinly populated with potential partner agencies? Does the service market tend to operate in a competitive context or are collaboration and cooperation the norm for peer organizations in the industry? Complexity of resource and service options also might foster

TABLE 11-6   External Contingencies and Preconditions

Factor	Example Issues
Industry conditions	Number and density of providers
	Resource features
	Rates of change and turbulence
Awareness	Knowledge of potential partners
	Sense of shared purpose and norms
Dominant players	Influence of funders
	Major providers
Social forces	Crisis response
	Public demand for increased coordination

collaboration as managers seek clarity and hope to minimize risk inherent in a turbulent environment. A number of factors that drive this include the rate of change and regulatory factors that drive or push service providers to work independently or cooperatively. Modest resource constraints are likely to foster collaboration while severe resource cuts can foster a need for contraction of partner relationships. Extreme resource constraints can also force mergers because organizations can no longer operate independently (Murray, 1998).

The existence of preexisting networks and relationships facilitates cooperative arrangements. Interorganizational relationships rely on trust and prior knowledge of partners, which facilitates planning and coordinated action (Hardy et al., 2003). Without modest awareness of potential partners it is very difficult to arrange and instigate cooperative action. The extent to which participating organizations share similar perceptions of the problem and the potential value of collaborative initiatives is also important. If participants harbor preferences for operating independently and there are not sufficient external controls or influences to guide cooperative action then the tendency is to devolve into individual action because cooperative initiatives require substantive support and management. Another factor relates to the existence of dominant providers and the extent to which those providers foster collaborative initiatives. The existence of a convening entity such as the United Way can be instrumental in bringing together divergent partners and uniting action toward a particular objective. The influence of funders also is a significant driver of collaborative initiatives. As discussed, funders often expect providers to operate collaboratively; while this pressure is likely to increase the likelihood of collaborative structures, it takes much more than funding requirements to support interorganizational relationships. The extent to which funders support the administration and monitoring of collaborative initiatives is potentially even more important than requirements that organizations submit joint proposals. The pressure or urgency for change is another factor that can instigate collaborative action. High-profile media attention to a tragedy, for instance, highlights weaknesses and instigates participants to coordinate and respond to those concerns. These institutional and social factors are very important and serve as preconditions that facilitate successful arrangements. The management activities described in the next section operate in the context of these factors, and the more elements that reinforce collaboration and cooperative initiatives, the more likely that such activities are going to be successful, especially if there is a systematic approach to developing and monitoring the collaborative initiatives.

Phases of Managing Interorganizational Arrangements

There are substantial variations in how interorganizational relationships are structured and operate, but there are three broad categories of activities that managers should ensure are addressed. The first is related to planning and negotiation with partners. The first phase also entails internal organizational self-assessment of interests and capabilities related to collective action. The second phase relates to the process of organizing and managing the collaboration. This includes tactical and operational challenges of shared initiatives as well as governance and oversight issues. The final area of management activities relates to evaluation and performance. This includes assessing organizational costs and benefits as well as collective impact and performance expectations of the collaborative overall.

Phase One: Initiate

In the context of the institutional and environmental factors just described, organizations need to undertake individual and collective planning regarding the objectives of the joint endeavor (see **Table 11-7**). Internally, an organization should clarify their objectives and evaluate the potential benefits that collective action is likely to produce. Internal planning facilitates the process of evaluating and selecting potential partner agencies. When looking for potential partners, managers should consider instrumental compatibilities, such as extending services and providing access to new customers, as well as cultural compatibilities. This includes similar outlooks on the social issues and perspectives on

TABLE 11-7   Phase One Planning Issues

Considerations	Issues
Organizational planning	Internal rationale for partnership arrangement and assessment of internal resources
Partner selection	Shared norms and purposes
	Resource and asset capabilities
Collective planning and negotiation	Developing collective goals and objectives
Leadership and resources	Identifying organizational and collective leaders
	Access to sufficient resources

how solutions should be implemented. While different perspectives might drive innovation, a lack of agreement on fundamental approaches is likely to lead to conflict. Once potential partner organizations have been identified there is a process of planning joint priorities and objectives. Depending on the nature of the interorganizational arrangement and level of engagement, planning might be modest or significant. For instance, multistakeholder collaboratives are going to require extended planning, involvement of various entities, and extensive analysis. Participation is partially contingent on the ability of managers to define collective objectives that meet institutional priorities. However, joining an existing peer-to-peer network is a modest investment, and typically the purposes of the network are specified. Although not always true, the rationales for a peer-to-peer network are often related to cooperation and planning future initiatives. So participation in a network might facilitate broader, more complex planning. The distinction is internal (organizational) planning versus collective planning. Both take place in the early stages of collective activities.

Another critical feature is the identification of leadership. This entails identifying lead organizations, if appropriate, and individuals. While this chapter discusses interorganizational relationships, these arrangements are built on the efforts and relationships of individuals (Bailey & Koney, 2000). So, while a peer-to-peer network may actively avoid appointing a lead organization, without some system for decision making the process can be quite cumbersome. Having influential individuals serve as champions both at partner entities and within the collaborative is recognized as an important feature for success (Crutchfield & Grant, 2008). A final feature that must be addressed in the early stages is identification of sufficient resources to underwrite some of the costs inherent in these collaborations. Support to bring constituents together, support to coordinate activities, and exploratory work are critical. It doesn't have to come from an external funding source, but identification of resource needs and sources is critical. If organizations enter a collective initiative without allocating sufficient resources (time and money) subsequent steps are likely to falter.

Phase Two: Implementation

There is a lot going on in these arrangements and the variety already described recognizes that it is difficult to speak uniformly about the features and steps needed to implement collective action. So this section identifies a few key principles and priorities that seem to be prevalent in many successful collaborative arrangements (see **Table 11-8**). Implementation is about the *management* of collective action and consequently entails structures, processes, and ongoing adaptation to changing circumstances (Bryson et al., 2006; Kelman, Hong, & Turbitt, 2012). Systems facilitate enactment of key features and control mechanisms to ascertain performance levels. The governance and oversight of collective activities is complicated due to the shared responsibilities and autonomy of partner entities. So there has to be structure and processes that allow for individual action and collective accountability (Chen, 2010). This is where leadership becomes very important, because without a perspective that reaches beyond an individual organization's interests it is difficult to coordinate activities. Beyond clarifying roles and communication channels, managers need to have confidence in partner capabilities to fulfill requirements. This assessment of risk potential is informed by past actions and interpersonal trust. A reoccurring

TABLE 11-8 Phase Two Planning and Management Issues

Consideration	Issues
Design of systems and structures	Based on planning objectives, the creation of systems that blend individual and joint assets
Governance	Develop mechanisms for accountability and oversight
Management and coordination	Attend to changes and conflict Overcome barriers Foster engagement Monitor risk and cost
Trust development	Regular and accurate communication Information sharing Personal relationships
Backbone and support entity	For complex collection action Robust and trusted support infrastructure

theme in successful collaborations is the recognition that *individuals* have to form successful working relationships (Bailey & Koney, 2000). It is the ability of representatives to negotiate and adjust on an ongoing basis that facilitates success. Part of what motivates participation is the sense that the collaborative action is producing value and that component parts are engaged in reinforcing activities (Austin, 2000). There is a role for participants, and they can perceive how the collective action is producing benefits beyond their individual contribution.

The more substantive and complex the collective goals, the more institutional support is required. The concept of collective impact reinforces that strong backbone entities are required for success (Kania & Kramer, 2011). Achieving social benefits in cooperative action is too complex without rigorous oversight that refines the vision, negotiates roles, and monitors performance. Initiatives that seek to address multifaceted social problems require creative and innovative solutions that blend assets from various entities and create interventions that are distinct from prior practices. This recognizes the collaborative entity as distinct and in many ways more complex than individual organizational activities. The collective requires its own set of management talents and resources (Provan & Kenis, 2008). Thinking about the collective as a unit requiring management and oversight distills the challenges that could be present in these contexts. Interorganizational arrangements are an extension of organizational activities that require separate and continued attention and communication. Success is contingent on the capabilities, responsiveness, and engagement of partner entities. Realistic open discussion of the risks and benefits builds trust as the motivations of partners are better understood, as are the perceptions of how the collaborative is facilitating organizational objectives. Effort to learn through the process is important, as is actively building organizational capabilities. Institutionalizing practices with partner agencies builds the sustainability of the collective because it is the strength of partners geared toward collective action that facilities success.

Phase Three: Sustain and Assess Impact

Monitoring performance is intricately linked to the management activities in phase two. There are multiple aspects of performance assessment that should be addressed. This includes assessment at the organizational level and with the collective (see **Table 11-9**). There are also different types of evaluation activity. There are formative activities that monitor individual and collective activities. There are also summative evaluation activities that draw judgment on the performance benefits both for the individual partner organization and the broader collective initiative.

TABLE 11-9   Types of Evaluation and Performance Assessment

Level	Organizational	Collaborative
Formative	Performance management Organizational capabilities	Assess inputs and outputs
Summative	Assessment of organizational priorities	Public benefit, impact

Formative assessment activities are concerned with monitoring inputs, activities, and outputs. This encompasses monitoring resource allocation for individual organizational activities as well as the activities of partner organizations. At the organizational level, managers should track activities and the intended outputs of those activities. While tracking organizational activities is fairly perfunctory it is often not done effectively. Beyond basic organizational monitoring of activities and the level of service provided, managers should monitor the challenges discussed earlier (see Table 11-5), perhaps by periodically considering how activities are creating dependency on partner organizations. Managers might consider how capabilities could be internalized so as to retain autonomy and foster long-term viability. Monitoring organizational activities is the easy part when compared to understanding the level of performance demonstrated by partner entities. In fairly tight interorganizational arrangements with few partner entities it might be possible to track the performance inputs of partners, but in more complex arrangements it can be very difficult to ascertain the contributions of particular partners. Managers are monitoring both performance expectations and trust expectations. Are partner entities oriented toward collective goods or do they orient toward private benefits? While this is difficult to ascertain, some attention to both factors facilitates successful relationships. Accountability is difficult, negotiated, and dependent on the good will of partner entities that are open and willing to share performance data. This type of assessment and monitoring is ongoing and is contingent on the whole variety of complexities already discussed. For instance, power and control dynamics might allow certain partner entities to dictate reporting expectations that are not necessarily reciprocated. Similarly, network structures might facilitate information flows to central entities that more distant entities do not benefit from. Formative evaluation is fundamentally about a participant's ability to understand the contributions of partner entities and the costs incurred as a result of the interorganizational relationship.

Summative evaluation is about determining the benefits of collective activities. Formative evaluation and monitoring helps to understand the direct outputs of organizational and collective

activities, while summative evaluation is concerned with knowing how the activities have benefited target groups. In what way is
the status of service beneficiaries and society better off as a result
of collective initiatives? There are two parts to this question, and
neither is necessarily easy to answer. The first is associated with
benefits and outcomes of service recipients. The fundamentals
discussed earlier suggest how collectives might be able to answer
this question. It has to do with tracking changes and understanding the way that benefits are revealed. The second part of the
question is even more difficult, and it has to do with understanding how the interventions *caused* the improvements. Given the
inherently messy context of collaborations, this really has to do
with increasing confidence in the link between activities and service recipient benefits. Various activities that seek to raise confidence include sophisticated tracking, established baselines, and
comparison opportunities.

In addition to the social and public benefits, organizations
should determine the extent to which they achieved some of the
organizational benefits they had hoped might develop through
the collaborative arrangement (see Table 11-4). There are numerous organizational benefits such as learning new service practices and gaining access to resource options. These benefits, as
well as the public benefits, should be assessed. Without monitoring these accomplishments (public and organizational), participant members will potentially lose interest. While trust is the
basis for successful partnerships and collaborations, there is still
a need for management markers that facilitate resource allocation
requirements for collective action. Without clear organizational
and social benefits, these initiatives are unlikely to be sustained.

Trust in Interorganizational Relationships

Interorganizational relationships are based on trust. Trust is
defined as a genuine concern for the interest of others (Mayer,
Davis, & Schoorman, 1995), and to be viable it must exist at the
interpersonal and the institutional level. It is the ability to act
knowing (trusting) that others will respond in an appropriate

manner. Fundamentally, trust is related to perceived risk. As trust increases, the sense of risk associated with particular actions is mitigated. Organizational trust is fundamental to the nature of nonprofit action (see **Table 11-10**). In interorganizational relationships it is worthwhile to discuss two broad types of risk: relational risk and performance risk (Das & Teng, 2001). Relational risk relates to the spirit of cooperation that is developed between individuals and organizations. It is the basis for engagement and relates to a sense of honest motivations and goodwill on the part of another. Performance risk relates to capabilities and the ability of partner entities to fulfill commitments. Relationship risk relates to trusting the intentions of partners, and performance risk relates to trusting the organization's *ability* to fulfill commitments. To maintain trust, organizations must communicate honestly about abilities and limitations. Performance trust is based on actions. The two are related but there are instances when we trust another to not exploit our weaknesses or expropriate resources, while we might have only modest confidence in their ability to generate benefit for the collaboration. Understanding both aspects of risk informs the management strategies that can be utilized to control risk exposure and to gain benefits from the aspects of trust that do exist.

TABLE 11-10   Trust in Interorganizational Relationships

Factors	Issues
Multilevel aspects	Individual/interpersonal trust
	Organizational trust
Relational risk	Potential for exploitation
	Limited cooperation
	Opportunistic behavior
	Private benefits vs. shared benefits
Performance risk	Inability of other to provide what is needed
	Inability to achieve economies of scale
	Anticipated benefits not created
	Inability to capitalize on benefits created
Control	Informal and formal

There are a limited number of control methods available to partner organizations. As discussed, there are methods to monitor and track performance behaviors. This is useful in instances when performance risk is a potential challenge. The problem is that it can be difficult to ascertain clear markers of performance expectations, especially when provided by an independent entity. The alternative is to track and monitor outputs or inputs so as to be indicative of performance expectations. Outputs tend to be more accessible than behavioral controls that attempt to track compliance with specific behaviors. In instances when measurement of either feature is difficult or inaccessible, organizations have to rely on normative controls. This entails social norms that foster compliance through expectations. Reliance on social controls is prevalent, but enforcement is problematic because of the potential for conflict. Ambiguous behavioral performance and outcome measures suggest a lack of clarity that makes control of partners very difficult. As with all control and monitoring activities, costs are balanced against potential benefits, hence, the fundamental role of trust in interorganizational relationships. If partners cannot cost-effectively monitor behavior, inputs, or output, reliance on indicators of a trusting dynamic then is the method to justify participation.

Conclusion

Interorganizational relationships are challenging to manage but an inevitable aspect of nonprofit management. If utilized appropriately, collaborative efforts provide the opportunity to achieve both organizational benefits and social impact priorities. Cross-sector collaborations provide significant promise to bring multiple participants together to address complex social problems. Building substantive support systems that value participation and negotiate priorities is not simple or inexpensive. Collaborative initiatives suffer from difficult accountability measures that frustrate participants and mute effectiveness. They are built on cooperative and trusting relationships that take significant time to develop and maintain.

Discussion Questions

1. What kinds of networks are you familiar with, and how do those networks operate? What benefits do you gain from participation in those networks? What are some of the costs you experience?
2. Think about the different types of collective action structures (see Table 11-1 and Table 11-2) and then work through the different phases of planning, implementation, and assessment. How might those phases be different for different types of collective action?
3. How do the paradoxes of interorganizational arrangements challenge the phases of management?
4. If interorganizational arrangements are so difficult to manage and support why are they utilized by nonprofit managers?

References

Austin, J. E. (2000). *The collaboration challenge: How nonprofits and businesses succeed through strategic alliances.* San Francisco, CA: Jossey-Bass.

Bailey, D., & Koney, K. M. (2000). *Strategic alliances among health and human service organizations.* Thousand Oaks, CA: Sage.

Barringer, B. R., & Harrison, J. S. (2000). Walking a tightrope: Creating value through interorganizational relationships. *Journal of Management, 26*(3), 367–403.

Bryson, J. M., Crosby, B. C., & Stone, M. M. (2006). The design and implementation of cross-sector collaborations: Propositions from the literature. *Public Administration Review, 66,* 44–55.

Chen, B. (2010). Antecedents or processes? Determinants of perceived effectiveness of interorganizational collaborations for public service delivery. *International Public Management Journal, 13*(4), 381–407.

Crutchfield, L. R., & Grant, H. M. (2008). *Forces for good: The six practices of high-impact nonprofits.* San Francisco, CA: Jossey-Bass.

Das, T. K., & Teng, B.-S. (2001). Trust, control, and risk in strategic alliances: An integrated framework. *Organization Studies, 22*(2), 251–283.

Guo, C., & Acar, M. (2005). Understanding collaboration among nonprofit organizations: Combining resource dependency, institutional, and network perspectives. *Nonprofit and Voluntary Sector Quarterly, 34*(3), 340–361.

Hallen, L., Johanson, J., & Seyed-Mohamed, N. (1991). Interform adaption in business relationships. *Journal of Marketing, 55*(2), 29–37.

Hanleybrown, F., Kania, J., & Kramer, M. (2012). Channeling change: Making collective impact work [Web blog post]. *Stanford Social Innovation Review.* Retrieved from http://www.ssireview.org/blog/entry/channeling_change_making_collective_impact_work

Hardy, C., Phillips, N., & Lawrence, T. B. (2003). Resources, knowledge and influence: The organizational effects of interorganizational collaboration. *Journal of Management Studies, 40*(2), 321–347.

Human, S. E., & Provan, K. G. (2000). Legitimacy building in the evolution of small-firm multilateral networks: A comparative study of success and demise. *Administrative Science Quarterly, 45*(2), 327–365.

Kania, J., & Kramer, M. (2011, Winter). Collective impact. *Stanford Social Innovation review, 36*–41.

Kelman, S., Hong, S., & Turbitt, I. (2012). Are there managerial practices associated with the outcomes of an interagency service delivery collaboration? Evidence from British crime and disorder reduction partnerships. *Journal of Public Administration Research and Theory.* doi: 10.1093/jopart/mus038

Mayer, R. C., Davis, J. H., & Schoorman, F. D. (1995). An integrative model of organizational trust. *The Academy of Management Review, 20*(3), 709–734.

Murray, V. (1998). Interorganizational collaborations in the nonprofit sector. *International Encyclopaedia of Public Policy and Administration, 2*, 1192–1196.

Phelps, C. C. (2010). A longitudinal study of the influence of alliance network structure and composition on firm exploratrory innovation. *Academy of Management Journal, 53*(4), 890–913.

Provan, K. G., & Kenis, P. (2008). Modes of network governance: Structure, management, and effectiveness. *Journal of Public Administration Research and Theory, 18*(2), 229–252.

Provan, K. G., & Milward, H. B. (2002). Do networks really work? A framework for evaluating public-sector organizational networks. *Peace Research Abstracts, 39*(5), 611–755.

Scearce, D., Kasper, G., & Grant, H. M. (2010, Summer). Working wikily. *Stanford Social Innovation Review,* 31–37.

Tjemkes, B., Vos, P., & Burgers, K. (2012). *Strategic alliance management.* Florance, KY: Routledge.

Strategic Leadership

Learning Objectives

- Define and explain the functions of strategic leadership in nonprofits
- Relate these functions to elements in the strategic management cycle

Leadership is discussed in hundreds of books, and countless studies have explored what it means to be an effective leader. Leadership is part vision, part message, and part influence (Bass & Bass, 2008). A great deal of effort has been put forward to define the traits, behaviors, and styles of effective leaders. The purpose here is to focus on key behaviors of successful strategic leadership in nonprofit organizations. The focus is on the leaders' role to interpret environmental uncertainties in relation to organizational assets and capabilities. Leadership is critical to organizational performance and success (Yukl, 2012). The senior staff, governing board, and occasionally other significant stakeholders (e.g., funders) share the responsibility for strategic leadership in nonprofits. The exact composition of the "dominant coalition"

(Miles & Snow, 1978) is unique to the organizational context and includes paid and unpaid individuals. The next section identifies some key areas for leadership functioning. The term *executive director* is used to refer to the highest-level "staff" member that has leadership responsibilities independent of the board's governing role. It is important to remember that for many organizations the executive team constitutes a number of individuals responsible for these functions. In fact, one of the conclusions is that effective executives diligently share power and leadership responsibilities (Crutchfield & Grant, 2008).

Executive Leadership

Nonprofit leadership entails a multitude of functions, such as raising support from key stakeholders, engaging key participants, and guiding decision making to select priorities that meet the needs of stakeholders. As Martha Golensky (2011) concludes, leadership is fundamentally the ability to operate in the political and resource environments while attending to the affairs of the organization to achieve public benefit objectives. The strategic management cycle is used to cluster key roles of strategic leadership in nonprofits. While it is impossible to capture all the important features of leadership in the sector, there do seem to be a few attributes that are particularly relevant to the nonprofit context and strategic leadership (see **Figure 12-1**). It is important to remember that there is no "one" style. Individuals enact these behaviors in a variety of ways. The chapter highlights some potentially important behaviors and functions for nonprofit leaders (Santora & Sarros, 2001; Thach & Thompson, 2007). How and when these behaviors are used is dependent on the context and the issues confronting the organization.

Defining and Exploiting Market Domains

There are three functions related to market domains that leaders should prioritize (see **Table 12-1**): clarifying the public benefit

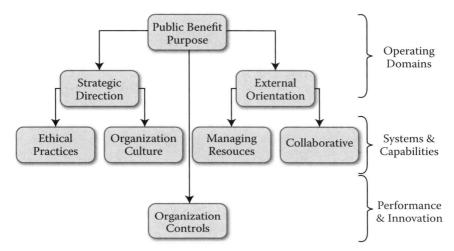

FIGURE 12-1   Strategic Leadership Functions

purpose, creating a strategic direction, and maintaining an external orientation. The *mission and public benefit purpose* of the
organization need to be central to decision making and thinking
for nonprofit executives. The mission is the emotional, inspirational, and tactical guide for the organization. Peter Drucker
states that "the mission comes first" in the role of the leader
(Drucker, 1990, p. 3). The mission captures why the organization
exists. It articulates the social value created by the organization;
as a result the mission should be the first guiding principle that
managers consider as they design and implement strategic priorities. Another analogy suggests that the mission is a bridge
to link the organization to real problems in society. This link is
inspirational and serves to create the vision for what the organization hopes to accomplish. Successful founding executives are
very good at articulating these needs and the benefits the organization will achieve. One more analogy compares the mission
to a touchstone that guides organizational activities. This talk of
the mission as preeminent is all well and good, but the tactical
translation of those ideals into action is the next test of an effective leader.

[handwritten margin note: need to manage strategic cycle]

TABLE 12-1   Leadership Functions Related to Defining Market Domains

Function	Key Elements
Public benefit purpose	• Define mission and purpose • Prioritize the public/member benefit purpose • Translate social need to organizational priorities (vision) • Use mission to guide activities
Strategic direction	• Position organizational purpose in relation to broader social context • Define priorities in multiple markets • Balance external forces with internal capabilities
External orientation	• Recognize issues of resource scarcity • Need for stakeholder support • Adapt to competing/pluralistic priorities

Creating a *strategic direction* that enacts the mission is critical. Drucker states that "action comes next" (Drucker, 1990, p. 5). It is the ability to shift that rather ambiguous ideal and inspirational principle into practical goals and strategies. This text is an attempt to capture the complexities of defining market features. Determining priorities in each market domain is difficult and tenuous. Leaders, along with others (dominant coalition), frame the boundaries of activity and suggest priorities to achieve objectives. There are various ways leaders can go about crafting strategic priorities (Kearns, 2000). The textbook suggests a logical sequential process that analyzes environmental features and internal capabilities to define strategic priorities. This is recognized as an analytic and logical framework that implies the need for detailed information and thoughtful analysis and interpretation. Another reality is that some leaders rely on inspirational visions. The logic of analysis is circumvented by interpretation of community need and intuition to develop guiding philosophies and tactical practices. While one may appear better than another, the reality is that leaders rely on intuition and insight to define priorities (Ritchie, Kolodinsky, & Eastwood, 2007), and these insights are valuable for success.

Leadership and even strategic direction are not solely analytic processes. They include coalition building to gain capacity and visionary ideas to inspire participation. Leaders can tap into human interest and deep motivations to achieve objectives, and successful leaders can interpret and define priorities. This ability to interpret comes from rich and deep experience (Ritchie & Eastwood, 2006). The third approach to developing a strategic orientation suggests an incremental approach (Johnson, 1988; Quinn, 1980). Recognizing the practicalities of organizational change, an incremental approach adjusts organizational priorities over time to accommodate changing environmental conditions. This sort of approach works well in fairly stable environmental conditions that allow modest change in organizational practices over time. Through robust feedback mechanisms, organizational practices are piloted and reviewed, then expanded, modified, or terminated based on results. Whatever the method, leaders need to help craft guidelines for organizational action.

The third function, related to defining market domains, is the need to be *externally oriented*. Given the resource-dependent nature of nonprofits, attention to external stakeholders and the resource environment is critical. This entails maintaining relationships and understanding the preferences and interests of key groups and individuals. Early seminal work by Bob Herman and others (Heimovics, Herman, & Jurkiewicz, 1995) found that effective executives enacted a "political" frame to understand and interpret the operating environment and organizational challenges (Bolman & Deal, 2008). The political frame is one of four models executives use to guide and focus their actions. The structural frame emphasizes specialized roles and the division of labor. The human resource lens prioritizes people and their feelings, while the symbolic frame recognizes the power of cultures and images. The political frame recognizes the potential conflict over resources and the need to build support. Executives using the political frame seek to gain power so as to move forward the purposes of the organization. Power is built through the goodwill and alignment with influential stakeholders.

These executives are adept at negotiating and compromise. They work for intermediate win-win situations that align with the goals of the organization. The executive views stakeholder preferences through the lens of the organization's mission and the competing interests of other stakeholders, while considering the benefit particular stakeholders can provide the organization. This responsiveness is also reflective of a market orientation toward the customers of the organization (Gainer & Padanyi, 2005; Slater & Narver, 1995). Market orientation is the organization's tendency to listen to customers and the various forces operating within the field that are likely to influence behaviors. It is critical to attend to task environment features, and leaders set the tone for how this is done successfully. Leaders then translate these definitions and interpretations of market features into organizational practices that operationalize the work of the organization.

Building Systems and Capabilities

Leaders should prioritize four functions in relation to building organizational systems and capabilities (see **Table 12-2**): ensuring ethical standards, managing organizational resources, nurturing an organizational culture, and seeking to be collaborative. The mission serves as a touchstone and agenda-setting method for the organization, and a deep personal commitment to *ethical practice* can guide organizational operations (Jeavons, 2010). Seeking to function with high integrity is an essential guidepost for nonprofit executives. These organizations operate in industries without clear measures of success. Consequently, stakeholders must be able to trust the work of the organization and, inherently, the leadership of the organization. This is especially true when you consider donors, who are often disconnected from actual service delivery. Thom Jeavons (2010) identifies key values of ethical organizations.

Organizations must operate with integrity, which entails consistency of words, appearances, and actions (Jensen, 2009). Integrity is fundamental to trustworthiness and reflects that organizations and individuals fulfill their promises. Erhard, Jensen, and Zaffron (2009) define integrity as "wholeness" or "completeness" and draw an analogy to systems and machines that

TABLE 12-2 Leadership Functions in Building Systems and Capabilities

Function	Key Elements
Ethical practices	• Builds trust and commitment • Consistency of message and action (integrity) • Openness to accountability
Managing resource portfolio	• Core competencies • Structuring, bundling, leveraging • Human and social capital
Organizational culture	• Articulates values of the organization • Guides management decisions • Entrepreneurial
Collaborative	• Shares leadership within and outside the organization *Stakeholders* • Engages board members

work ineffectively unless they are whole and complete. Integrity requires that leaders consistently fulfill spoken and implied commitments, and honestly address those who have expectations beyond organizational capabilities. Without an ability to trust someone's word, the work of the organization is compromised and inherently limited in achieving its full potential. Integrity is a powerful cultural and behavioral norm that is fundamental to effective organizational operations. Another important concept is a prioritization of openness. Nonprofits and nonprofit leaders should strive to build cultures that are open to review. Accountability is the natural extension of this idea, and it is the responsibility of the leadership to demonstrate that the organization is a good steward of resources (Ebrahim, 2010).

The resource portfolio is the set of assets that are critical for operational success. Leaders *manage the resource portfolio* so as to weave together competencies, which allow the organization to efficiently produce public benefit outcomes (Nadler & Tushman, 1999). Competencies are a mix of asset elements and organizational systems (often related to human resources), which create value. Leaders should utilize core competencies in all three market domains (public benefit, resource, and sociopolitical), to provide value to each customer type. In the resource market, well-designed fundraising systems that tap donor interests are an example of a core competency. This stitching together of resources into a set of core competencies creates systems that help the organization be more successful and operate with a comparative advantage. How and what competencies are created is dependent on internal and external factors, guided by the preferences of leaders. Leaders assume the role of building these capabilities and utilizing them in strategic choices.

There are various ways to develop competencies. Sirmon, Hitt, Ireland, and Gilbert (2011) suggest three useful clusters of management activities (structuring, bundling, and leveraging). Structuring entails the range of activities related to acquiring and accumulating necessary resources. Such management activities depend upon the resource market, and leaders must ensure that the organization can acquire financial, human, and physical capital. The acquisition of resources improves stability. Bundling and integrating these asset elements creates the potential for distinctive advantage. Bundling is the act of integrating organizational assets to create core competencies within distinctive market domains. So managers should be clear on the logic that blends assets and talents to achieve optimal service delivery. The third cluster of activities link core competencies to market opportunities. It is the strategic utilization of resource competencies to exploit market opportunities. Managers ask, "How can we best deploy these capabilities in our market domains?" This might entail growth into new service areas. Not only do managers blend assets to create capabilities within specific market spheres (e.g., service delivery) but leaders also integrate competencies across market domains. Leaders might or might not be hands-on in all these areas. There is some argument that leaders should attend to the structuring function while fostering creativity and entrepreneurial perspectives among organizational participants so they can seek how best to bundle and leverage resources toward market opportunities. In the resource-poor context of nonprofits, stability might be the most salient strategic asset.

Managers can do quite a bit to ensure that the organization has good, viable, and useful resources. Managers should especially attend to people engaged in supporting the organization. This includes those who work for the organization (volunteers and paid) (Cappelli & Crocker-Hefter, 1996) and the social relationships maintained by the organization (Nahapiet & Ghoshal, 1998). Who are the people that are willing to work toward our objectives, and what relationships facilitate success? Nonprofits fundamentally function on the capabilities of the people associated with the organization. Leaders actively work to strengthen the commitments of employees and volunteers. Social capital is critical to what nonprofits try to do, especially in the resource and sociopolitical domains. By their very nature, these domains are reliant on relationships as a key feature of success. Social capital within the organization is also likely to facilitate the utilization of resource elements. It is familiarity and positive working relationships within the organization that allow leaders to leverage resource capabilities across organizational divisions.

There are numerous human resource practices (compensation, decision authority) that managers can use to support performance (Akingbola, 2012). Scholars emphasize *organizational culture* in particular because it reflects how leaders can influence organizational behavior (Schein, 1995). Organizational culture relates to the defining assumptions about how the organizational should and does operate (Schein, 1990). It is a mix of values, symbols, and beliefs that develop over time. These shared assumptions are reinforced by leaders and organizational practices. While difficult to manipulate because culture operates on multiple levels, leaders can adjust cultural assumptions over time with consistent practices that address each level. This includes artifacts and symbols that are used to reinforce espoused values. Undergirding these elements are the realities of organizational behavior. If a leader wants to foster an entrepreneurial culture there has to be consistent reinforcement of those behaviors throughout the organization. Fundamentally, organizational participants need to perceive that acting according to those values is instrumental to success. Does the espoused value align with what it takes to be successful from the standpoint of an organizational participant? Mission orientation is another example of a cultural norm that can help guide action. Managers can remind organizational participants about the mission, they can utilize the mission prominently in organizational materials, but that orientation must also guide decisions that are supported by performance success. Organizational participants adopt cultural assumptions because those assumptions are instrumental to getting the work done.

The last area that seems particularly important in the nonprofit context is the ability to *share power* and leadership responsibilities (Crutchfield & Grant, 2008). In their review of high-impact nonprofits, Crutchfield and Grant found a distinctive pattern of how executives led organizations. In many instances, they had an "inside" manager who administered the day-to-day activities of the organization, and there was an "outside" director who attended to relationships with external stakeholders. This reflects the multiple market demands that nonprofits confront. The outside director is particularly attuned to the resource and political market, while the inside director builds organizational systems to achieve social impact. This dual-power arrangement reflects authentic shared power. Leonard Berry (Berry & Seltman, 2008) discovered a similar pattern in the Mayo Clinic, where all major administrative positions are shared between a medical professional and an executive administrator. This shared power structure allowed for skilled individuals to assume more responsibility and authority while balancing the weaknesses of the other. The shared power orientation also extends to the board (Herman, 2010). Executives ultimately have responsibility for engaging board members and helping them to fulfill their leadership responsibilities. It is not uncommon for a nonprofit board to be nothing more than a rubber stamp that approves all administrative initiatives, or they are perceived only as a method to raise funds. The executive has significant responsibility to help build the capacity of the board and to support their engagement in the work of the organization.

Ensuring Performance and Innovation

The final area of leadership relates to performance and innovation—the third aspect of the strategic management cycle. The performance areas are drawn from a balanced scorecard approach

(Kaplan, 2001), which recognizes financial and nonfinancial measures (see **Table 12-3**). These dimensions are "balanced" in the sense that each has contributes a holistic view of performance in the organization. While the creation of performance measures can be difficult and at times bureaucratic, thoughtful systems that balance information needs with operational realities are critical. Consequently, leaders attend to both the limitations of information demands that can burden frontline workers while seeking systems that facilitate informed decision making.

Performance measures related to social value creation and the fulfillment of public benefit purpose is critical. Mission and public benefit purpose are *the* rationale for organizational existence and the guiding philosophy of the organization. The measurement of social impact is particularly problematic and difficult. Nevertheless, attention to objectives in this area requires honest effort. The theory of change used by an organization to explain and link services to outcomes provides opportunities to assess incremental aspects of performance. So, while measurement may never be able to *prove* the impact of services, there are sequential indicators that suggest fulfillment of public benefit purposes. It is these indicators that guide action and suggest opportunities for improvement.

TABLE 12-3 Leadership Functions to Ensure Performance and Innovation

Function	Key Elements
Organizational controls related to:	
Social value, public benefit	• Program quality, outputs, and outcomes
Finance and resources	• Budgeting and financial controls • Forecasts and tracking of key revenue sources
Stakeholder relations	• Awareness of key stakeholder perspectives and attitudes regarding the nonprofit
Internal processes	• Concern for efficiency and operational practices
Learning and growing	• Attending to human capital • Facilitating innovations and development of new programs and processes

Financial performance measures are more objective, and there are several aspects to which managers should attend. Cash flow is a critical issue for many nonprofits, so the day-to-day monitoring and forecasting of cash flow is a key aspect of leadership in this area. Systematic budgeting and tracking of expenses, as well, facilitate operations and allow the financial controls to be disbursed throughout the organization to allow departmental and divisional managers the information required for independent decision making. Revenue forecasting is another aspect of financial performance that needs accurate information. Leaders might expect growth or stability in revenue depending on performance objectives. Nonprofits are inherently sensitive to fluctuations in donated income, so attending to donor attitudes is as important as quarterly revenue reports. This leads to the third area that managers should monitor—stakeholder relationships. Leaders should be cognizant of significant relationship dynamics in all markets of the organization. Prioritizing the management of these relationships is a critical responsibility and should be a component of any feedback system.

The last two areas (internal processes and learning and growth) reflect a range of information needs and tracking challenges. Managers should assess key process features such as those related to services, communications, and the like. If these measures can be quantified, it facilitates monitoring trends over time. Sometimes monitoring might entail the specification of learning opportunities utilized and trainings attended. It is reasonable for leaders to seek information and report on key processes. The specifics of those reports are dependent on the context and the decision-making requirements. The creation of some unified, balanced reporting system is very useful for board members as well.

Conclusion

Leadership in nonprofit organizations attends to all aspects of the strategic management cycle. Starting with a focus on the mission, leaders attend to external forces so as to help design and set a strategic direction. Organizational operations are guided by ethical management practices that prioritize individual integrity. Emphasizing ethical practices lends to creating a culture that defines the logic of operational practices. Leaders support the development of core competencies that effectively utilize human and social capital features. Core competencies emerge from a shared leadership model that seeks engagement of board members. Attending to the multiple priorities and operational forces is facilitated by a balanced performance management system that recognizes the various priorities operating in the nonprofit context.

Discussion Questions

1. Leaders and the dominant coalition must balance competing priorities that are encapsulated in the strategic management cycle. How might you, as a leader of a small nonprofit, seek to prioritize these different demands?
2. What areas, do you suspect, would be the most pressing for managers in small- to modest-sized nonprofits?

References

Akingbola, K. (2013). A model of strategic nonprofit human resource management. *Voluntas: International Journal of Voluntary and Nonprofit Organizations, 24*(1), 1–27.

Bass, B. M., & Bass, R. (2008). *The Bass handbook of leadership: Theory, research and managerial applications.* New York, NY: Free Press.

Berry, L. L., & Seltman, K. D. (2008). *Management lessons from the Mayo Clinic.* New York, NY: McGraw-Hill.

Bolman, L. G., & Deal, T. E. (2008). *Reframing organizations: Artistry, choice and leadership* (4th ed.). San Francisco, CA: Jossey-Bass.

Cappelli, P., & Crocker-Hefter, A. (1996). Distinctive human resources are firms' core competencies. *Organizational Dynamics, 24*(3), 7–22.

Crutchfield, L. R., & Grant, H. M. (2008). *Forces for good: The six practices of high-impact nonprofits.* San Francisco, CA: Jossey-Bass.

Drucker, P. F. (1990). *Managing the nonprofit organization*. New York, NY: Harper Collins.

Ebrahim, A. (2010). *The many faces of nonprofit accountability*. Harvard University. Retrieved from http://hbswk.hbs.edu/item/6387.html

Erhard, W. H., Jensen, M. C., & Zaffron, S. (2009). *Integrity: A positive model that incorporates the normative phenomena of morality, ethics and legality*. Harvard University. Retrieved from http://ssrn.com/abstract=920625

Gainer, B., & Padanyi, P. (2005). The relationship between market-oriented activities and market-oriented culture: Implications for the development of market orientation in nonprofit service organizations. *Journal of Business Research, 58*(6), 854–862.

Golensky, M. (2011). *Strategic leadership and management in nonprofit organizations*. Chicago, IL: Lyceum.

Heimovics, R. D., Herman, R. D., & Jurkiewicz, C. L. (1995). The political dimension of effective nonprofit executive leadership. *Nonprofit Management & Leadership, 5*(3), 233–248.

Herman, R. D. (2010). Executive leadership. In D. O. Renz (Ed.), *The Jossey-Bass handbook of nonprofit leadership and management* (3rd ed., pp. 157–177). San Francisco, CA: Jossey-Bass.

Jeavons, T. (2010). Ethical nonprofit management: Core values and key practices. In D. O. Renz (Ed.), *The Jossey-Bass handbook of nonprofit management* (3rd ed., pp. 178–205). San Francisco, CA: Jossey-Bass.

Jensen, M. C. (2009). Integrity: Without it nothing works. *Rotman: The Magzine of the Rotman School of Management*, 16–20. Retrieved from http://ssrn.com/abstract=1511274

Johnson, G. (1988). Rethinking incrementalism. *Strategic Management Journal, 9*(1), 75–91.

Kaplan, R. S. (2001). Strategic performance measurement and management in nonprofit organizations. *Nonprofit Management and Leadership, 11*(3), 353–370.

Kearns, K. P. (2000). *Private sector strategies for social sector success*. San Francisco, CA: Jossey-Bass.

Miles, R. E., & Snow, C. C. (1978). *Organizational strategy structure and process*. New York, NY: McGraw-Hill.

Nadler, D. A., & Tushman, M. L. (1999). The organization of the future: Strategic imperatives and core competencies for the 21st century. *Organizational Dynamics, 28*(1), 45–60.

Nahapiet, J., & Ghoshal, S. (1998). Social capital, intellectual capital, and the organizational advantage. *The Academy of Management Review, 23*(2), 242–266.

Quinn, J. B. (1980). *Strategies for change: Logical incrementalism.* Homewood, IL: Irwin.

Ritchie, W. J., & Eastwood, K. (2006). Executive functional experience and its relationship to the financial performance of nonprofit organizations. *Nonprofit Management & Leadership, 17*(1), 67–82.

Ritchie, W. J., Kolodinsky, R. W., & Eastwood, K. (2007). Does executive intuition matter? An empirical analysis of its relationship with nonprofit organization financial performance. *Nonprofit and Voluntary Sector Quarterly, 36*(1), 140–155.

Santora, J. C., Sarros, J. C. (2001). CEO tenure in nonprofit community-based organizations: A multiple case study. *Career Development International, 6*(1), 56–60.

Schein, E. H. (1990). Organizational culture. *American Psychologist, 45*(2), 109–119.

Schein, E. H. (1995). The role of the founder in creating organizational culture. *Family Business Review, 8*(3), 221–238.

Sirmon, D. G., Hitt, M. A., Ireland, R. D., & Gilbert, B. A. (2011). Resource orchestration to create competitive advantage: Breadth, depth, and life cycle effects. *Journal of Management, 37*(5), 1390–1412.

Slater, S. F., & Narver, J. C. (1995). Market orientation and the learning organization. *Journal of Marketing, 59*(3), 63–74.

Thach, E., & Thompson, K. J. (2007). Trading places: Examining leadership competencies between for-profit vs. public and non-profit leaders. *Leadership & Organization Development Journal, 28*(4), 356–375.

Yukl, G. (2012). Effective leadership behavior: What we know and what questions need more attention. *The Academy of Management Perspectives, 26*(4), 66–85.

Index

Note: Page numbers followed by *f* and *t* indicate material in figures and tables, respectively.

E